VAULT

PUBLISHER
DAMIAN A. WASSEL

EDITOR-IN-CHIEF
ADRIAN F. WASSEL

ART DIRECTOR
NATHAN C. GOODEN

VP VISUAL BRANDING & DESIGN
TIM DANIEL

DIRECTOR OF MARKETING
KIM MCLEAN

PRINCIPAL
DAMIAN A. WASSEL, SR.

DIRECTOR PR & RETAILER RELATIONS
DAVID DISSANAYAKE

OPERATIONS MANAGER
IAN BALDESSARI

D1158734

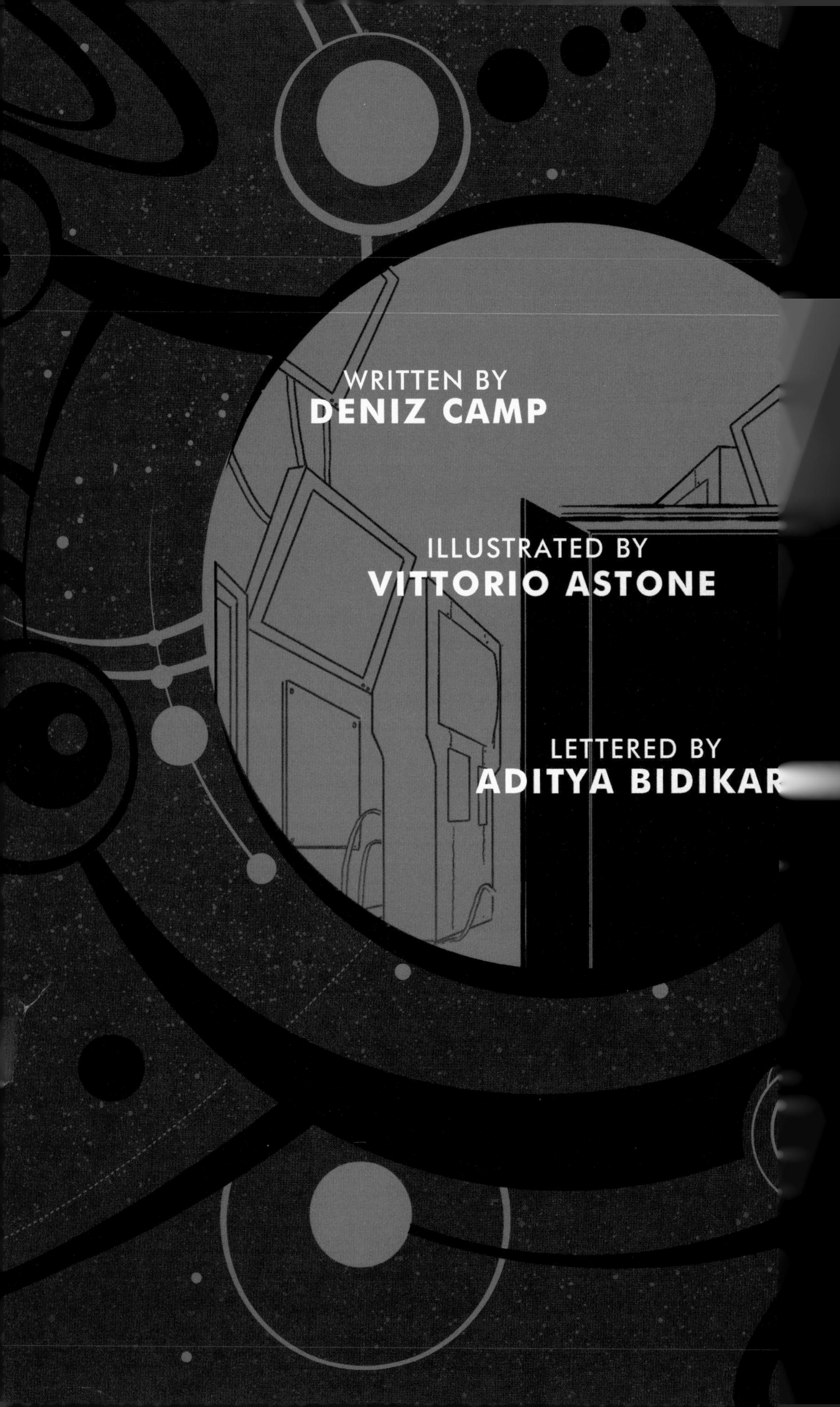
WRITTEN BY
DENIZ CAMP
ILLUSTRATED BY
VITTORIO ASTONE
LETTERED BY
ADITYA BIDIKAR

VAULT COMICS
PRESENTS

MAXWELL'S
DEMONS

FORGIVE HIM HIS GENUIS.

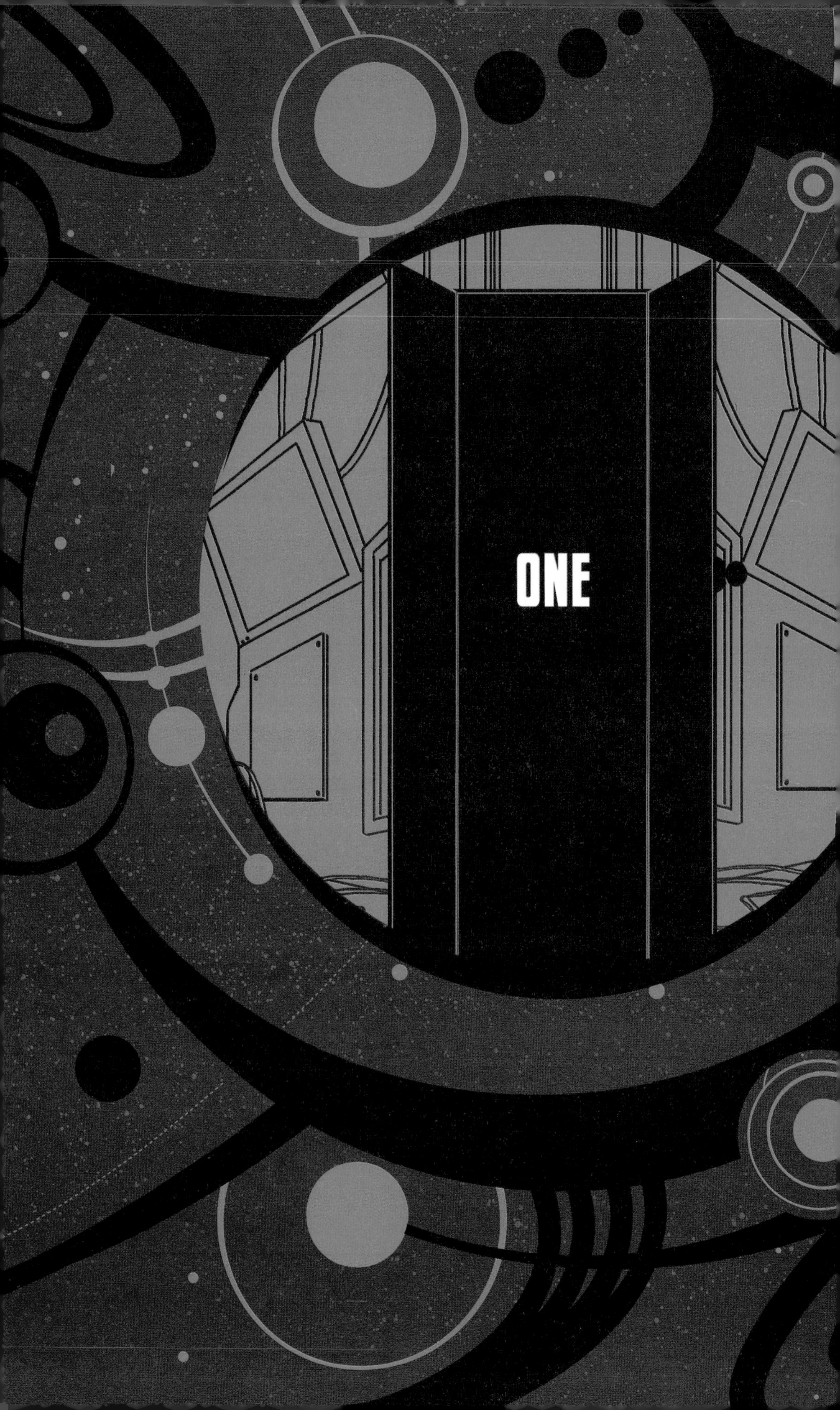

ONE

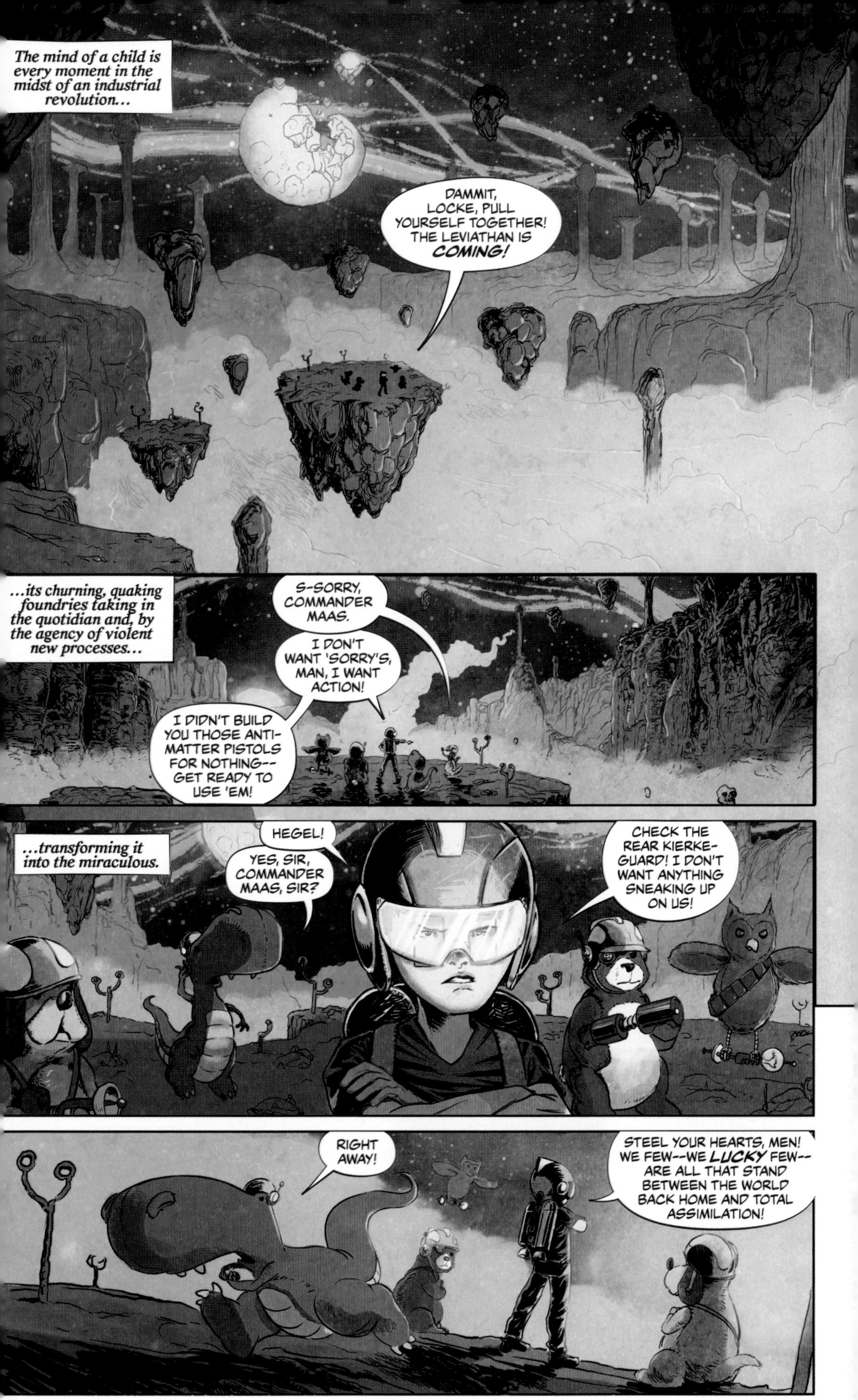

The mind of a child is every moment in the midst of an industrial revolution...
DAMMIT, LOCKE, PULL YOURSELF TOGETHER! THE LEVIATHAN IS COMING!
...its churning, quaking foundries taking in the quotidian and, by the agency of violent new processes...
S-SORRY, COMMANDER MAAS.
I DON'T WANT 'SORRY'S, MAN, I WANT ACTION!
I DIDN'T BUILD YOU THOSE ANTI-MATTER PISTOLS FOR NOTHING--GET READY TO USE 'EM!
...transforming it into the miraculous.
HEGEL!
YES, SIR, COMMANDER MAAS, SIR?
CHECK THE REAR KIERKE-GUARD! I DON'T WANT ANYTHING SNEAKING UP ON US!
RIGHT AWAY!
STEEL YOUR HEARTS, MEN! WE FEW--WE LUCKY FEW--ARE ALL THAT STAND BETWEEN THE WORLD BACK HOME AND TOTAL ASSIMILATION!

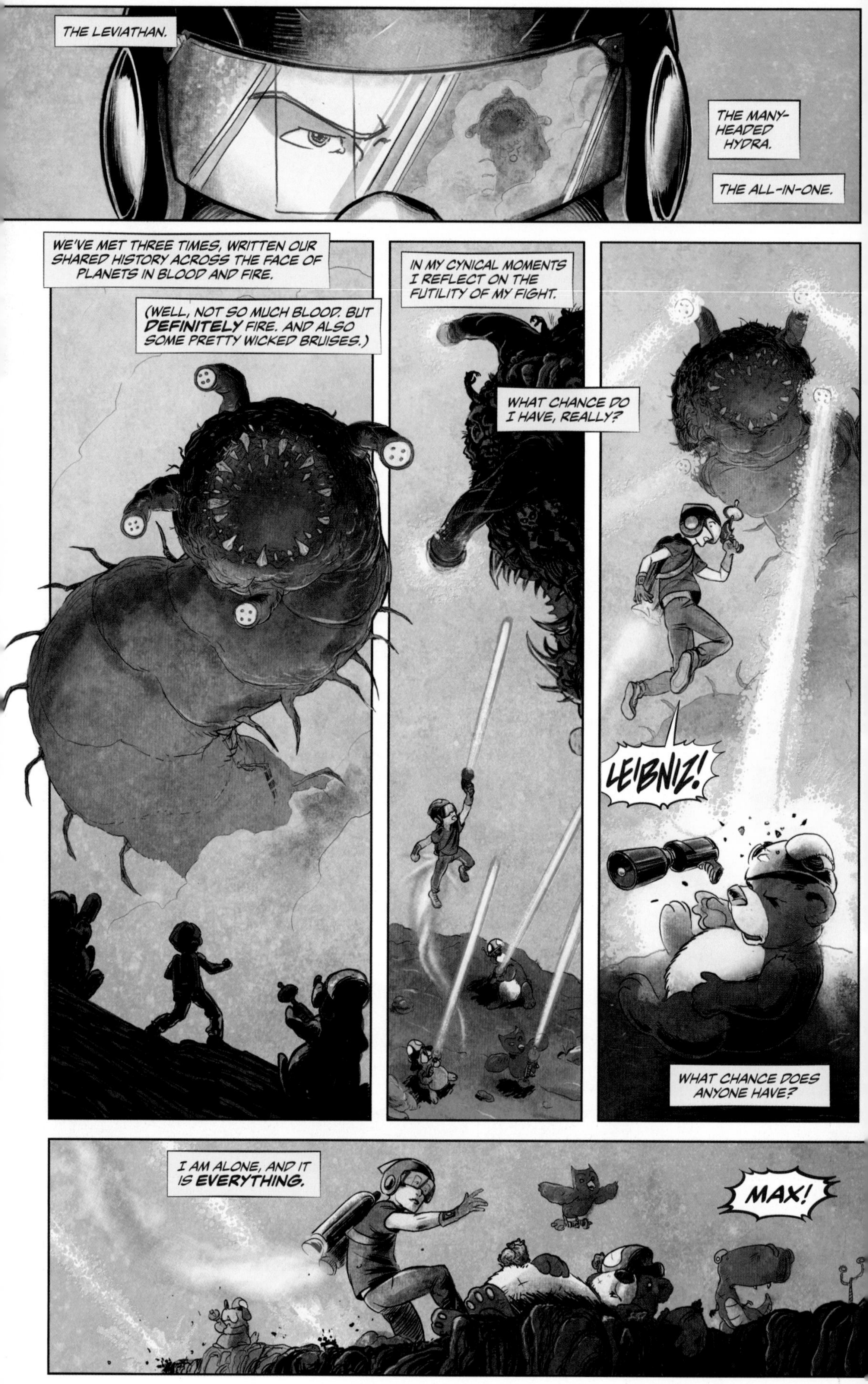

THE LEVIATHAN.
THE MANY-HEADED HYDRA.
THE ALL-IN-ONE.
WE'VE MET THREE TIMES, WRITTEN OUR SHARED HISTORY ACROSS THE FACE OF PLANETS IN BLOOD AND FIRE.
(WELL, NOT SO MUCH BLOOD. BUT DEFINITELY FIRE. AND ALSO SOME PRETTY WICKED BRUISES.)
IN MY CYNICAL MOMENTS I REFLECT ON THE FUTILITY OF MY FIGHT.
WHAT CHANCE DO I HAVE, REALLY?
LEIBNIZ!
WHAT CHANCE DOES ANYONE HAVE?
I AM ALONE, AND IT IS EVERYTHING.
MAX!

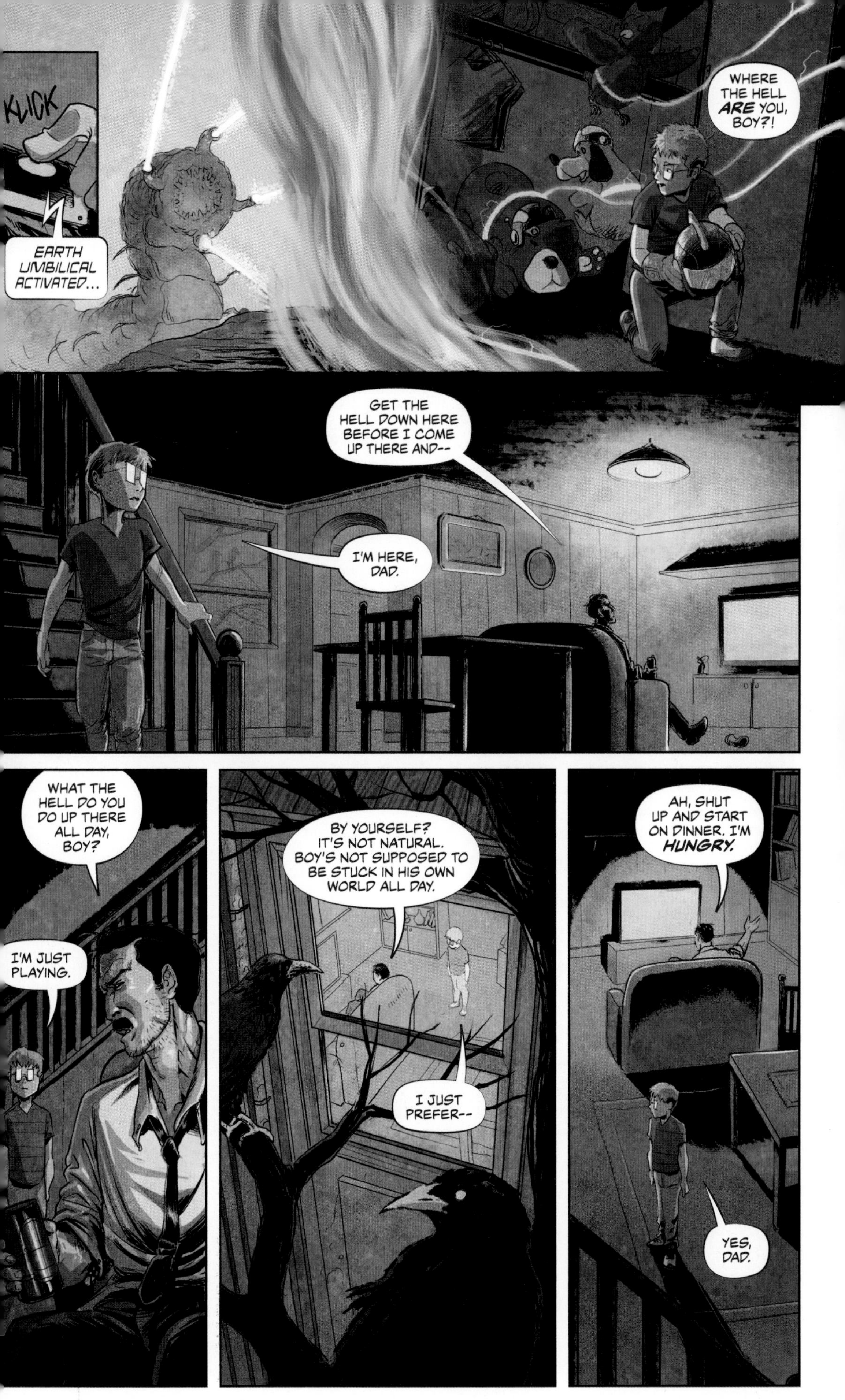
KLICK
EARTH UMBILICAL ACTIVATED...
WHERE THE HELL ARE YOU, BOY?!
GET THE HELL DOWN HERE BEFORE I COME UP THERE AND--
I'M HERE, DAD.
WHAT THE HELL DO YOU DO UP THERE ALL DAY, BOY?
I'M JUST PLAYING.
BY YOURSELF? IT'S NOT NATURAL. BOY'S NOT SUPPOSED TO BE STUCK IN HIS OWN WORLD ALL DAY.
I JUST PREFER--
AH, SHUT UP AND START ON DINNER. I'M HUNGRY.
YES, DAD.

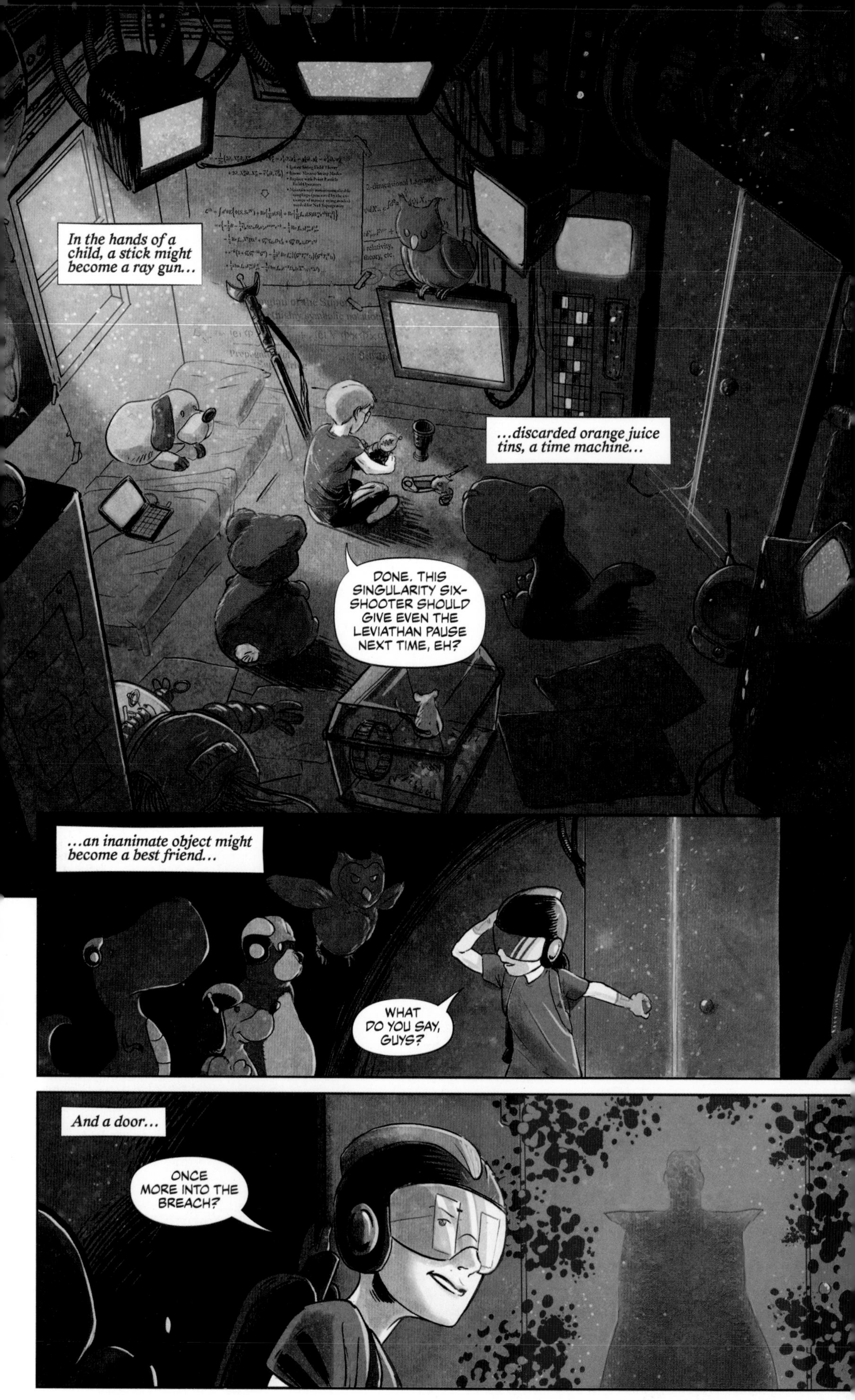
In the hands of a child, a stick might become a ray gun…
…discarded orange juice tins, a time machine…
DONE. THIS SINGULARITY SIX-SHOOTER SHOULD GIVE EVEN THE LEVIATHAN PAUSE NEXT TIME, EH?
…an inanimate object might become a best friend…
WHAT DO YOU SAY, GUYS?
And a door…
ONCE MORE INTO THE BREACH?

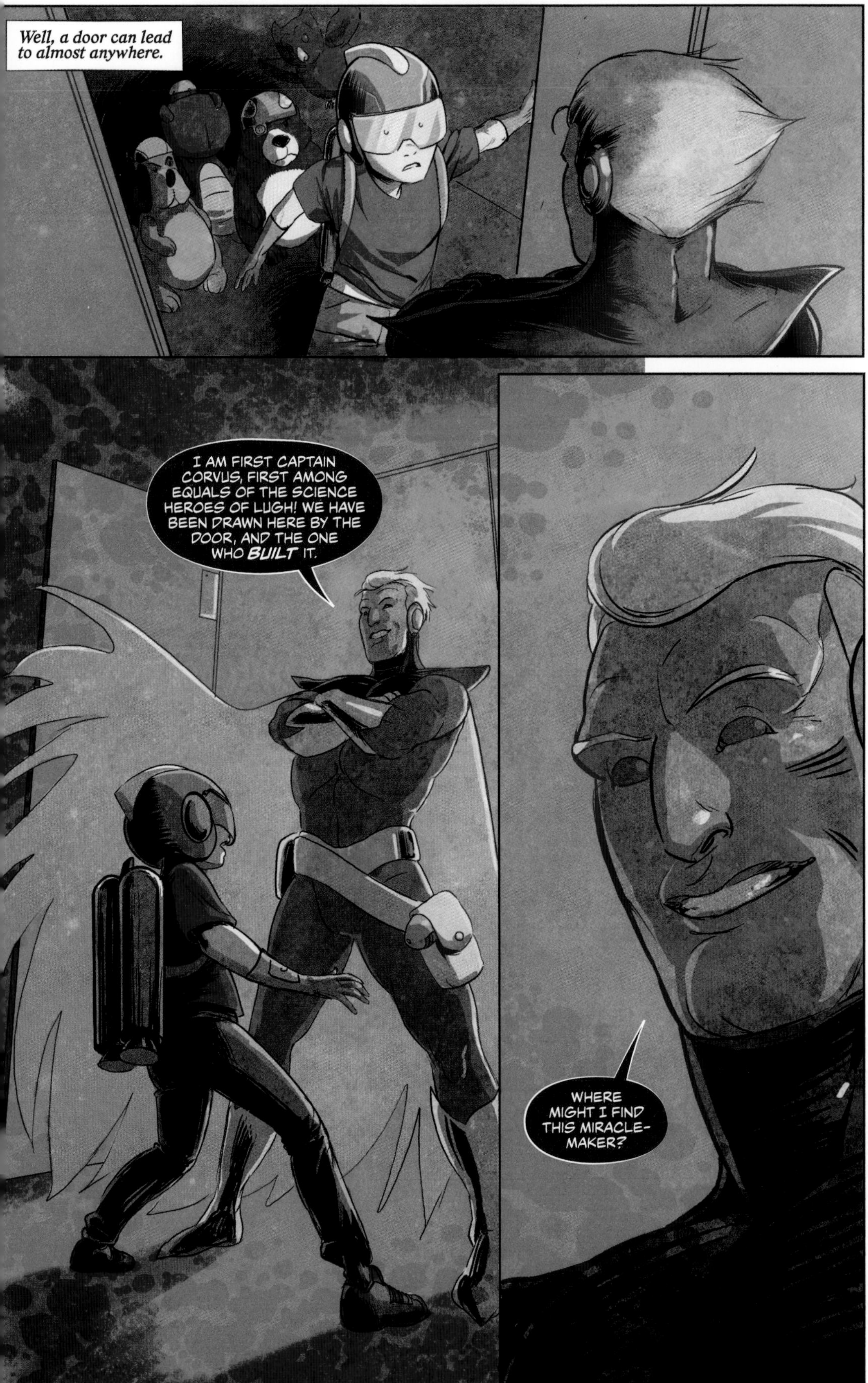
Well, a door can lead to almost anywhere.
I AM FIRST CAPTAIN CORVUS, FIRST AMONG EQUALS OF THE SCIENCE HEROES OF LUGH! WE HAVE BEEN DRAWN HERE BY THE DOOR, AND THE ONE WHO BUILT IT.
WHERE MIGHT I FIND THIS MIRACLE-MAKER?

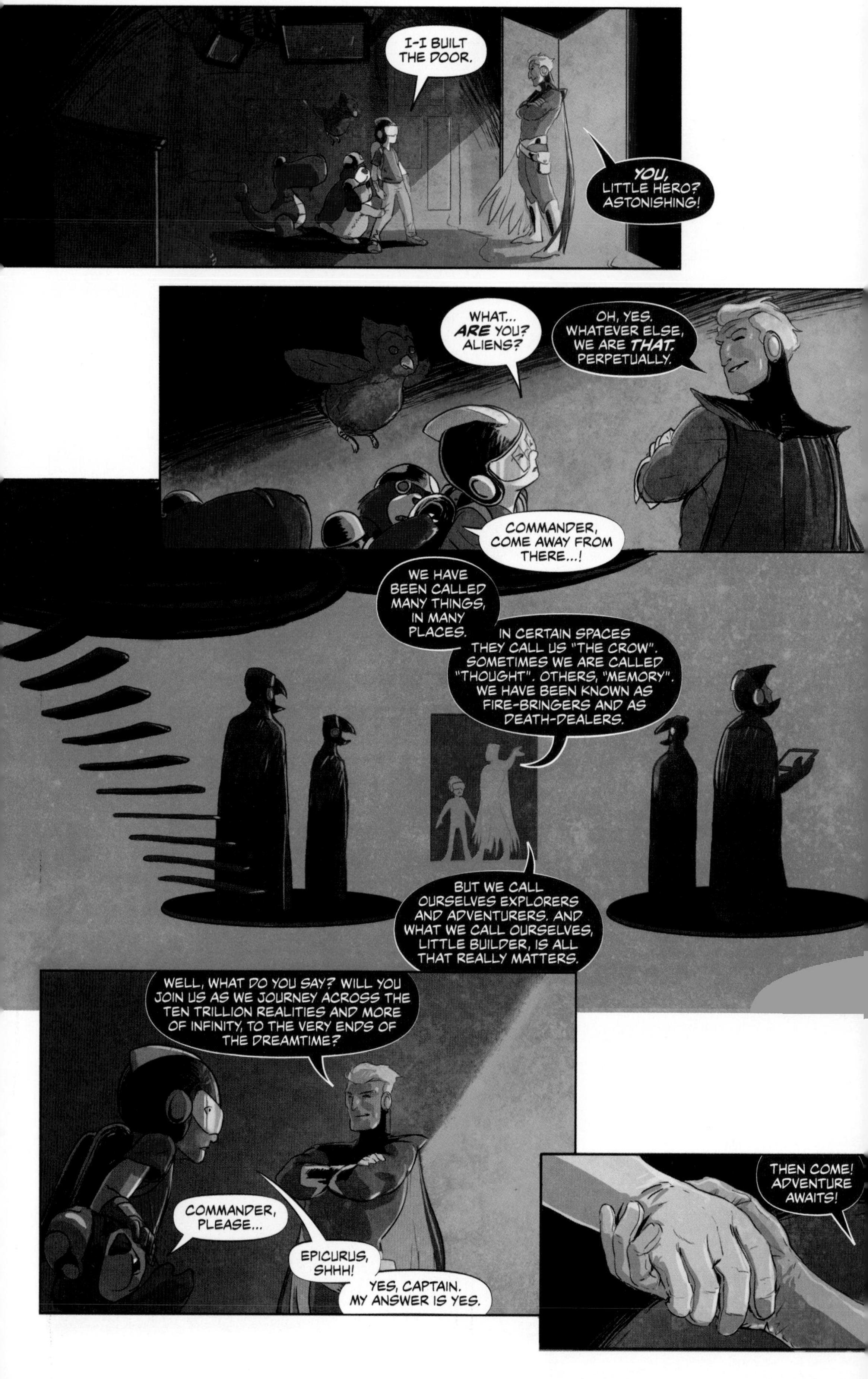
I-I BUILT THE DOOR.
YOU, LITTLE HERO? ASTONISHING!
WHAT... ARE YOU? ALIENS?
OH, YES. WHATEVER ELSE, WE ARE THAT. PERPETUALLY.
COMMANDER, COME AWAY FROM THERE...!
WE HAVE BEEN CALLED MANY THINGS, IN MANY PLACES.
IN CERTAIN SPACES THEY CALL US "THE CROW". SOMETIMES WE ARE CALLED "THOUGHT". OTHERS, "MEMORY". WE HAVE BEEN KNOWN AS FIRE-BRINGERS AND AS DEATH-DEALERS.
BUT WE CALL OURSELVES EXPLORERS AND ADVENTURERS. AND WHAT WE CALL OURSELVES, LITTLE BUILDER, IS ALL THAT REALLY MATTERS.
WELL, WHAT DO YOU SAY? WILL YOU JOIN US AS WE JOURNEY ACROSS THE TEN TRILLION REALITIES AND MORE OF INFINITY, TO THE VERY ENDS OF THE DREAMTIME?
COMMANDER, PLEASE...
EPICURUS, SHHH!
YES, CAPTAIN. MY ANSWER IS YES.
THEN COME! ADVENTURE AWAITS!

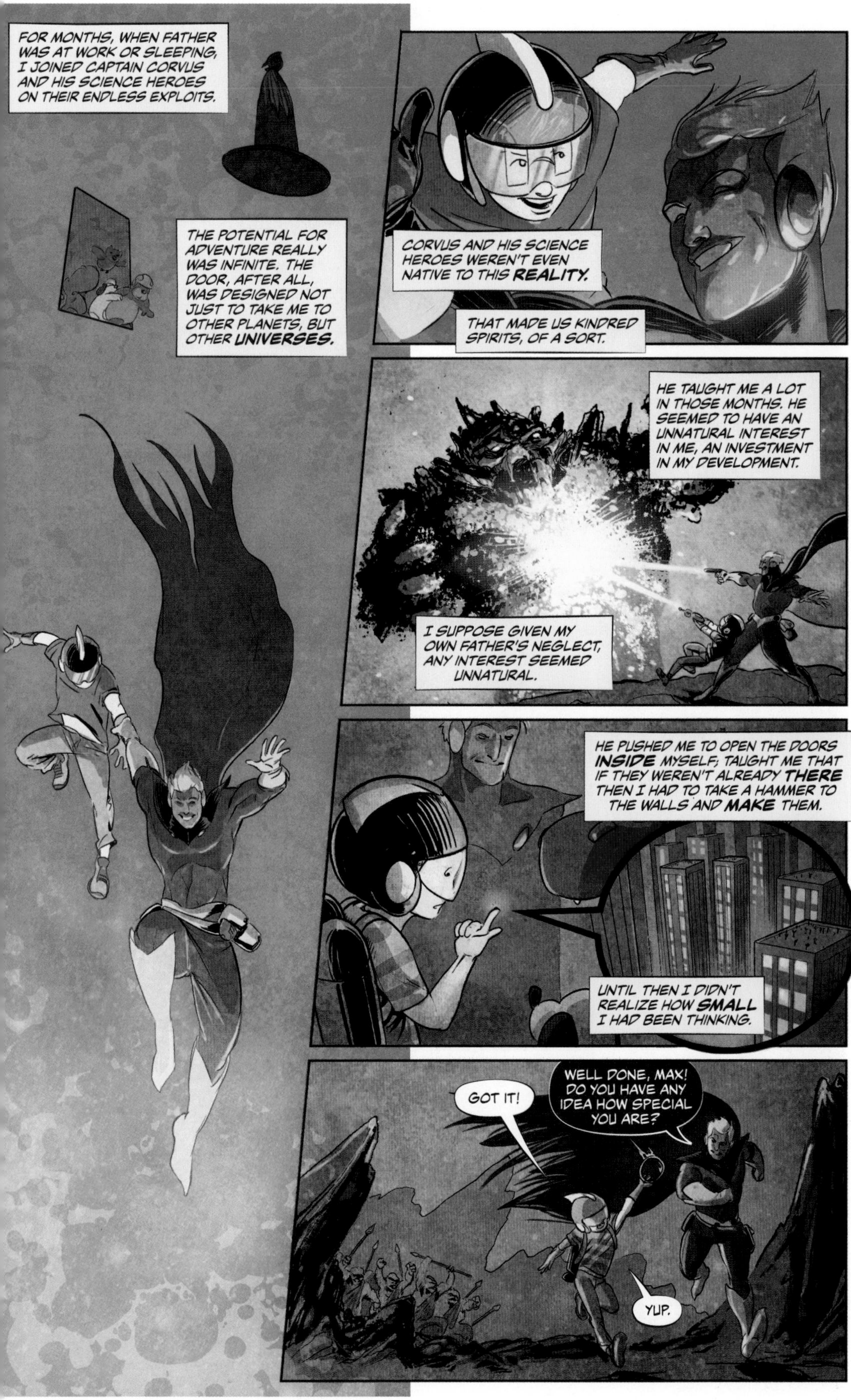

FOR MONTHS, WHEN FATHER WAS AT WORK OR SLEEPING, I JOINED CAPTAIN CORVUS AND HIS SCIENCE HEROES ON THEIR ENDLESS EXPLOITS.
THE POTENTIAL FOR ADVENTURE REALLY WAS INFINITE. THE DOOR, AFTER ALL, WAS DESIGNED NOT JUST TO TAKE ME TO OTHER PLANETS, BUT OTHER **UNIVERSES.**
CORVUS AND HIS SCIENCE HEROES WEREN'T EVEN NATIVE TO THIS **REALITY.**
THAT MADE US KINDRED SPIRITS, OF A SORT.
HE TAUGHT ME A LOT IN THOSE MONTHS. HE SEEMED TO HAVE AN UNNATURAL INTEREST IN ME, AN INVESTMENT IN MY DEVELOPMENT.
I SUPPOSE GIVEN MY OWN FATHER'S NEGLECT, ANY INTEREST SEEMED UNNATURAL.
HE PUSHED ME TO OPEN THE DOORS **INSIDE** MYSELF; TAUGHT ME THAT IF THEY WEREN'T ALREADY **THERE** THEN I HAD TO TAKE A HAMMER TO THE WALLS AND **MAKE** THEM.
UNTIL THEN I DIDN'T REALIZE HOW **SMALL** I HAD BEEN THINKING.
GOT IT!
WELL DONE, MAX! DO YOU HAVE ANY IDEA HOW SPECIAL YOU ARE?
YUP.

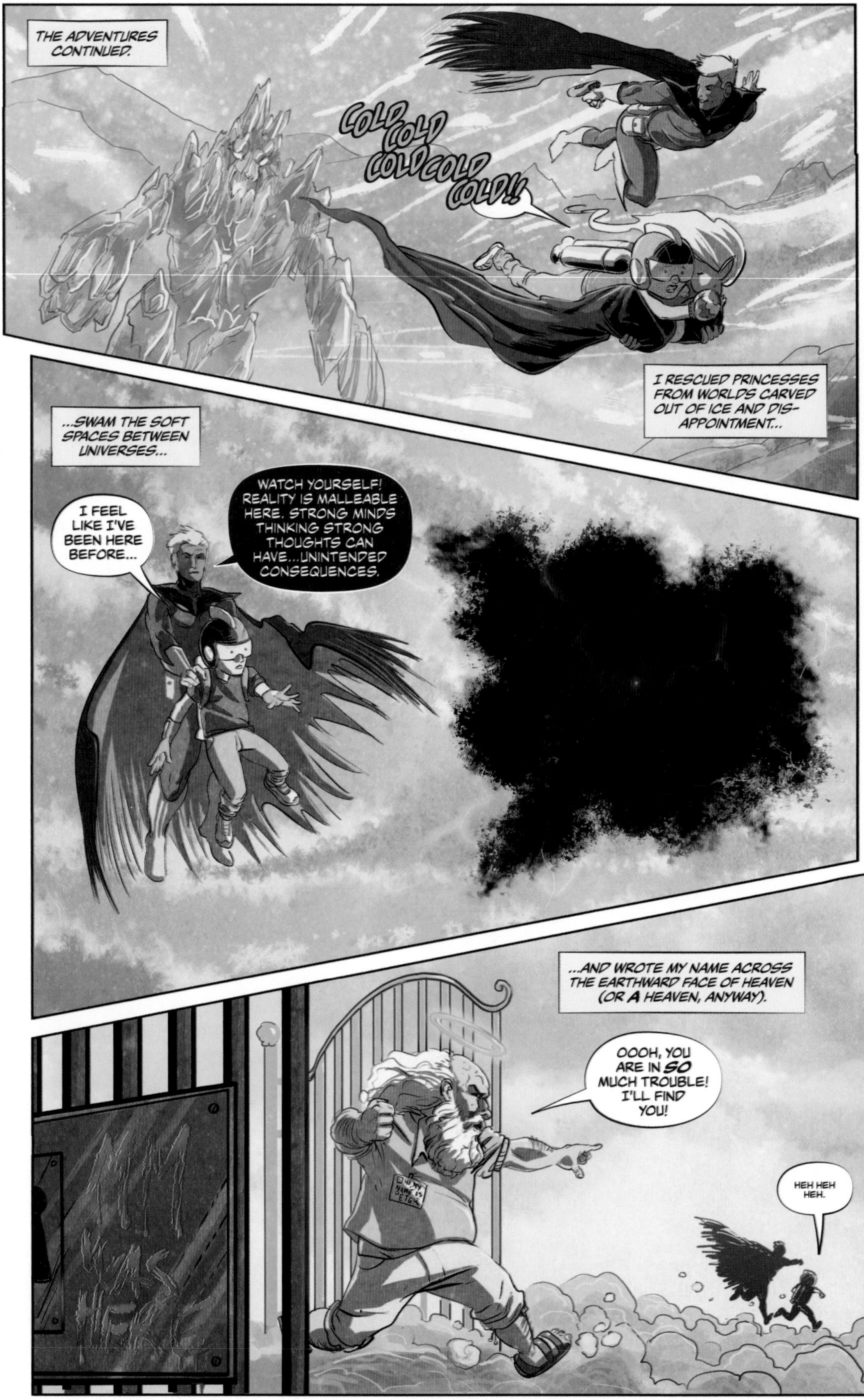
THE ADVENTURES CONTINUED.
COLD COLD COLD COLD COLD COLD!!
I RESCUED PRINCESSES FROM WORLDS CARVED OUT OF ICE AND DIS-APPOINTMENT...
...SWAM THE SOFT SPACES BETWEEN UNIVERSES...
I FEEL LIKE I'VE BEEN HERE BEFORE...
WATCH YOURSELF! REALITY IS MALLEABLE HERE. STRONG MINDS THINKING STRONG THOUGHTS CAN HAVE...UNINTENDED CONSEQUENCES.
...AND WROTE MY NAME ACROSS THE EARTHWARD FACE OF HEAVEN (OR A HEAVEN, ANYWAY).
OOOH, YOU ARE IN SO MUCH TROUBLE! I'LL FIND YOU!
HEH HEH HEH.

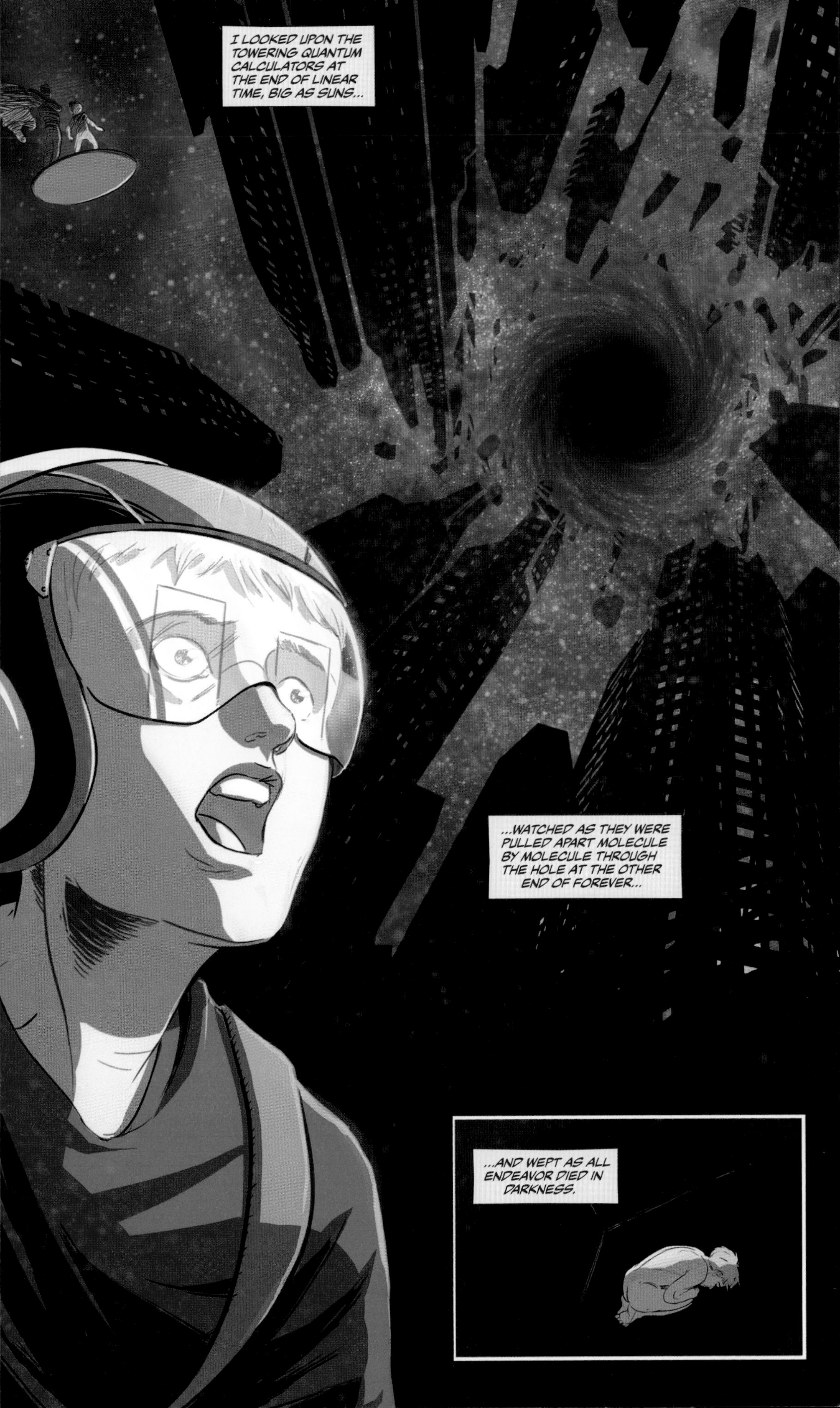
I LOOKED UPON THE TOWERING QUANTUM CALCULATORS AT THE END OF LINEAR TIME, BIG AS SUNS...
...WATCHED AS THEY WERE PULLED APART MOLECULE BY MOLECULE THROUGH THE HOLE AT THE OTHER END OF FOREVER...
...AND WEPT AS ALL ENDEAVOR DIED IN DARKNESS.

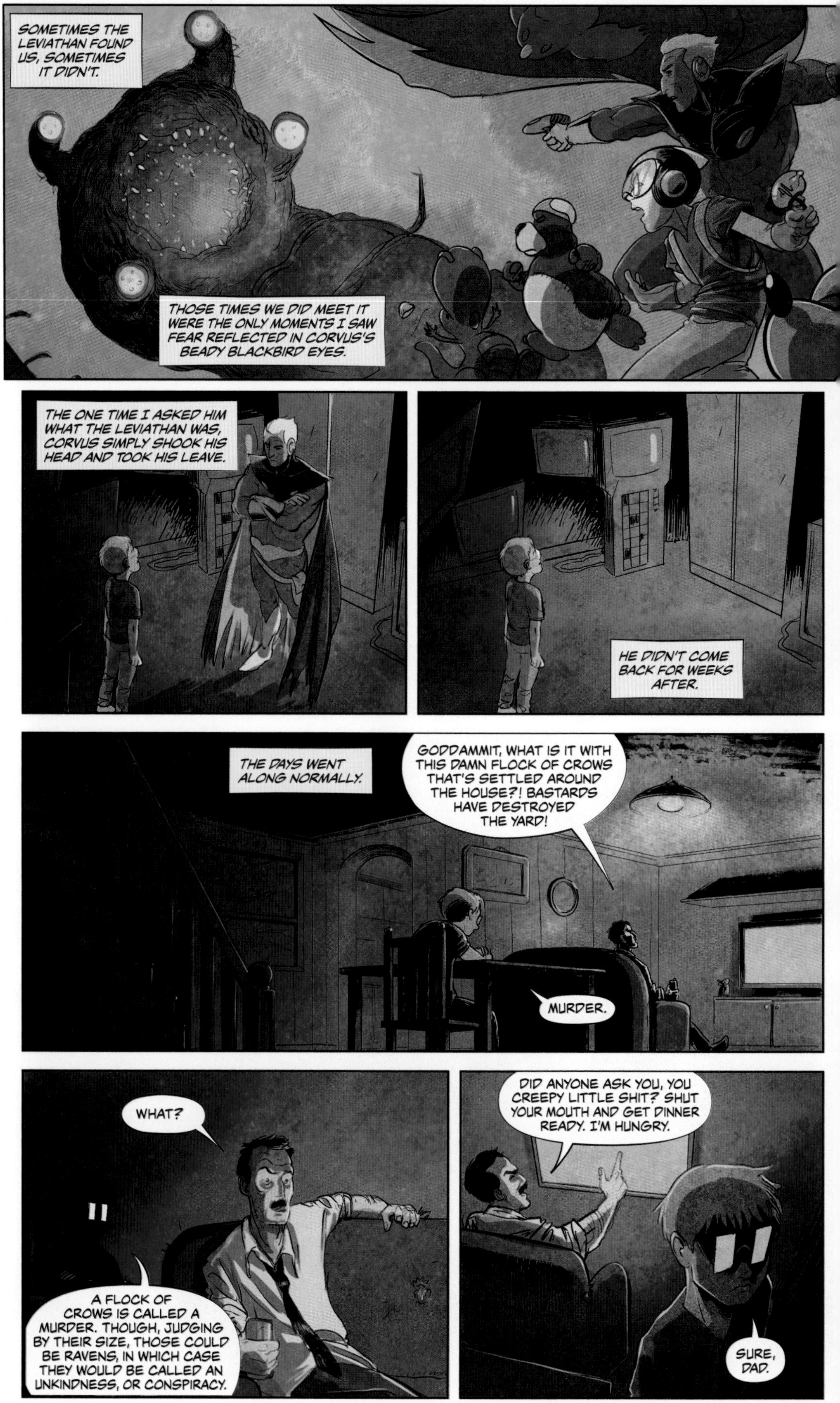
SOMETIMES THE LEVIATHAN FOUND US, SOMETIMES IT DIDN'T.
THOSE TIMES WE DID MEET IT WERE THE ONLY MOMENTS I SAW FEAR REFLECTED IN CORVUS'S BEADY BLACKBIRD EYES.
THE ONE TIME I ASKED HIM WHAT THE LEVIATHAN WAS, CORVUS SIMPLY SHOOK HIS HEAD AND TOOK HIS LEAVE.
HE DIDN'T COME BACK FOR WEEKS AFTER.
THE DAYS WENT ALONG NORMALLY.
GODDAMMIT, WHAT IS IT WITH THIS DAMN FLOCK OF CROWS THAT'S SETTLED AROUND THE HOUSE?! BASTARDS HAVE DESTROYED THE YARD!
MURDER.
WHAT?
A FLOCK OF CROWS IS CALLED A MURDER. THOUGH, JUDGING BY THEIR SIZE, THOSE COULD BE RAVENS, IN WHICH CASE THEY WOULD BE CALLED AN UNKINDNESS, OR CONSPIRACY.
DID ANYONE ASK YOU, YOU CREEPY LITTLE SHIT? SHUT YOUR MOUTH AND GET DINNER READY. I'M HUNGRY.
SURE, DAD.

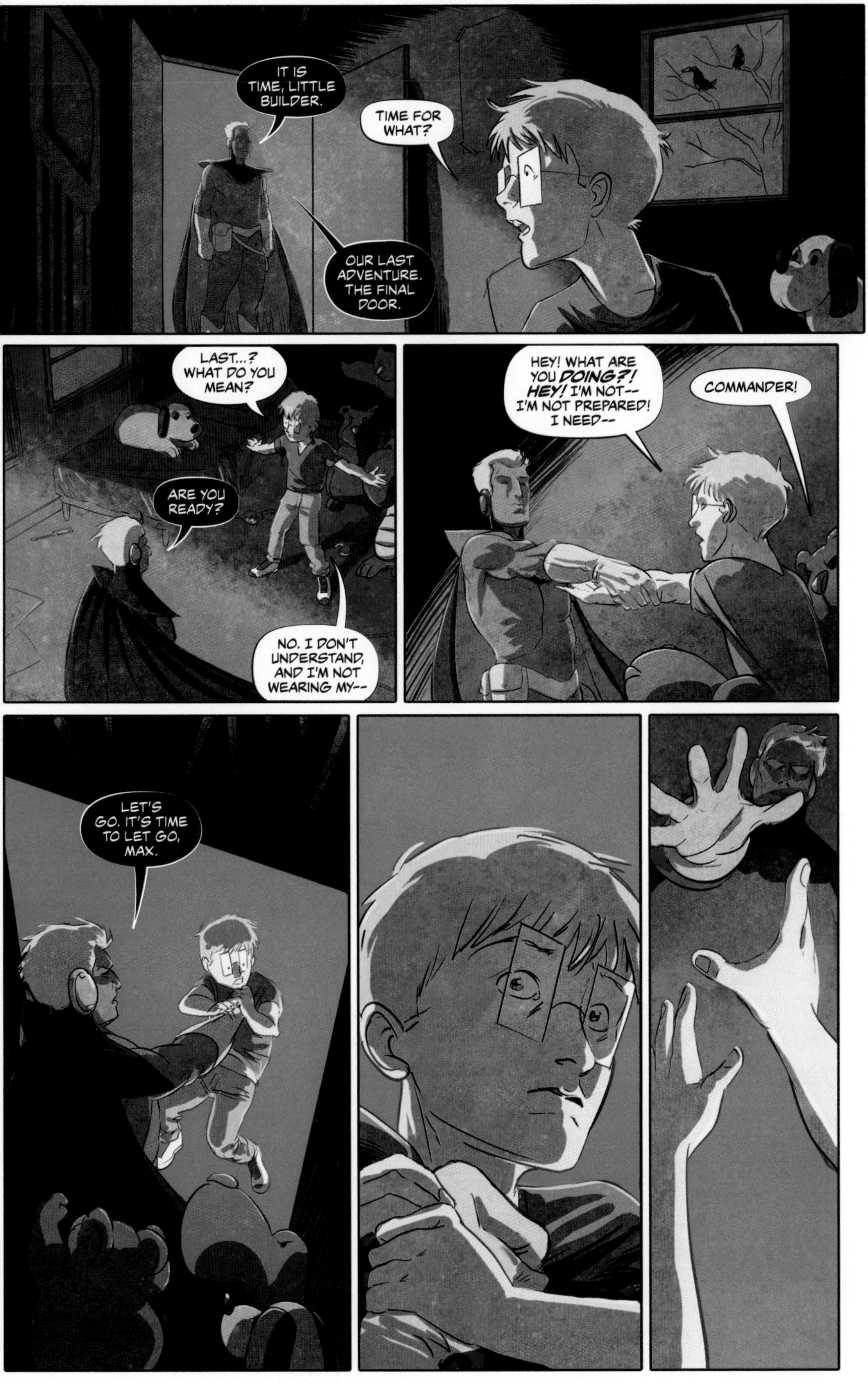
IT IS TIME, LITTLE BUILDER.
TIME FOR WHAT?
OUR LAST ADVENTURE. THE FINAL DOOR.
LAST...? WHAT DO YOU MEAN?
ARE YOU READY?
NO. I DON'T UNDERSTAND, AND I'M NOT WEARING MY--
HEY! WHAT ARE YOU DOING?! HEY! I'M NOT-- I'M NOT PREPARED! I NEED--
COMMANDER!
LET'S GO. IT'S TIME TO LET GO, MAX.

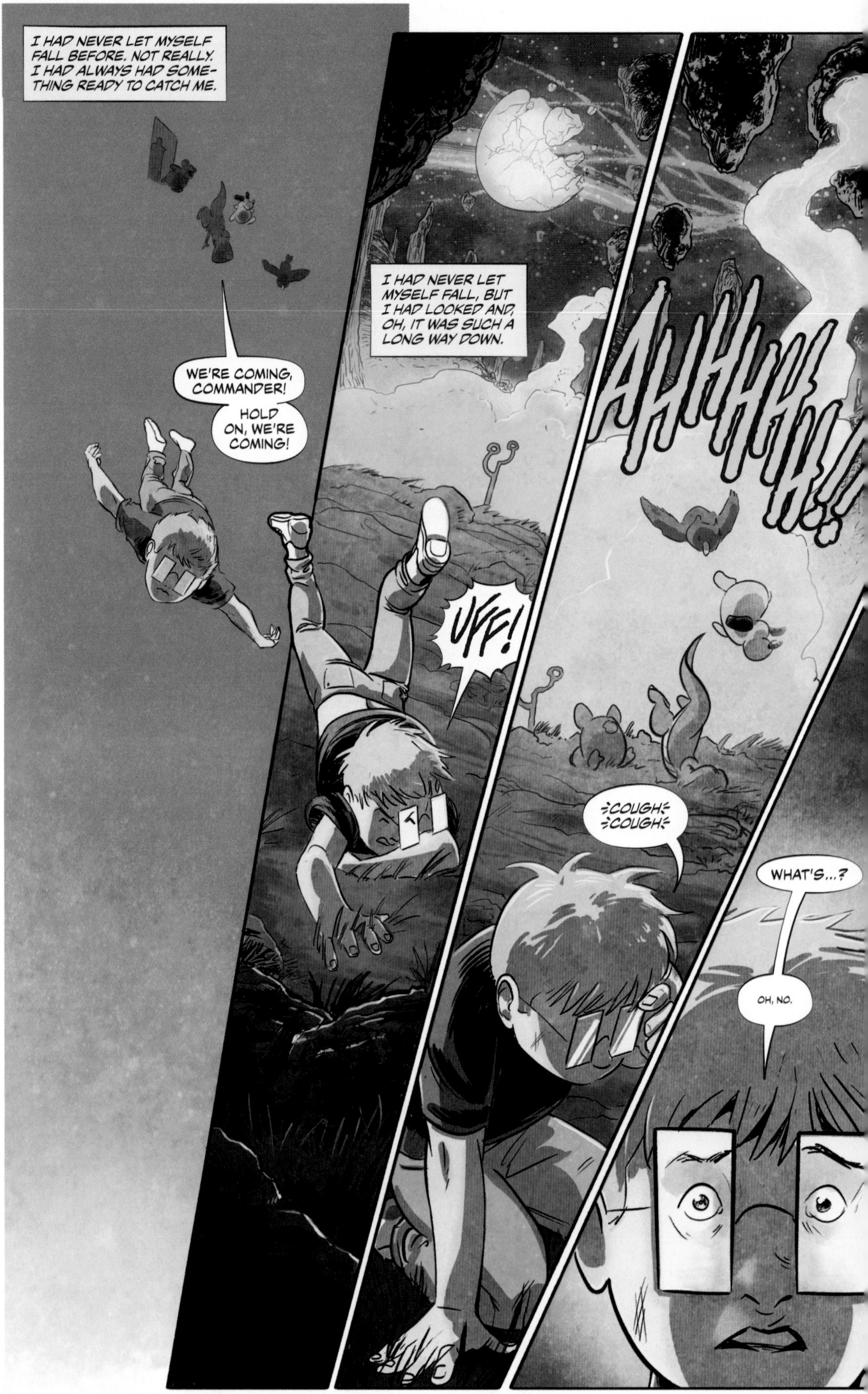
I HAD NEVER LET MYSELF FALL BEFORE. NOT REALLY. I HAD ALWAYS HAD SOMETHING READY TO CATCH ME.
WE'RE COMING, COMMANDER!
HOLD ON, WE'RE COMING!
I HAD NEVER LET MYSELF FALL, BUT I HAD LOOKED AND, OH, IT WAS SUCH A LONG WAY DOWN.
UFF!
AHHHH!!
COUGH COUGH
WHAT'S...?
OH, NO.

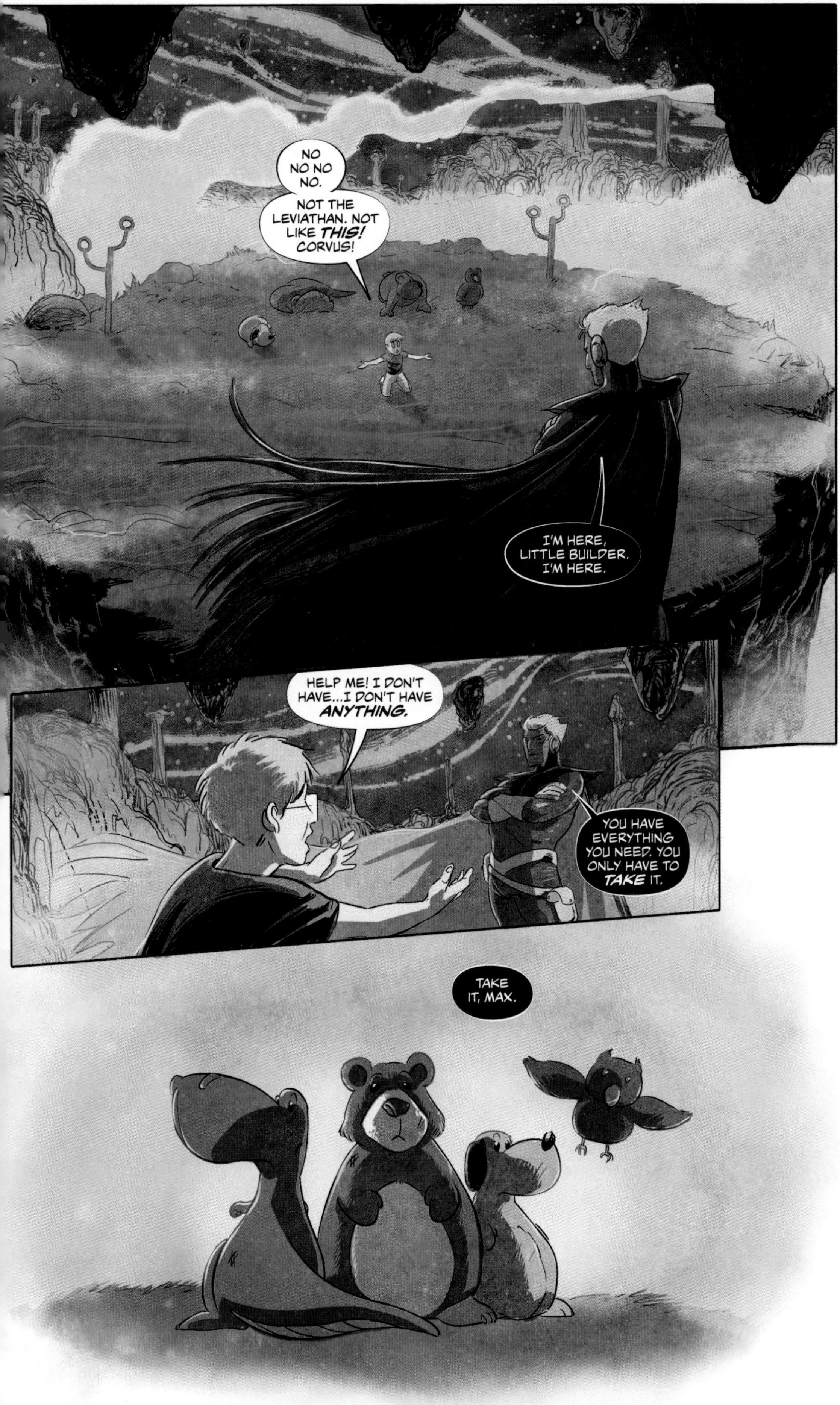

NO NO NO NO.
NOT THE LEVIATHAN. NOT LIKE *THIS!* CORVUS!
I'M HERE, LITTLE BUILDER. I'M HERE.
HELP ME! I DON'T HAVE...I DON'T HAVE *ANYTHING.*
YOU HAVE EVERYTHING YOU NEED. YOU ONLY HAVE TO *TAKE* IT.
TAKE IT, MAX.

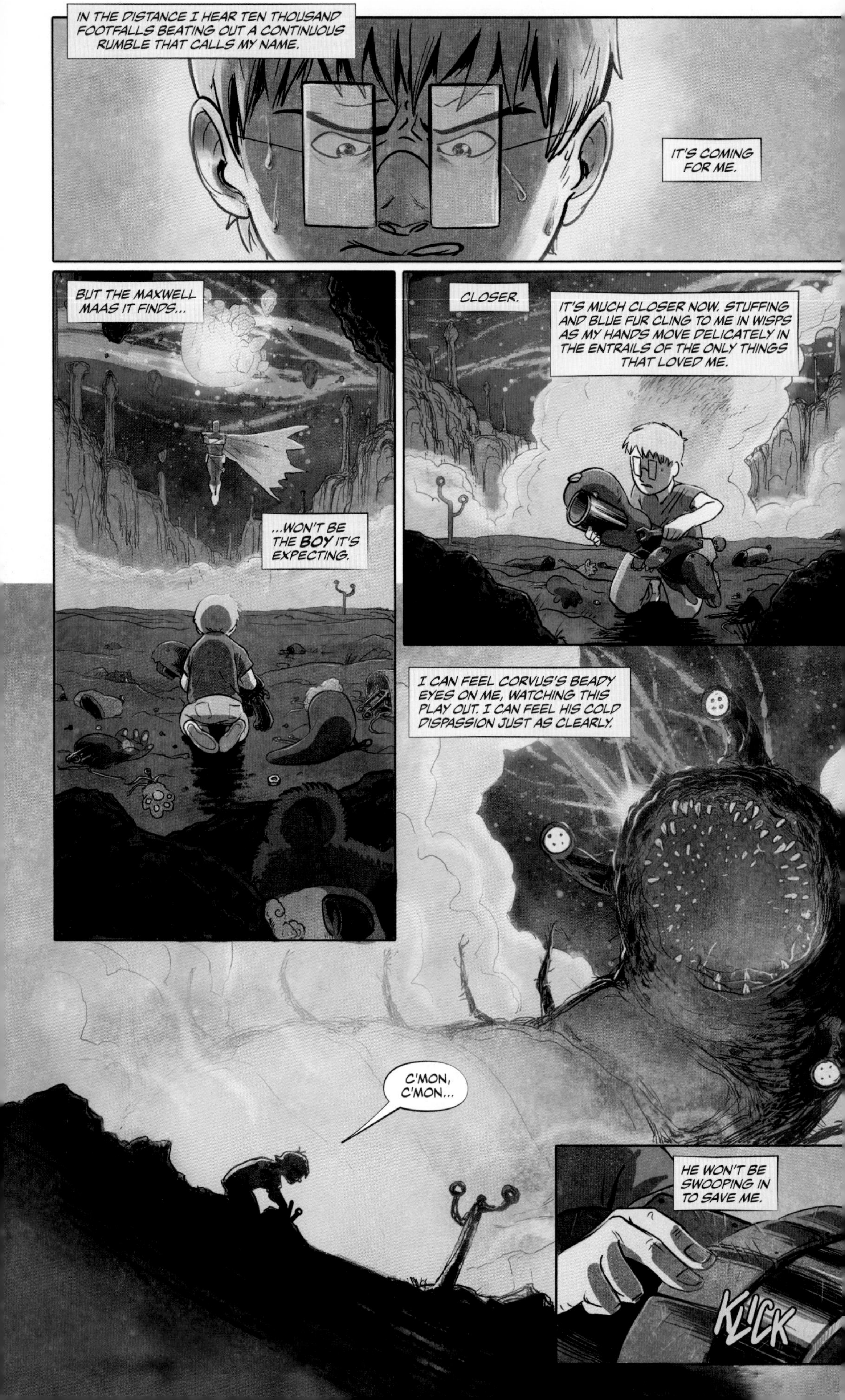
IN THE DISTANCE I HEAR TEN THOUSAND FOOTFALLS BEATING OUT A CONTINUOUS RUMBLE THAT CALLS MY NAME.
IT'S COMING FOR ME.
BUT THE MAXWELL MAAS IT FINDS...
...WON'T BE THE **BOY** IT'S EXPECTING.
CLOSER.
IT'S MUCH CLOSER NOW. STUFFING AND BLUE FUR CLING TO ME IN WISPS AS MY HANDS MOVE DELICATELY IN THE ENTRAILS OF THE ONLY THINGS THAT LOVED ME.
I CAN FEEL CORVUS'S BEADY EYES ON ME, WATCHING THIS PLAY OUT. I CAN FEEL HIS COLD DISPASSION JUST AS CLEARLY.
C'MON, C'MON...
HE WON'T BE SWOOPING IN TO SAVE ME.
KLICK

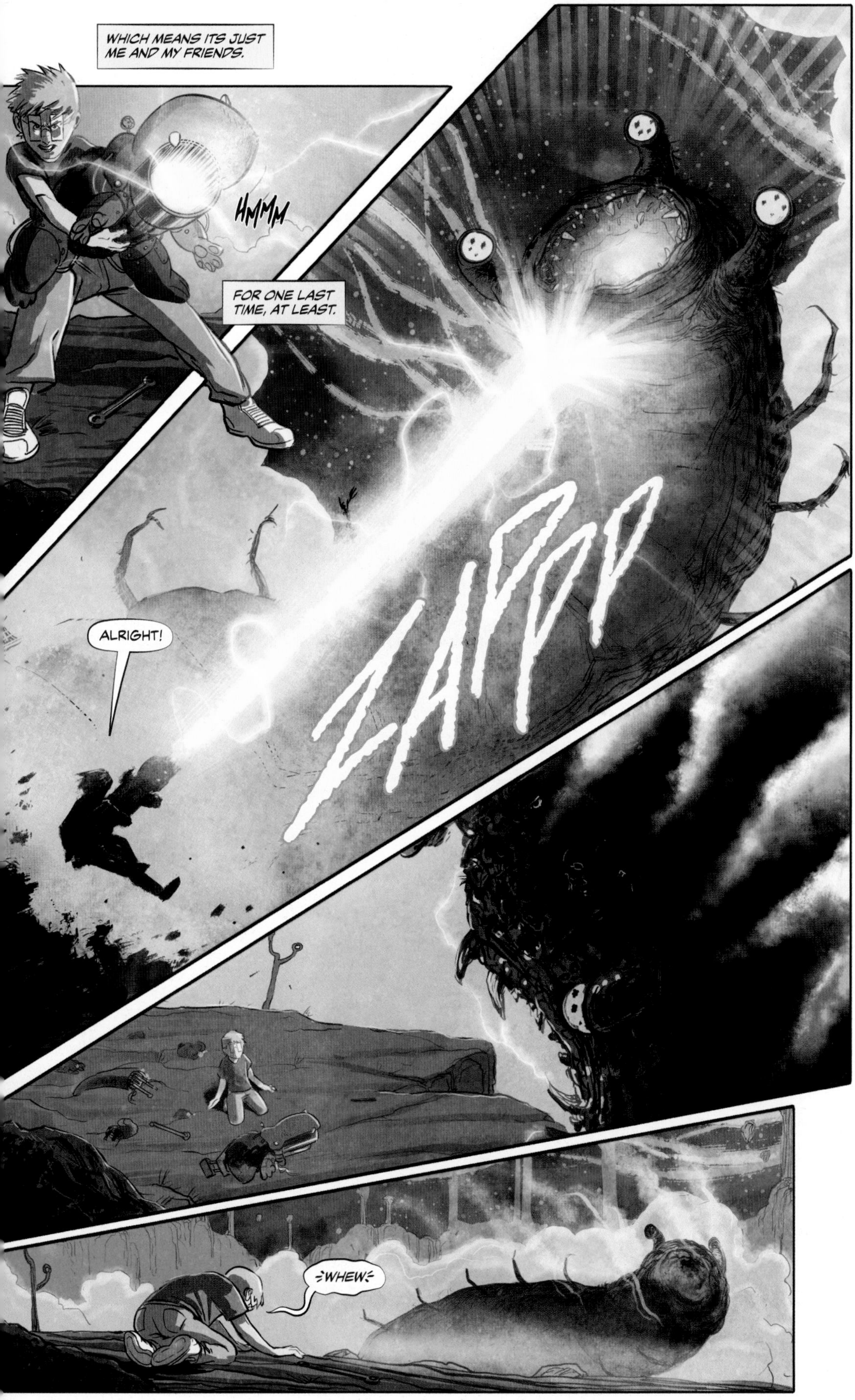
WHICH MEANS ITS JUST ME AND MY FRIENDS.
HMMM
FOR ONE LAST TIME, AT LEAST.
ALRIGHT!
ZAPPP
WHEW

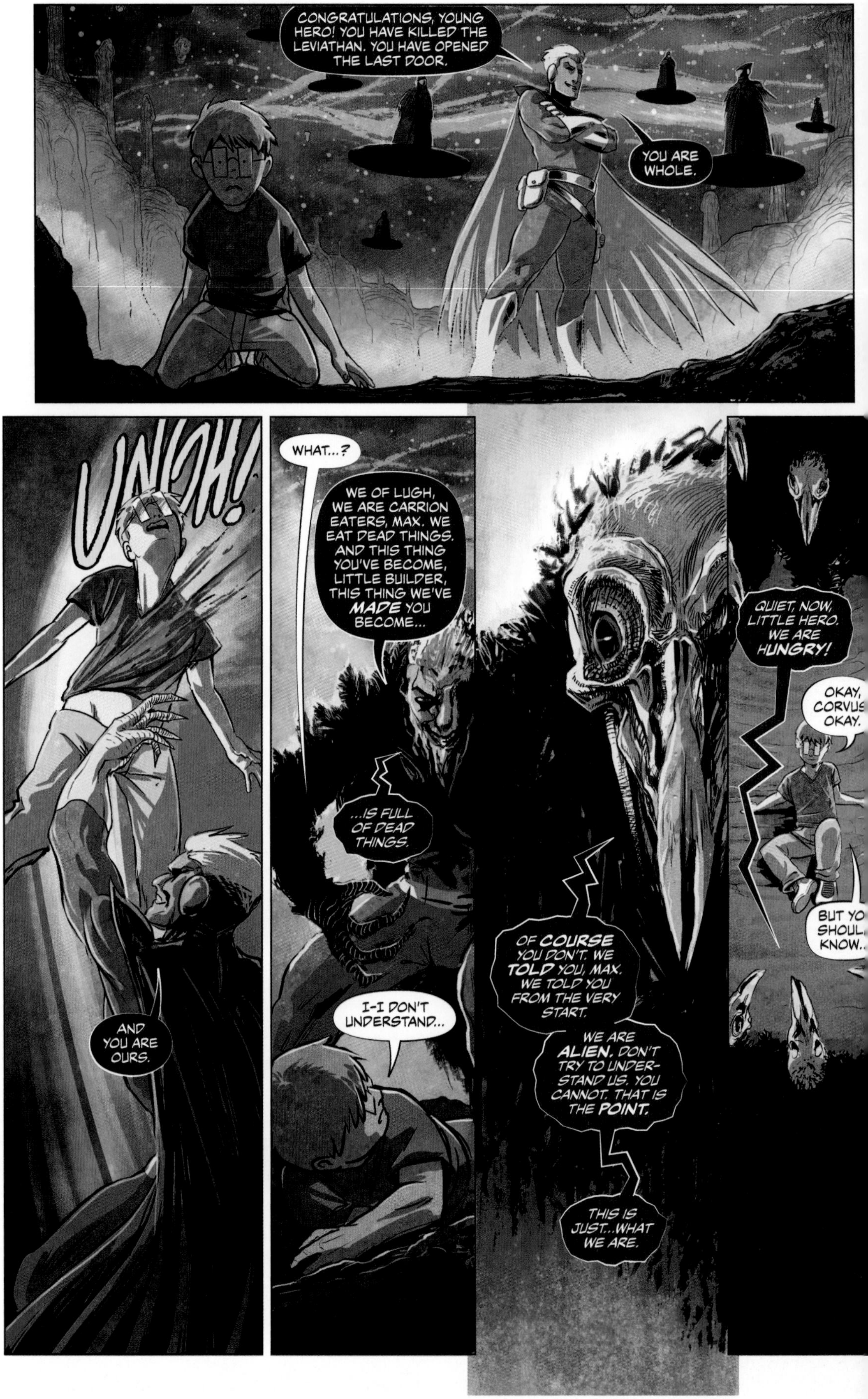
CONGRATULATIONS, YOUNG HERO! YOU HAVE KILLED THE LEVIATHAN. YOU HAVE OPENED THE LAST DOOR.
YOU ARE WHOLE.
UNGH!
AND YOU ARE OURS.
WHAT...?
WE OF LUGH, WE ARE CARRION EATERS, MAX. WE EAT DEAD THINGS. AND THIS THING YOU'VE BECOME, LITTLE BUILDER, THIS THING WE'VE MADE YOU BECOME...
...IS FULL OF DEAD THINGS.
I-I DON'T UNDERSTAND...
OF COURSE YOU DON'T. WE TOLD YOU, MAX. WE TOLD YOU FROM THE VERY START.
WE ARE ALIEN. DON'T TRY TO UNDERSTAND US. YOU CANNOT. THAT IS THE POINT.
THIS IS JUST...WHAT WE ARE.
QUIET, NOW, LITTLE HERO. WE ARE HUNGRY!
OKAY, CORVUS OKAY.
BUT YO SHOUL KNOW...

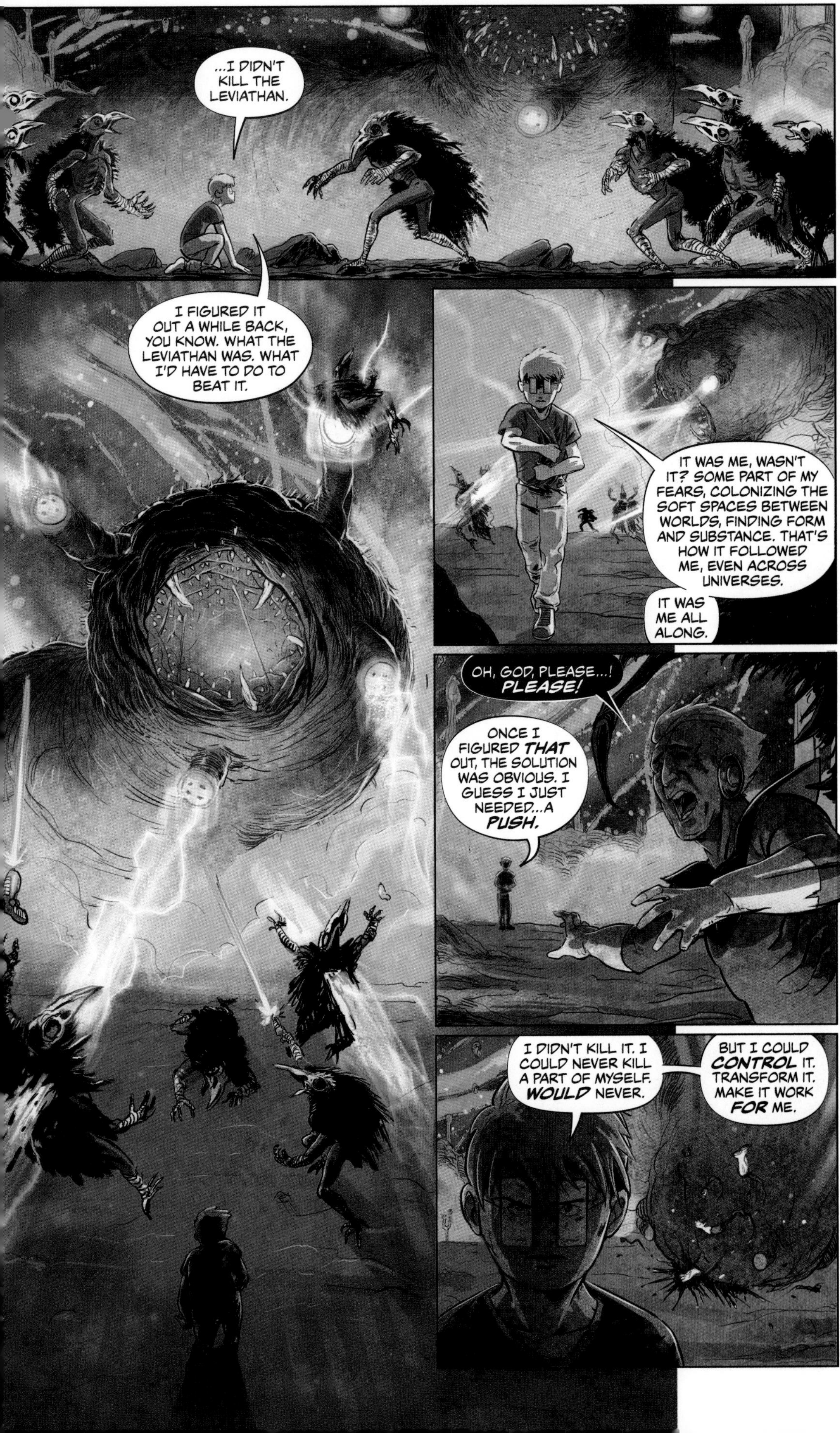
...I DIDN'T KILL THE LEVIATHAN.
I FIGURED IT OUT A WHILE BACK, YOU KNOW. WHAT THE LEVIATHAN WAS. WHAT I'D HAVE TO DO TO BEAT IT.
IT WAS ME, WASN'T IT? SOME PART OF MY FEARS, COLONIZING THE SOFT SPACES BETWEEN WORLDS, FINDING FORM AND SUBSTANCE. THAT'S HOW IT FOLLOWED ME, EVEN ACROSS UNIVERSES.
IT WAS ME ALL ALONG.
OH, GOD, PLEASE...! PLEASE!
ONCE I FIGURED THAT OUT, THE SOLUTION WAS OBVIOUS. I GUESS I JUST NEEDED...A PUSH.
I DIDN'T KILL IT. I COULD NEVER KILL A PART OF MYSELF. WOULD NEVER.
BUT I COULD CONTROL IT. TRANSFORM IT. MAKE IT WORK FOR ME.

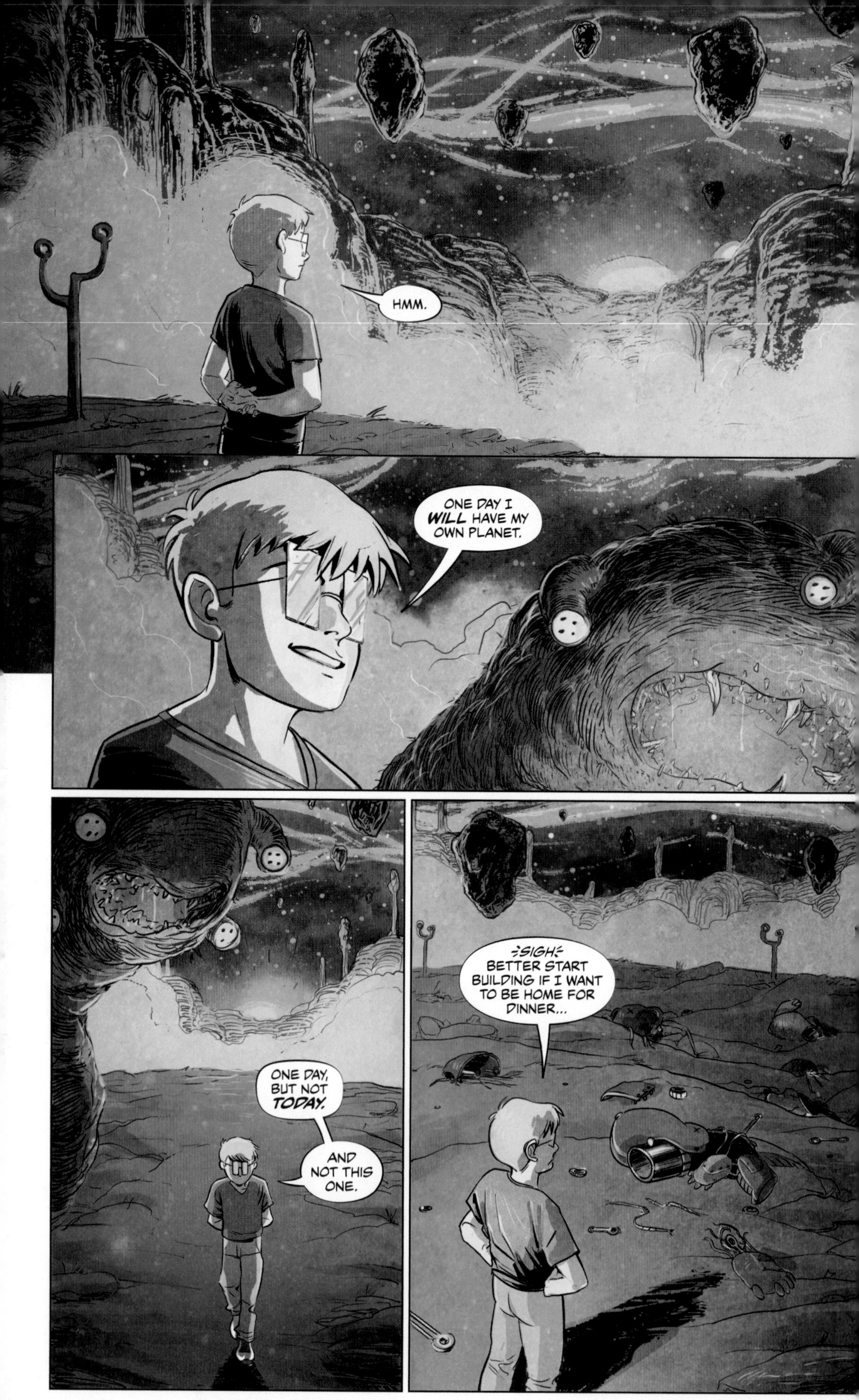
HMM.
ONE DAY I WILL HAVE MY OWN PLANET.
ONE DAY, BUT NOT TODAY.
AND NOT THIS ONE.
SIGH
BETTER START BUILDING IF I WANT TO BE HOME FOR DINNER...

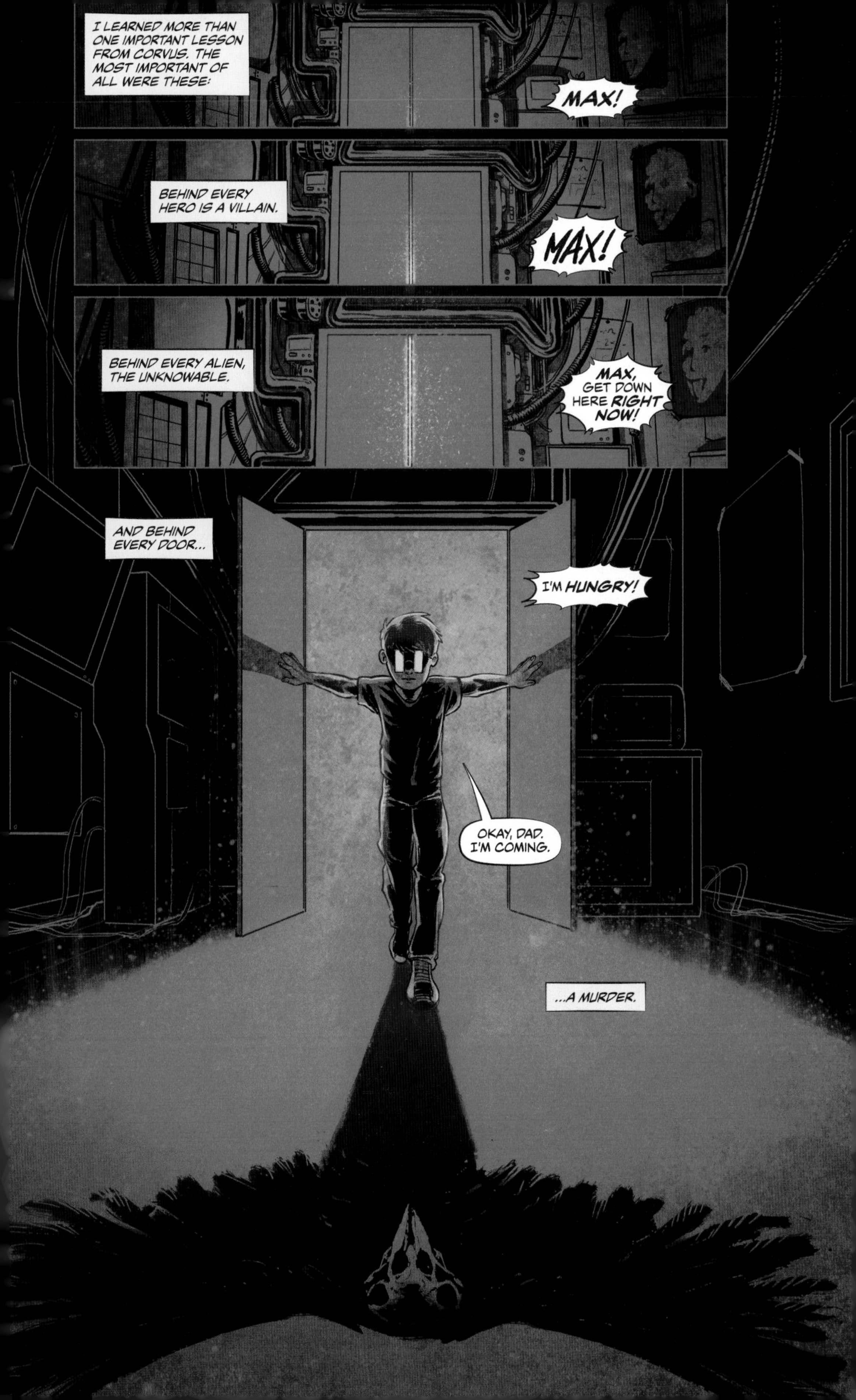

I LEARNED MORE THAN ONE IMPORTANT LESSON FROM CORVUS. THE MOST IMPORTANT OF ALL WERE THESE:
MAX!
BEHIND EVERY HERO IS A VILLAIN.
MAX!
BEHIND EVERY ALIEN, THE UNKNOWABLE.
MAX, GET DOWN HERE RIGHT NOW!
AND BEHIND EVERY DOOR...
I'M HUNGRY!
OKAY, DAD. I'M COMING.
...A MURDER.

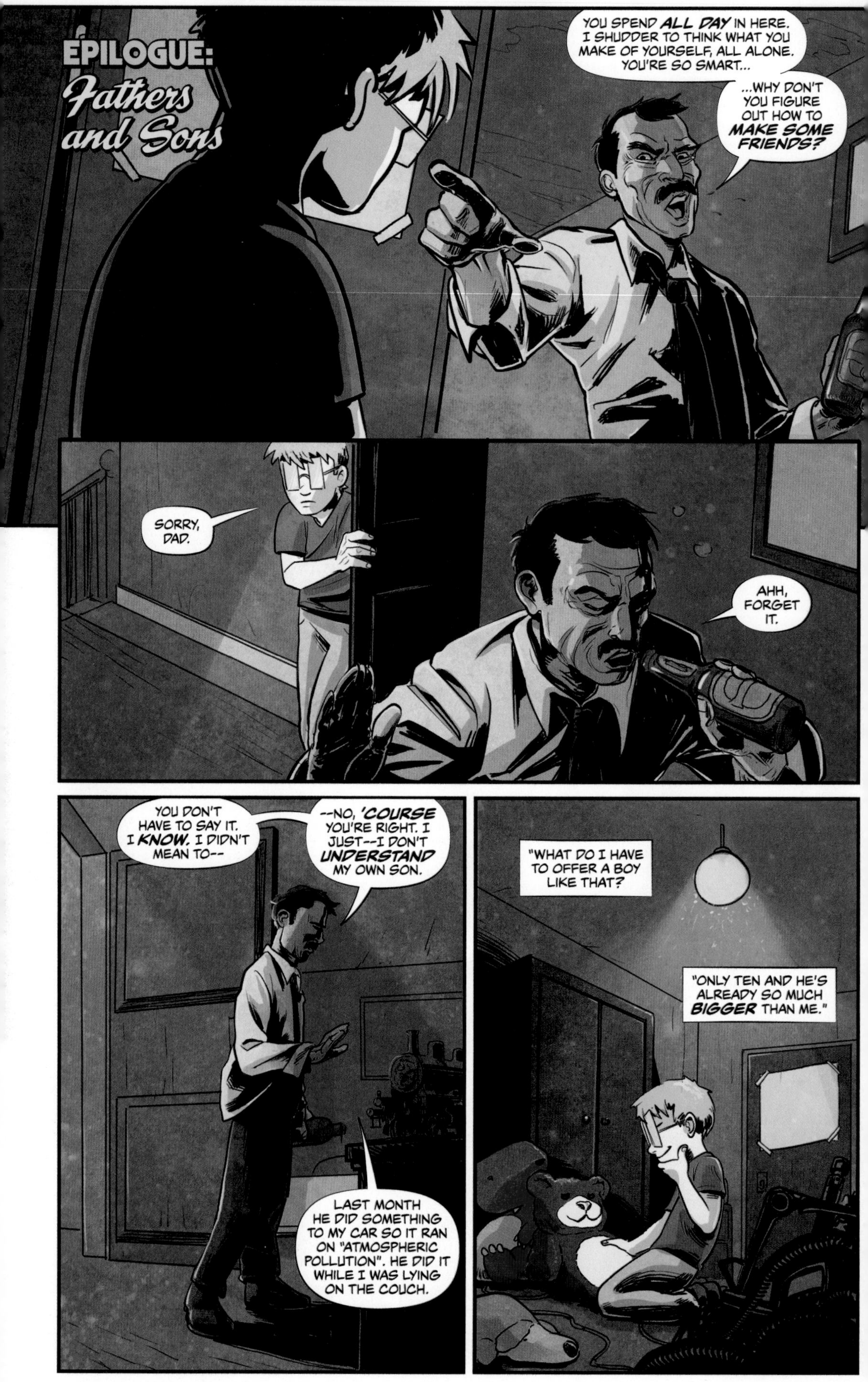
EPILOGUE:
Fathers and Sons
YOU SPEND ALL DAY IN HERE. I SHUDDER TO THINK WHAT YOU MAKE OF YOURSELF, ALL ALONE. YOU'RE SO SMART...
...WHY DON'T YOU FIGURE OUT HOW TO MAKE SOME FRIENDS?
SORRY, DAD.
AHH, FORGET IT.
YOU DON'T HAVE TO SAY IT. I KNOW. I DIDN'T MEAN TO--
--NO, 'COURSE YOU'RE RIGHT. I JUST--I DON'T UNDERSTAND MY OWN SON.
LAST MONTH HE DID SOMETHING TO MY CAR SO IT RAN ON "ATMOSPHERIC POLLUTION". HE DID IT WHILE I WAS LYING ON THE COUCH.
"WHAT DO I HAVE TO OFFER A BOY LIKE THAT?
"ONLY TEN AND HE'S ALREADY SO MUCH BIGGER THAN ME."

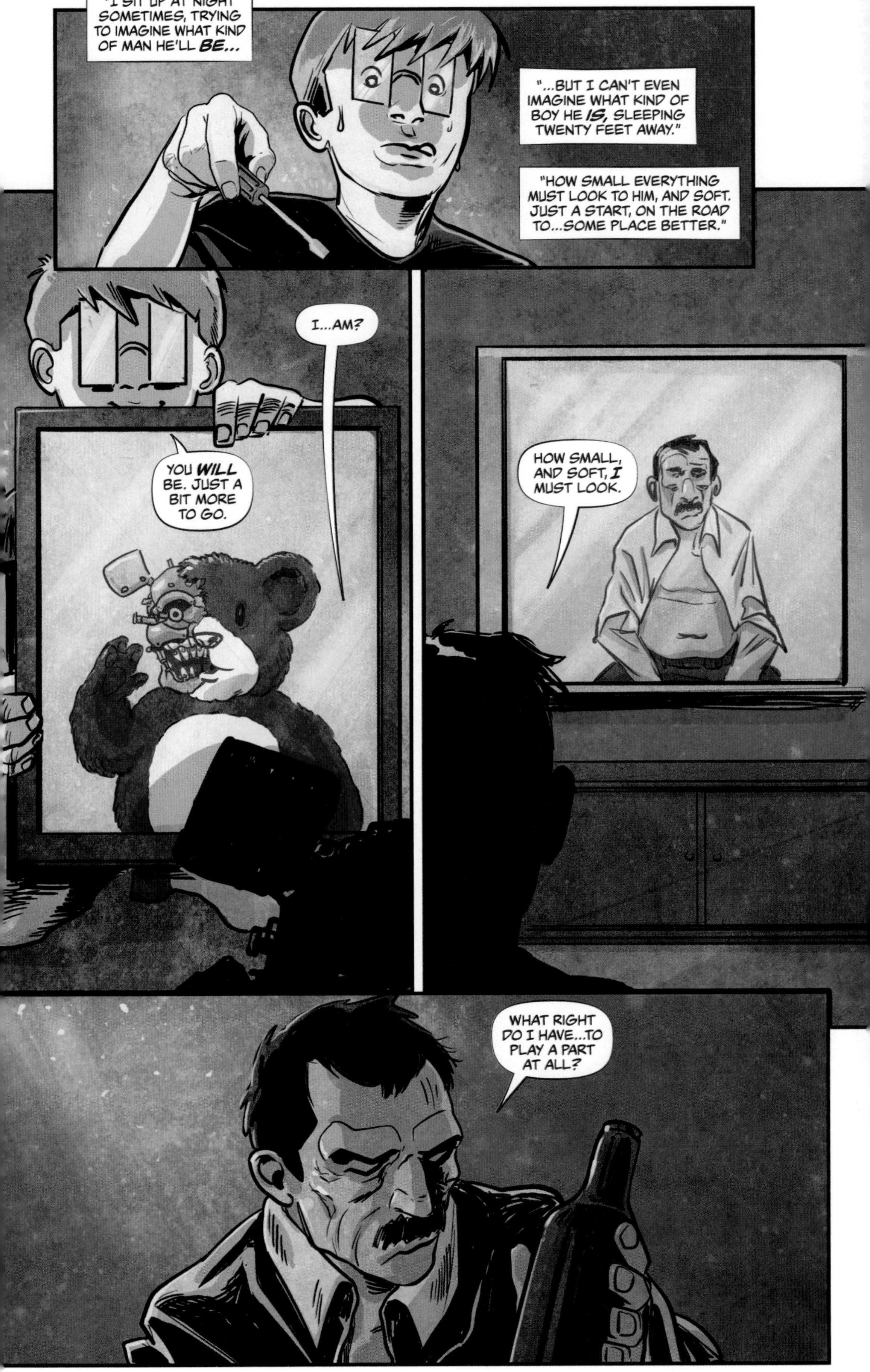
"I SIT UP AT NIGHT SOMETIMES, TRYING TO IMAGINE WHAT KIND OF MAN HE'LL BE...
"...BUT I CAN'T EVEN IMAGINE WHAT KIND OF BOY HE IS, SLEEPING TWENTY FEET AWAY."
"HOW SMALL EVERYTHING MUST LOOK TO HIM, AND SOFT. JUST A START, ON THE ROAD TO...SOME PLACE BETTER."
I...AM?
YOU WILL BE. JUST A BIT MORE TO GO.
HOW SMALL, AND SOFT, I MUST LOOK.
WHAT RIGHT DO I HAVE...TO PLAY A PART AT ALL?

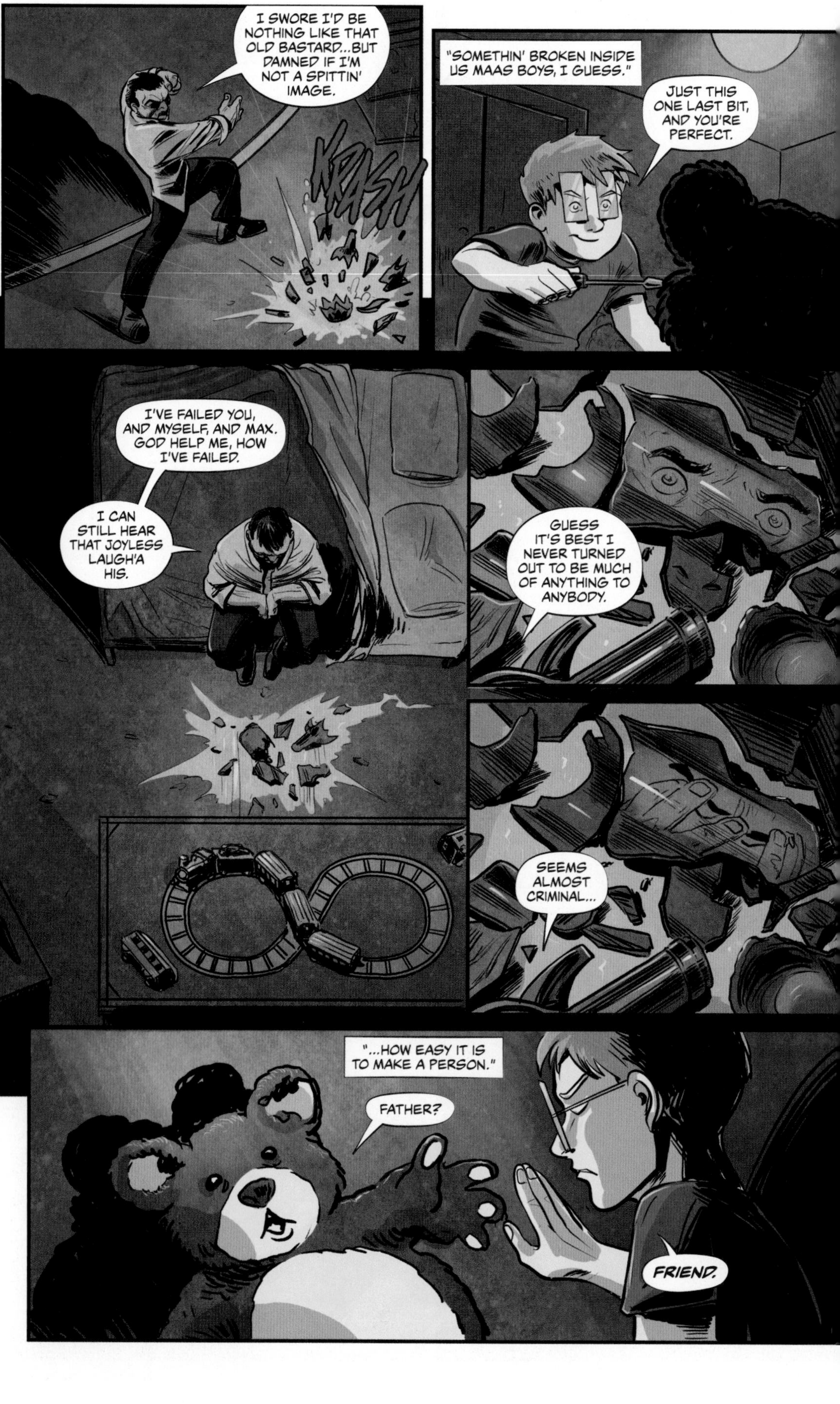
I SWORE I'D BE NOTHING LIKE THAT OLD BASTARD...BUT DAMNED IF I'M NOT A SPITTIN' IMAGE.
KRASH
"SOMETHIN' BROKEN INSIDE US MAAS BOYS, I GUESS."
JUST THIS ONE LAST BIT, AND YOU'RE PERFECT.
I'VE FAILED YOU, AND MYSELF, AND MAX. GOD HELP ME, HOW I'VE FAILED.
I CAN STILL HEAR THAT JOYLESS LAUGH'A HIS.
GUESS IT'S BEST I NEVER TURNED OUT TO BE MUCH OF ANYTHING TO ANYBODY.
SEEMS ALMOST CRIMINAL...
"...HOW EASY IT IS TO MAKE A PERSON."
FATHER?
FRIEND.

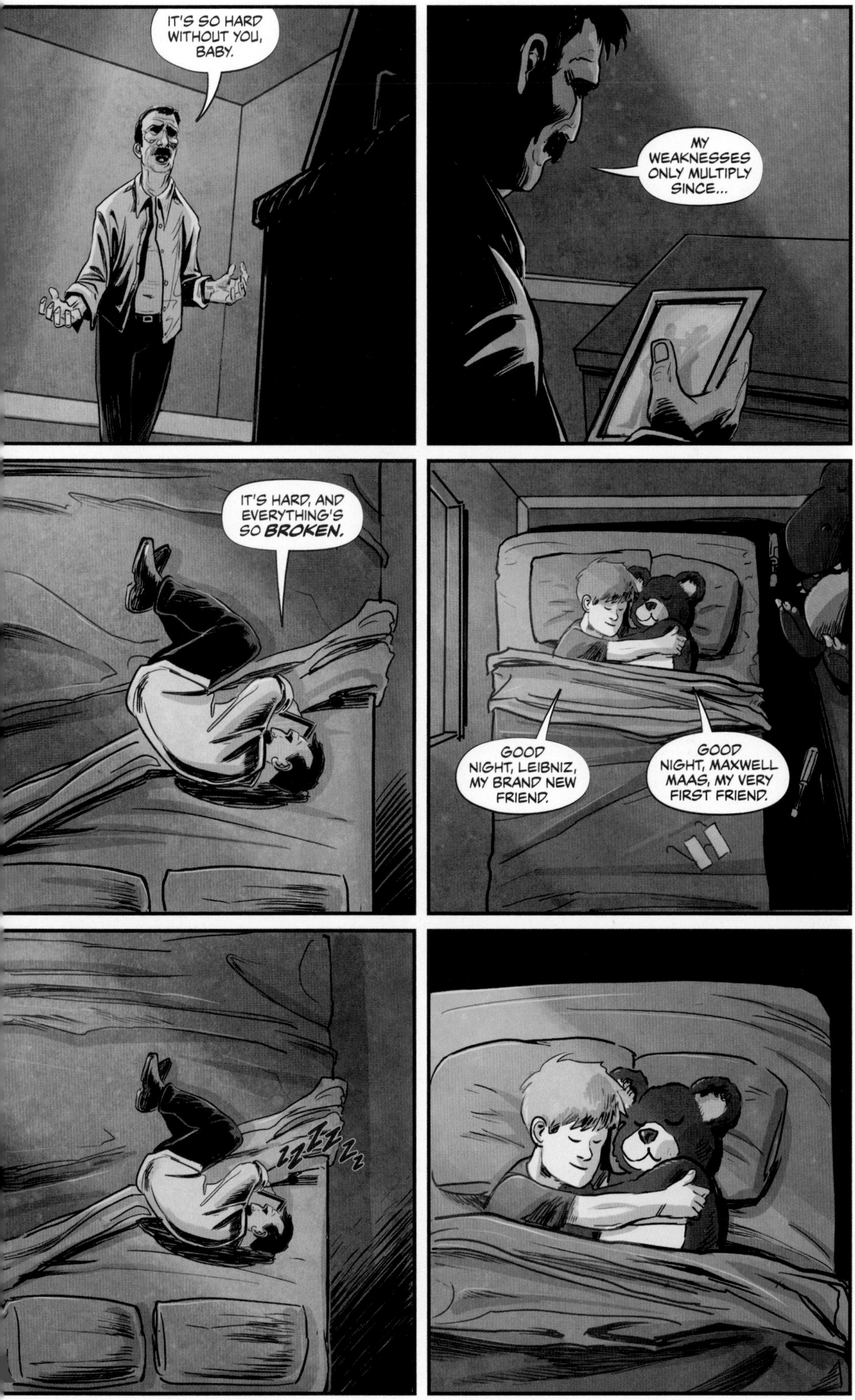
IT'S SO HARD WITHOUT YOU, BABY.
MY WEAKNESSES ONLY MULTIPLY SINCE...
IT'S HARD, AND EVERYTHING'S SO BROKEN.
GOOD NIGHT, LEIBNIZ, MY BRAND NEW FRIEND.
GOOD NIGHT, MAXWELL MAAS, MY VERY FIRST FRIEND.
ZZZZZZ

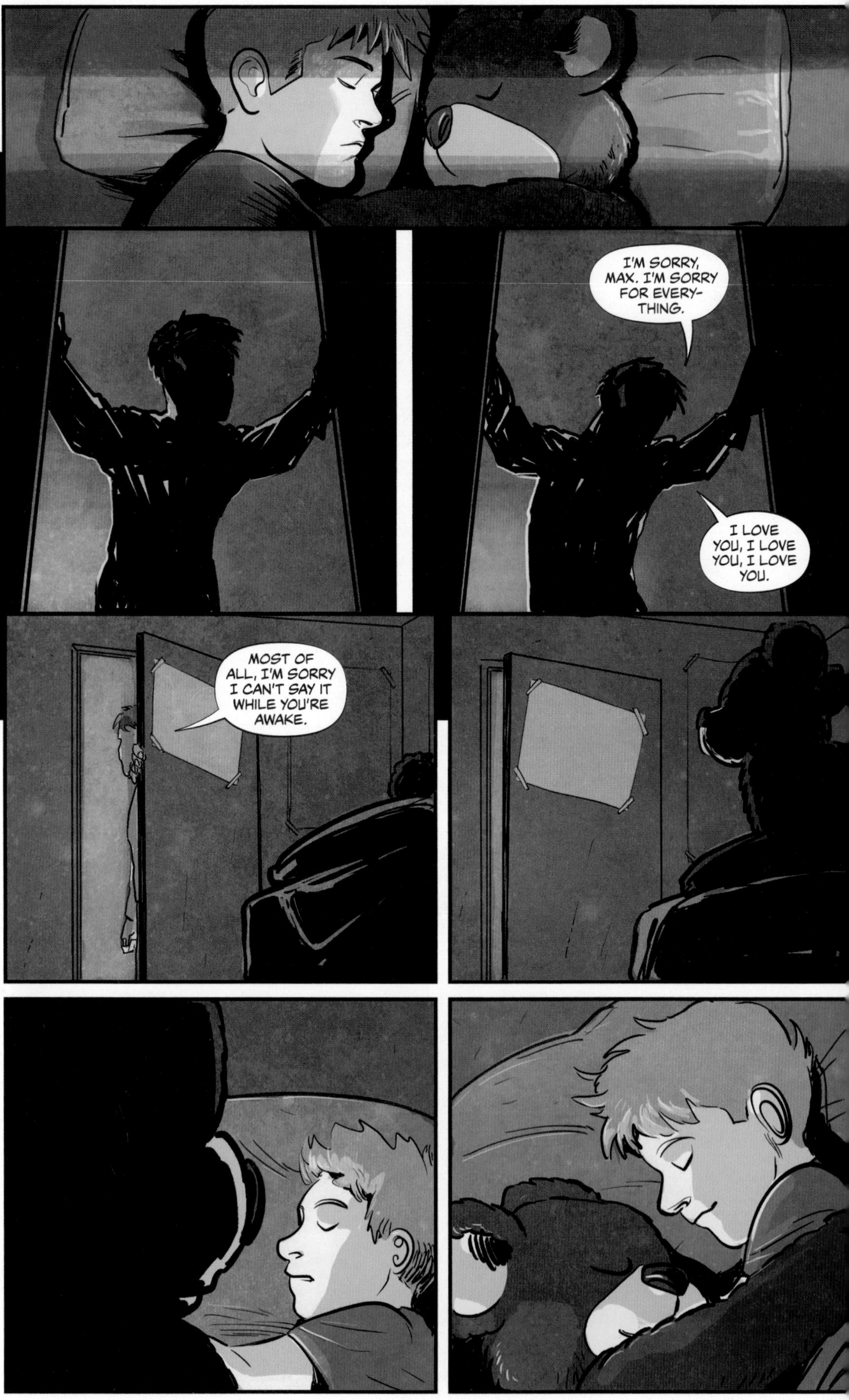
I'M SORRY, MAX. I'M SORRY FOR EVERY-THING.
I LOVE YOU, I LOVE YOU, I LOVE YOU.
MOST OF ALL, I'M SORRY I CAN'T SAY IT WHILE YOU'RE AWAKE.

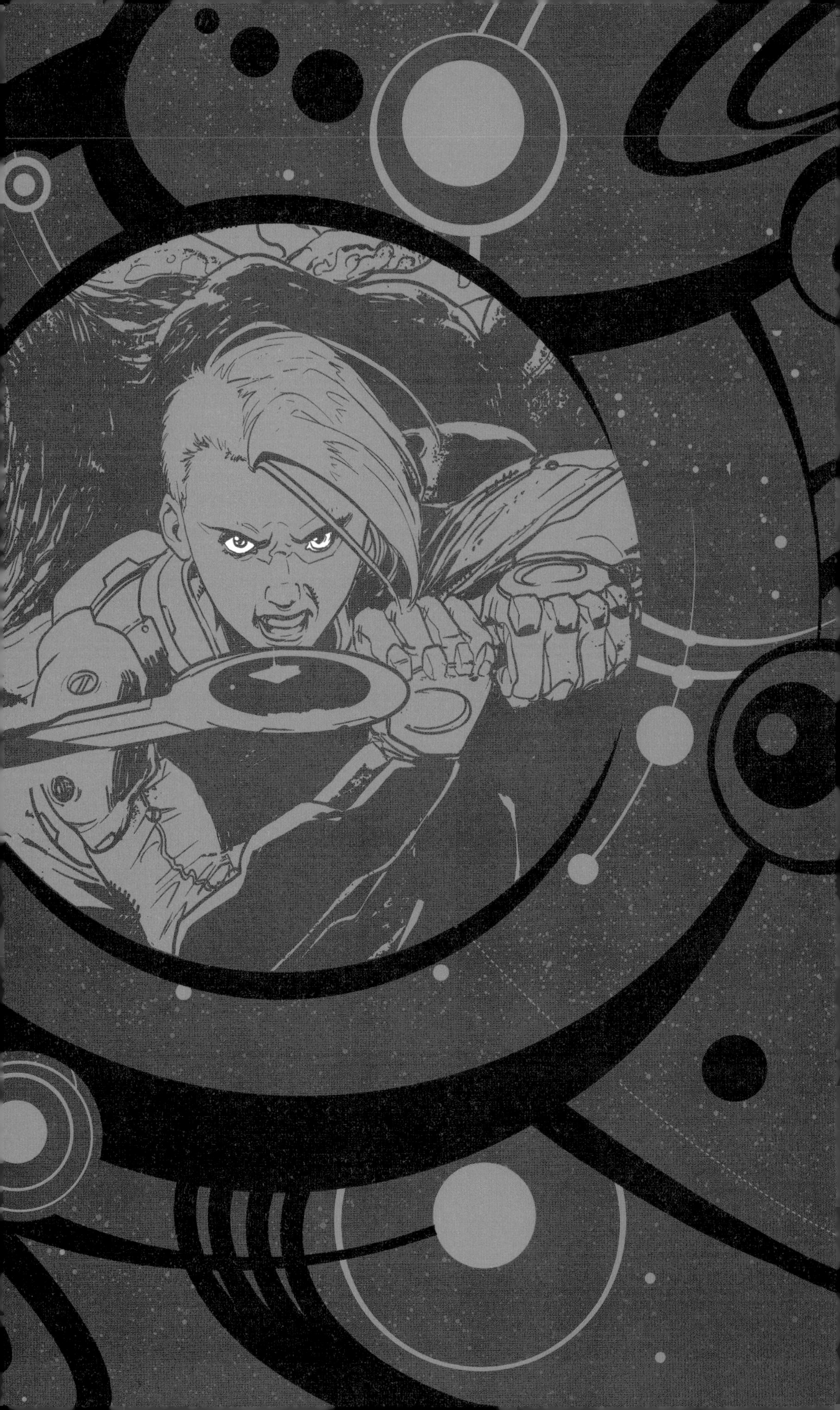

TWO

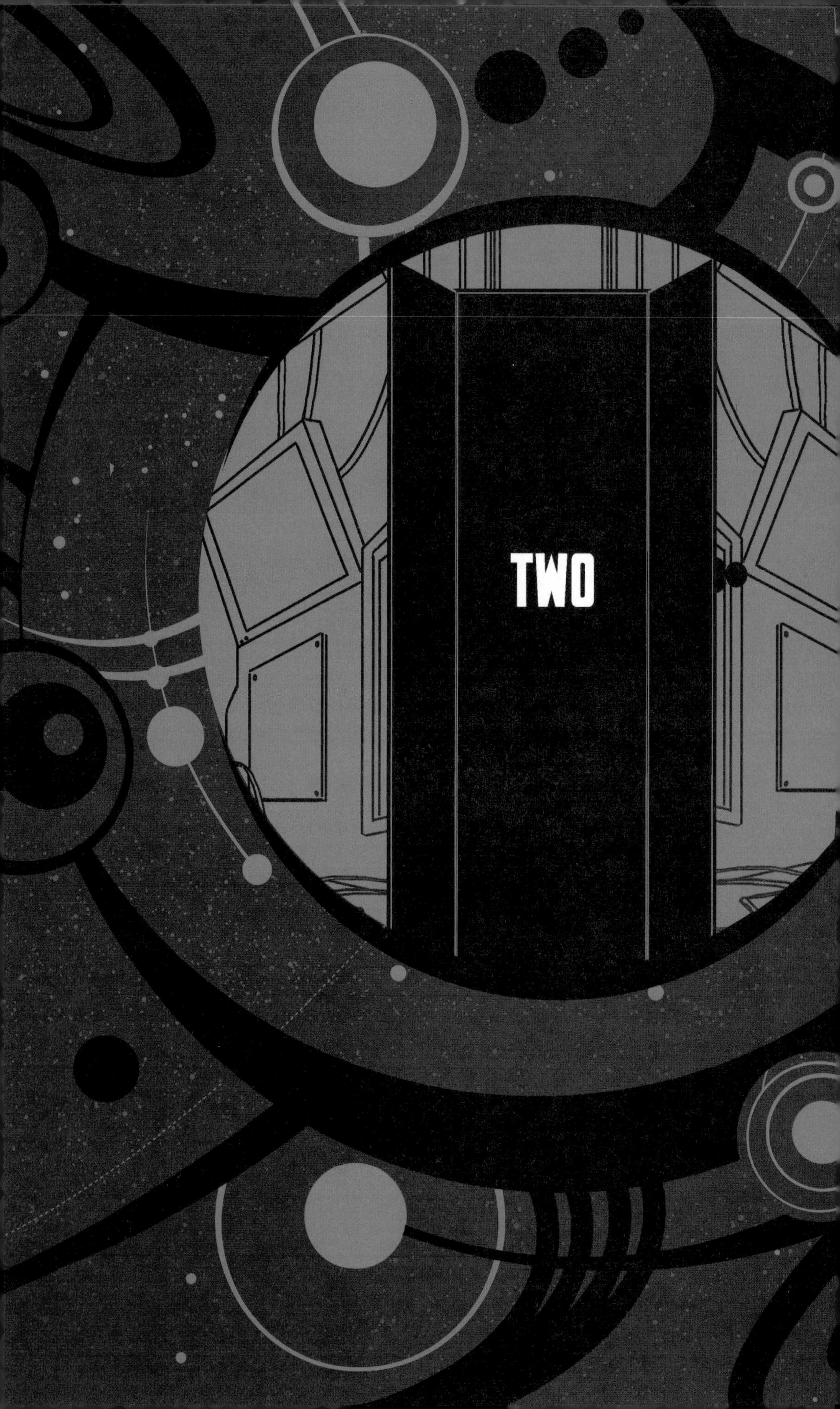

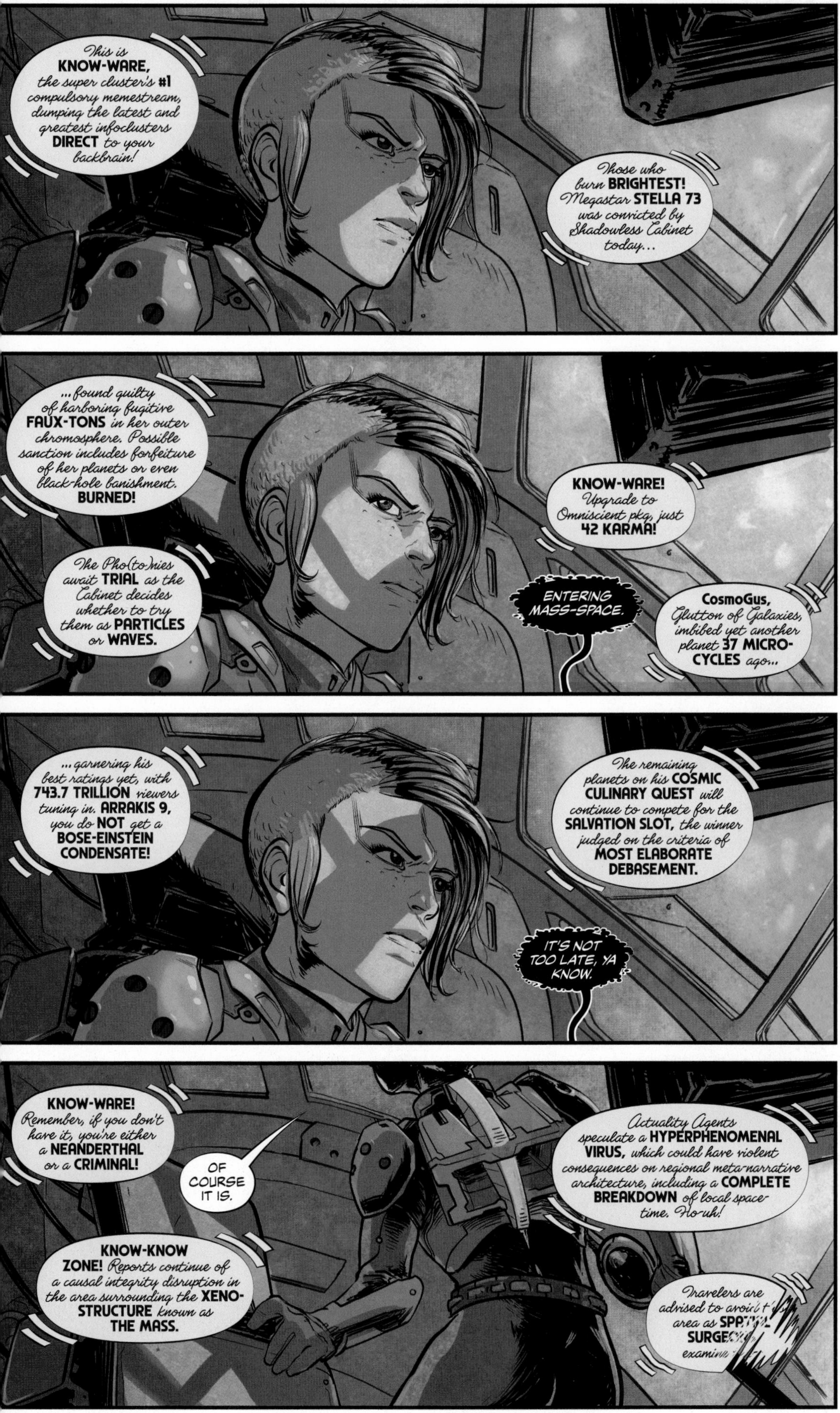

This is KNOW-WARE, the super cluster's #1 compulsory memestream, dumping the latest and greatest infoclusters DIRECT to your backbrain!
Those who burn BRIGHTEST! Megastar STELLA 73 was convicted by Shadowless Cabinet today...
...found guilty of harboring fugitive FAUX-TONS in her outer chromosphere. Possible sanction includes forfeiture of her planets or even black-hole banishment. BURNED!
KNOW-WARE! Upgrade to Omniscient pkg, just 42 KARMA!
The Pho(to)nies await TRIAL as the Cabinet decides whether to try them as PARTICLES or WAVES.
ENTERING MASS-SPACE.
CosmoGus, Glutton of Galaxies, imbibed yet another planet 37 MICRO-CYCLES ago...
...garnering his best ratings yet, with 743.7 TRILLION viewers tuning in. ARRAKIS 9, you do NOT get a BOSE-EINSTEIN CONDENSATE!
The remaining planets on his COSMIC CULINARY QUEST will continue to compete for the SALVATION SLOT, the winner judged on the criteria of MOST ELABORATE DEBASEMENT.
IT'S NOT TOO LATE, YA KNOW.
KNOW-WARE! Remember, if you don't have it, you're either a NEANDERTHAL or a CRIMINAL!
OF COURSE IT IS.
Actuality Agents speculate a HYPERPHENOMENAL VIRUS, which could have violent consequences on regional meta-narrative architecture, including a COMPLETE BREAKDOWN of local space-time. Ho-uh!
KNOW-KNOW ZONE! Reports continue of a causal integrity disruption in the area surrounding the XENO-STRUCTURE known as THE MASS.
Travelers are advised to avoid area as SURGE

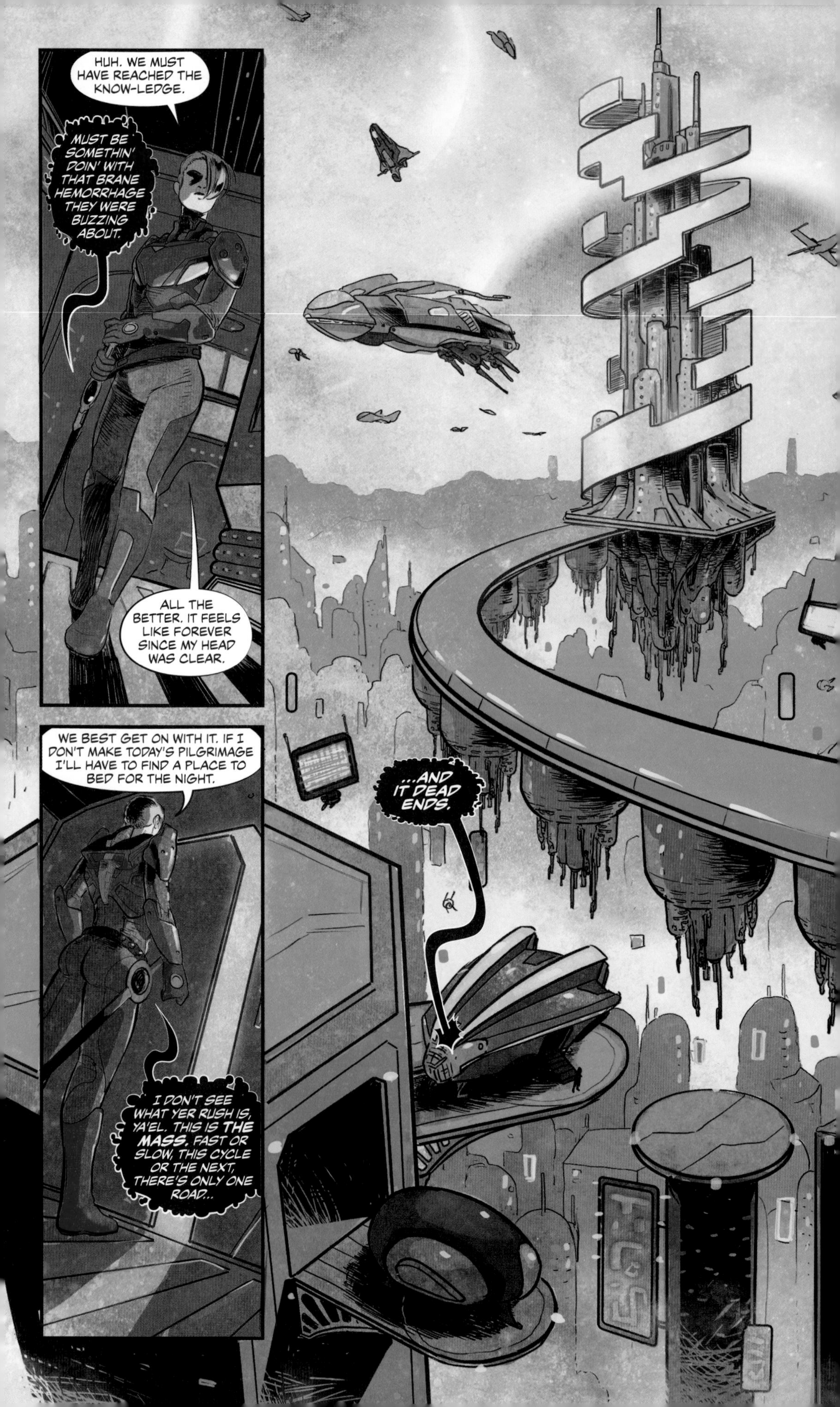
HUH. WE MUST HAVE REACHED THE KNOW-LEDGE.
MUST BE SOMETHIN' DOIN' WITH THAT BRANE HEMORRHAGE THEY WERE BUZZING ABOUT.
ALL THE BETTER. IT FEELS LIKE FOREVER SINCE MY HEAD WAS CLEAR.
WE BEST GET ON WITH IT. IF I DON'T MAKE TODAY'S PILGRIMAGE I'LL HAVE TO FIND A PLACE TO BED FOR THE NIGHT.
I DON'T SEE WHAT YER RUSH IS, YA'EL. THIS IS THE MASS. FAST OR SLOW, THIS CYCLE OR THE NEXT, THERE'S ONLY ONE ROAD...
...AND IT DEAD ENDS.

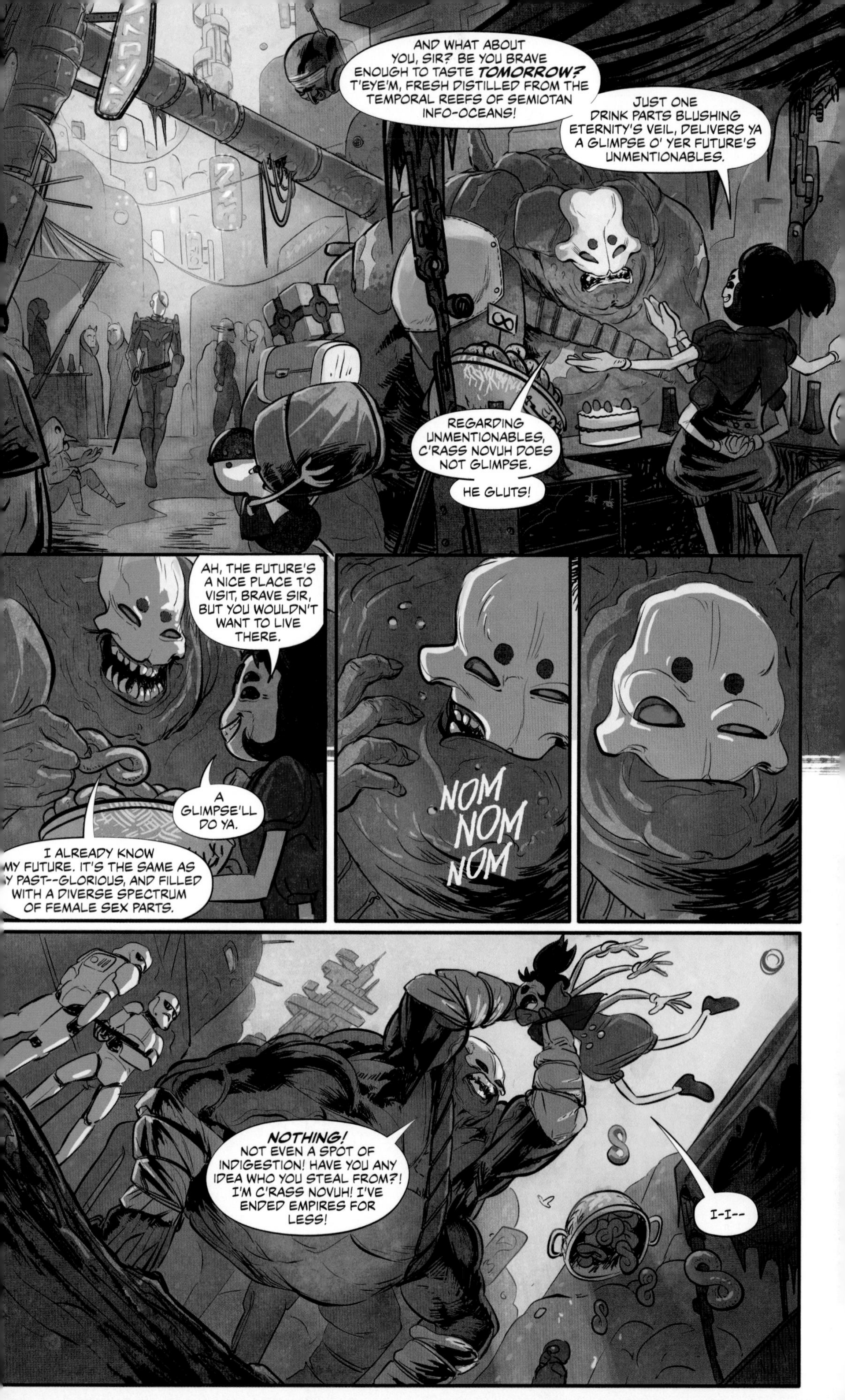
AND WHAT ABOUT YOU, SIR? BE YOU BRAVE ENOUGH TO TASTE *TOMORROW?* T'EYE'M, FRESH DISTILLED FROM THE TEMPORAL REEFS OF SEMIOTAN INFO-OCEANS!
JUST ONE DRINK PARTS BLUSHING ETERNITY'S VEIL, DELIVERS YA A GLIMPSE O' YER FUTURE'S UNMENTIONABLES.
REGARDING UNMENTIONABLES, C'RASS NOVUH DOES NOT GLIMPSE.
HE GLUTS!
AH, THE FUTURE'S A NICE PLACE TO VISIT, BRAVE SIR, BUT YOU WOULDN'T WANT TO LIVE THERE.
A GLIMPSE'LL DO YA.
I ALREADY KNOW MY FUTURE. IT'S THE SAME AS Y PAST--GLORIOUS, AND FILLED WITH A DIVERSE SPECTRUM OF FEMALE SEX PARTS.
NOM NOM NOM
NOTHING! NOT EVEN A SPOT OF INDIGESTION! HAVE YOU ANY IDEA WHO YOU STEAL FROM?! I'M C'RASS NOVUH! I'VE ENDED EMPIRES FOR LESS!
I-I--

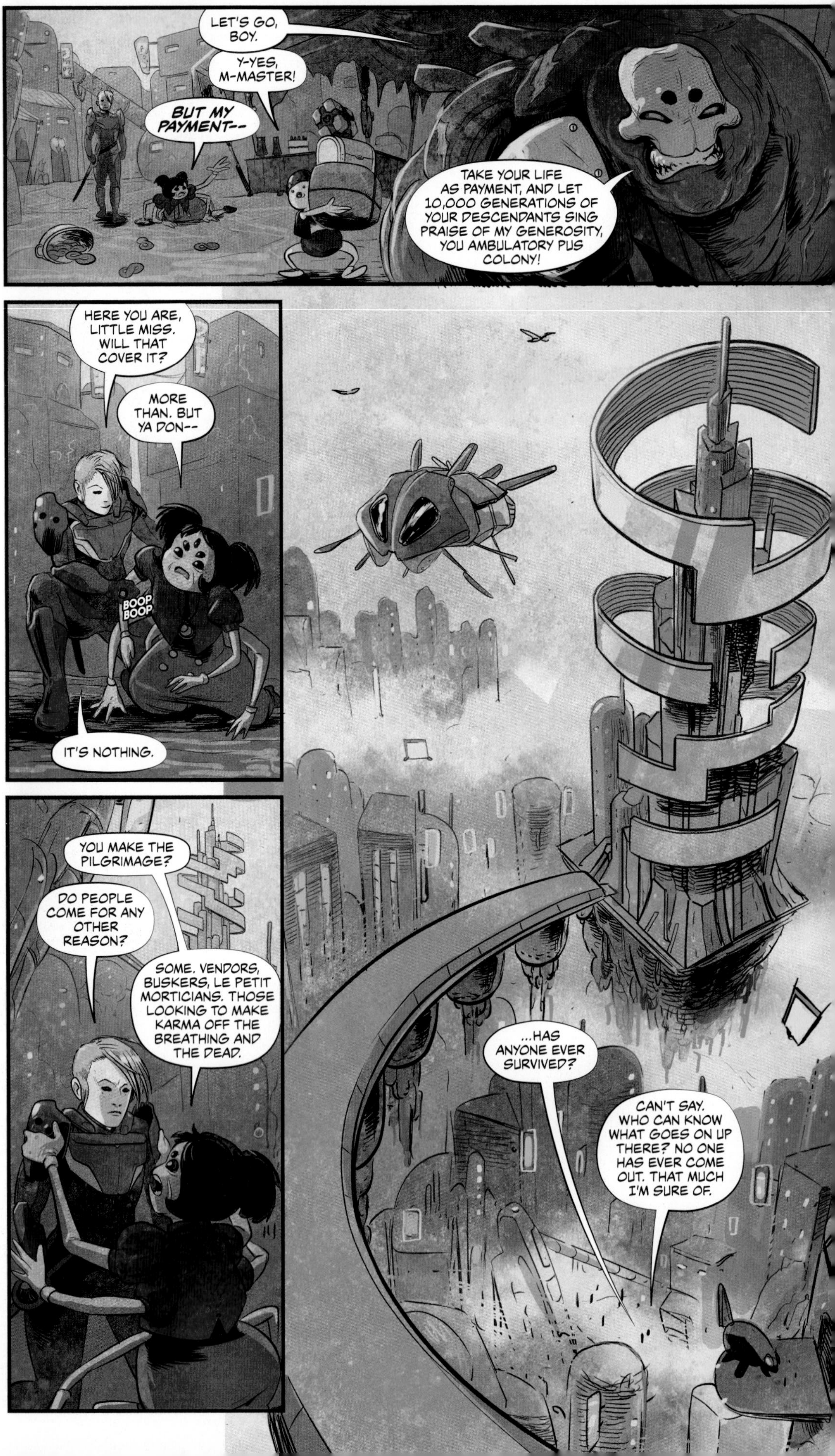
LET'S GO, BOY.
Y-YES, M-MASTER!
BUT MY PAYMENT--
TAKE YOUR LIFE AS PAYMENT, AND LET 10,000 GENERATIONS OF YOUR DESCENDANTS SING PRAISE OF MY GENEROSITY, YOU AMBULATORY PUS COLONY!
HERE YOU ARE, LITTLE MISS. WILL THAT COVER IT?
MORE THAN. BUT YA DON--
BOOP BOOP
IT'S NOTHING.
YOU MAKE THE PILGRIMAGE?
DO PEOPLE COME FOR ANY OTHER REASON?
SOME. VENDORS, BUSKERS, LE PETIT MORTICIANS. THOSE LOOKING TO MAKE KARMA OFF THE BREATHING AND THE DEAD.
...HAS ANYONE EVER SURVIVED?
CAN'T SAY. WHO CAN KNOW WHAT GOES ON UP THERE? NO ONE HAS EVER COME OUT. THAT MUCH I'M SURE OF.

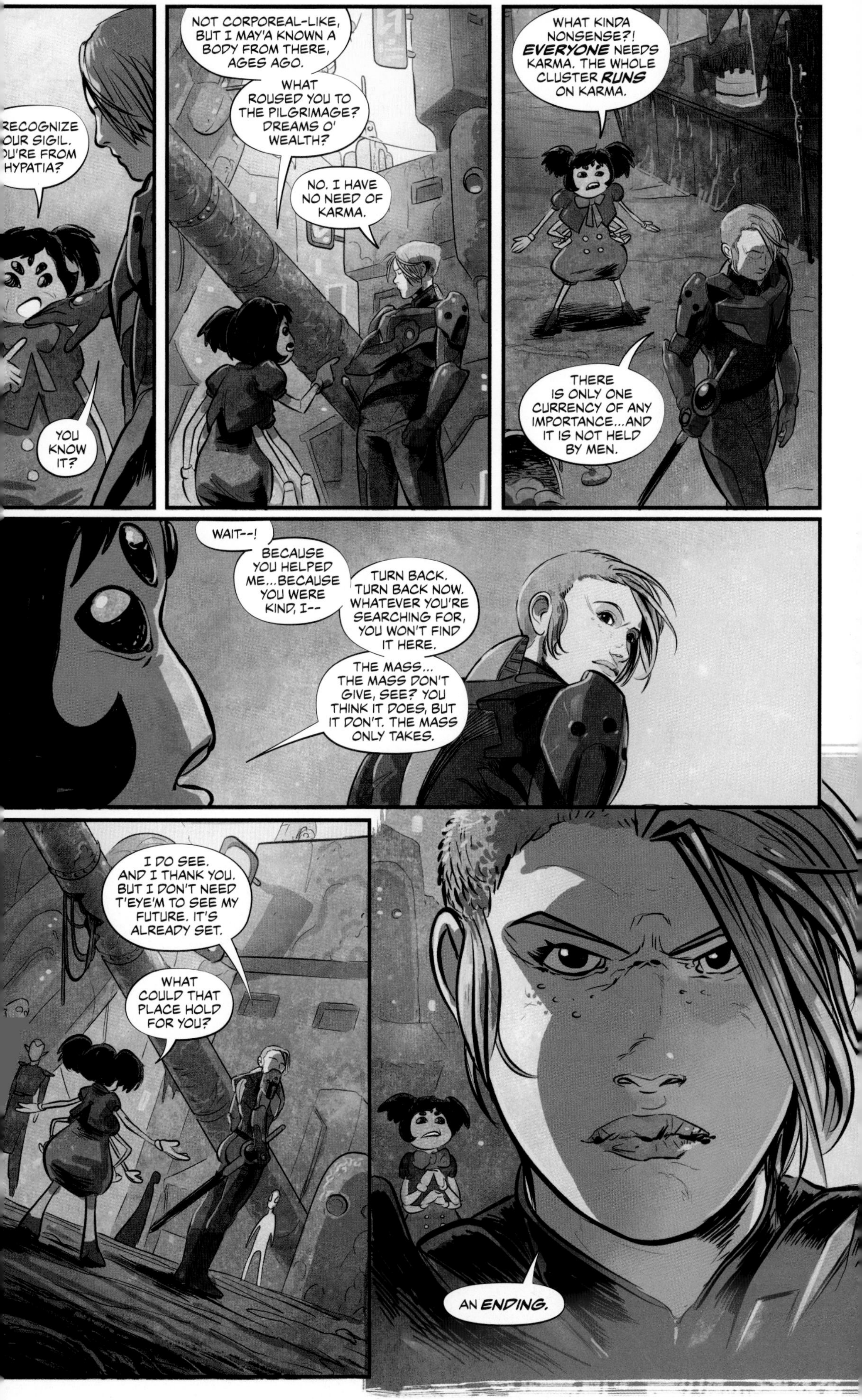

RECOGNIZE OUR SIGIL. YOU'RE FROM HYPATIA?
YOU KNOW IT?
NOT CORPOREAL-LIKE, BUT I MAY'A KNOWN A BODY FROM THERE, AGES AGO.
WHAT ROUSED YOU TO THE PILGRIMAGE? DREAMS O' WEALTH?
NO. I HAVE NO NEED OF KARMA.
WHAT KINDA NONSENSE?! EVERYONE NEEDS KARMA. THE WHOLE CLUSTER RUNS ON KARMA.
THERE IS ONLY ONE CURRENCY OF ANY IMPORTANCE...AND IT IS NOT HELD BY MEN.
WAIT--!
BECAUSE YOU HELPED ME...BECAUSE YOU WERE KIND, I--
TURN BACK. TURN BACK NOW. WHATEVER YOU'RE SEARCHING FOR, YOU WON'T FIND IT HERE.
THE MASS... THE MASS DON'T GIVE, SEE? YOU THINK IT DOES, BUT IT DON'T. THE MASS ONLY TAKES.
I DO SEE. AND I THANK YOU. BUT I DON'T NEED T'EYE'M TO SEE MY FUTURE. IT'S ALREADY SET.
WHAT COULD THAT PLACE HOLD FOR YOU?
AN ENDING.

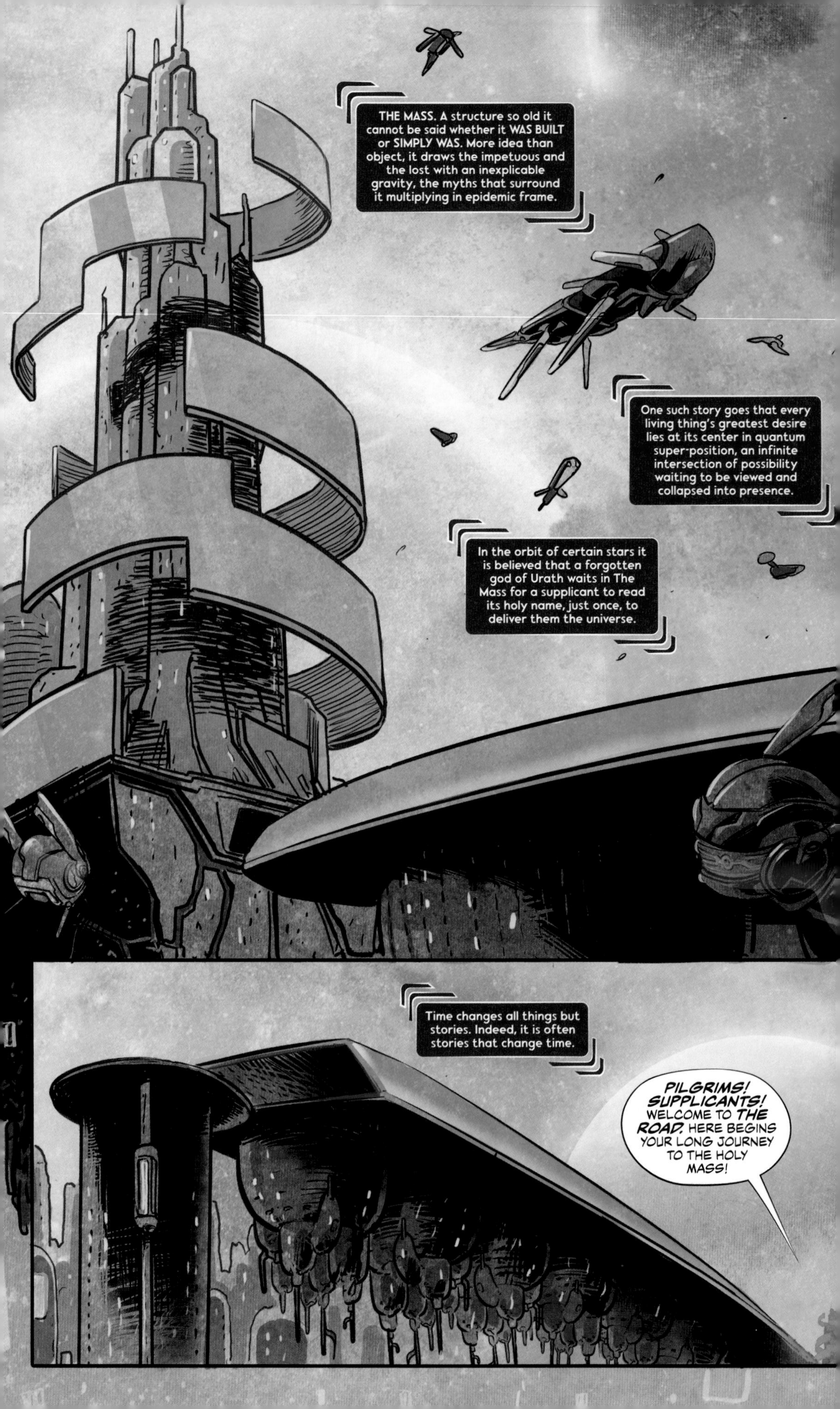

THE MASS. A structure so old it cannot be said whether it WAS BUILT or SIMPLY WAS. More idea than object, it draws the impetuous and the lost with an inexplicable gravity, the myths that surround it multiplying in epidemic frame.
One such story goes that every living thing's greatest desire lies at its center in quantum super-position, an infinite intersection of possibility waiting to be viewed and collapsed into presence.
In the orbit of certain stars it is believed that a forgotten god of Urath waits in The Mass for a supplicant to read its holy name, just once, to deliver them the universe.
Time changes all things but stories. Indeed, it is often stories that change time.
PILGRIMS! SUPPLICANTS! WELCOME TO THE ROAD. HERE BEGINS YOUR LONG JOURNEY TO THE HOLY MASS!

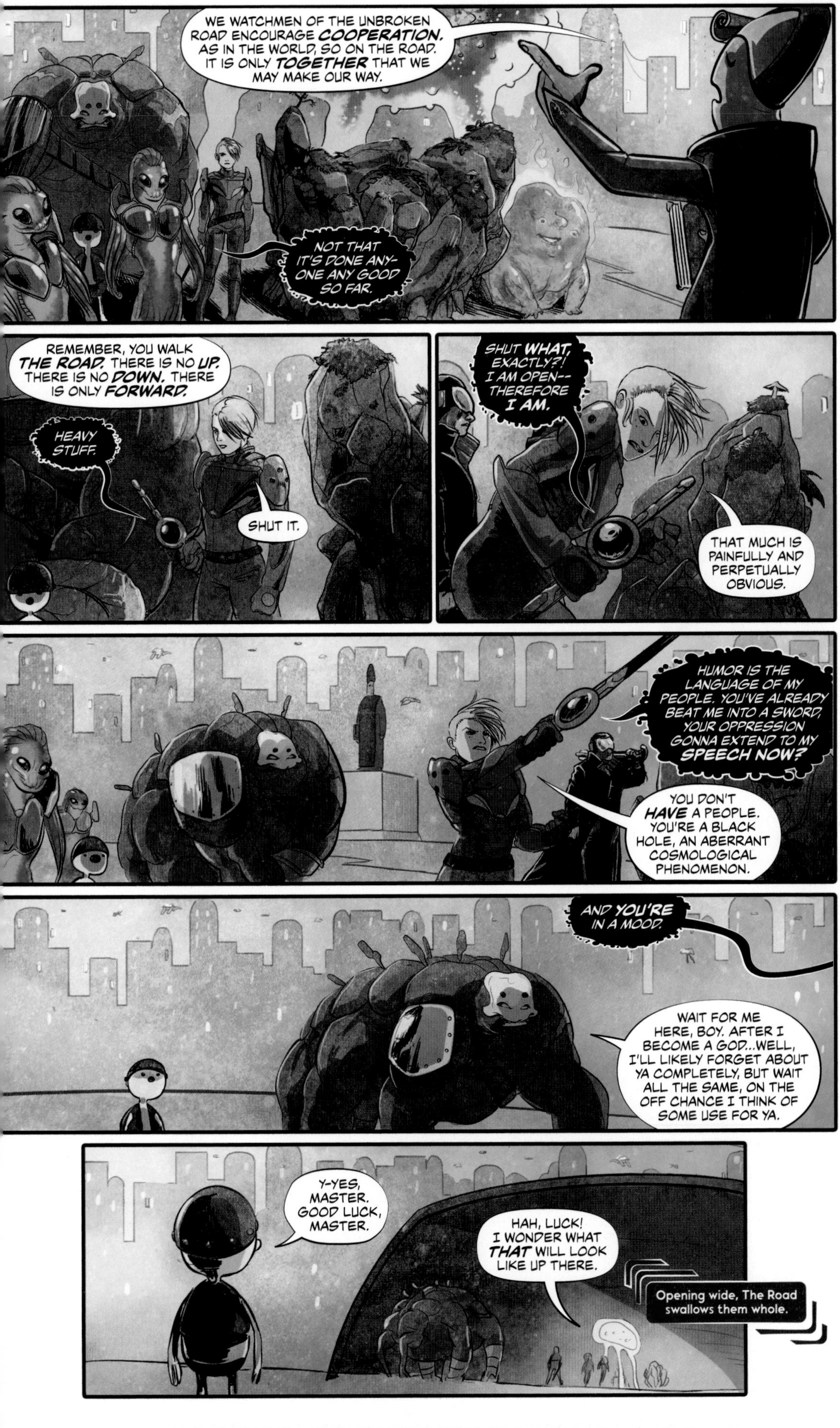
WE WATCHMEN OF THE UNBROKEN ROAD ENCOURAGE COOPERATION. AS IN THE WORLD, SO ON THE ROAD. IT IS ONLY TOGETHER THAT WE MAY MAKE OUR WAY.
NOT THAT IT'S DONE ANY-ONE ANY GOOD SO FAR.
REMEMBER, YOU WALK THE ROAD. THERE IS NO UP. THERE IS NO DOWN. THERE IS ONLY FORWARD.
HEAVY STUFF.
SHUT IT.
SHUT WHAT, EXACTLY?! I AM OPEN--THEREFORE I AM.
THAT MUCH IS PAINFULLY AND PERPETUALLY OBVIOUS.
HUMOR IS THE LANGUAGE OF MY PEOPLE. YOU'VE ALREADY BEAT ME INTO A SWORD, YOUR OPPRESSION GONNA EXTEND TO MY SPEECH NOW?
YOU DON'T HAVE A PEOPLE. YOU'RE A BLACK HOLE, AN ABERRANT COSMOLOGICAL PHENOMENON.
AND YOU'RE IN A MOOD.
WAIT FOR ME HERE, BOY. AFTER I BECOME A GOD...WELL, I'LL LIKELY FORGET ABOUT YA COMPLETELY, BUT WAIT ALL THE SAME, ON THE OFF CHANCE I THINK OF SOME USE FOR YA.
Y-YES, MASTER. GOOD LUCK, MASTER.
HAH, LUCK! I WONDER WHAT THAT WILL LOOK LIKE UP THERE.
Opening wide, The Road swallows them whole.

Crrsszzhhh is a silicon-based lifeform. His perceptions synched to geological tempos, in movements solemn and inevitable he has been making his way here for centuries.

He's dead without knowing it.

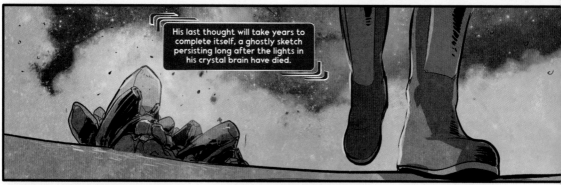

His last thought will take years to complete itself, a ghostly sketch persisting long after the lights in his crystal brain have died.

Somewhere, a very old man watches, and chuckles at the anachronism. A ghost in this bright age of reason.

Ya'el thinks, sadly, of twin setting suns seen through the soaring quartz orchards of her youth, then walks on.

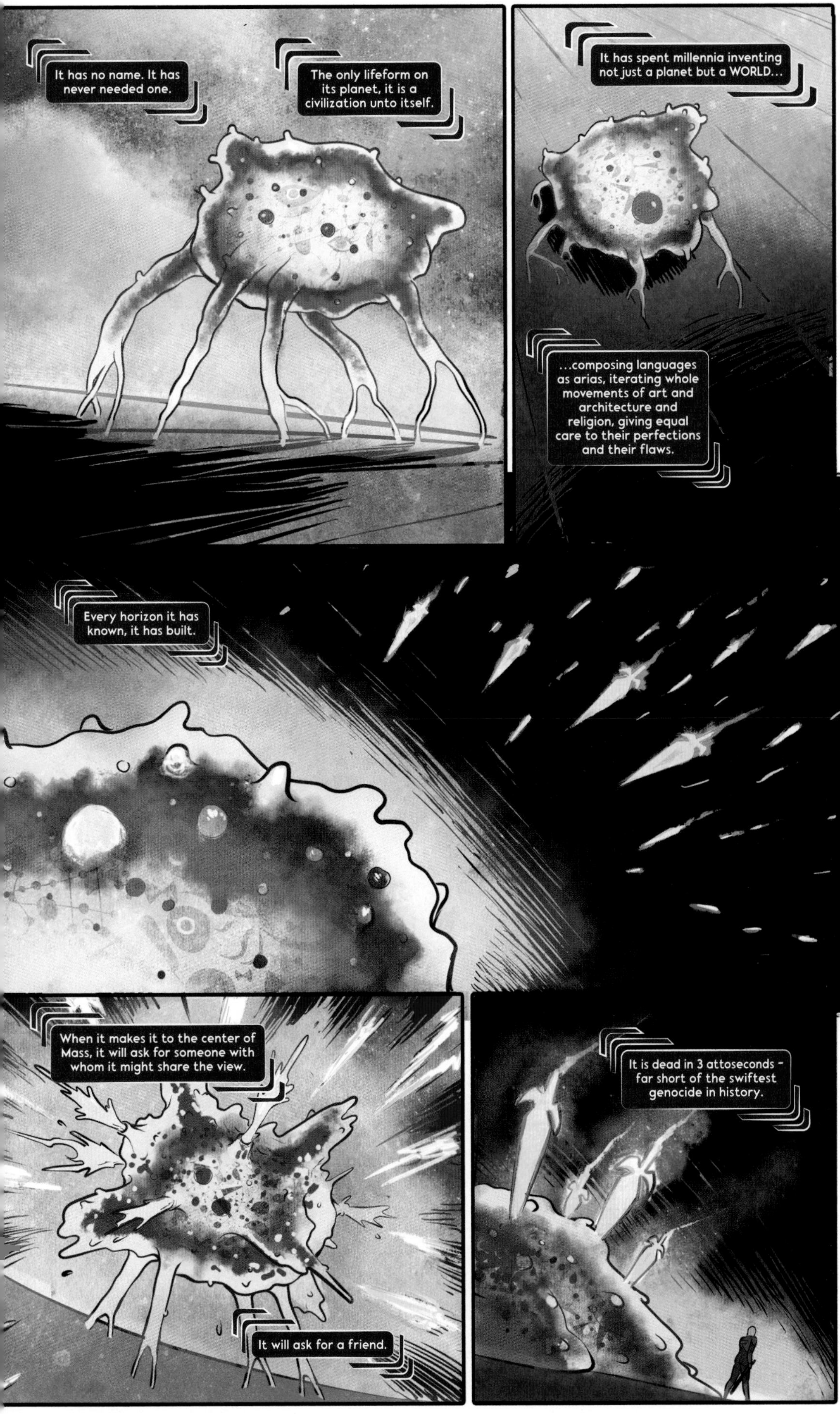
It has no name. It has never needed one.
The only lifeform on its planet, it is a civilization unto itself.
It has spent millennia inventing not just a planet but a WORLD...
...composing languages as arias, iterating whole movements of art and architecture and religion, giving equal care to their perfections and their flaws.
Every horizon it has known, it has built.
When it makes it to the center of Mass, it will ask for someone with whom it might share the view.
It will ask for a friend.
It is dead in 3 attoseconds - far short of the swiftest genocide in history.

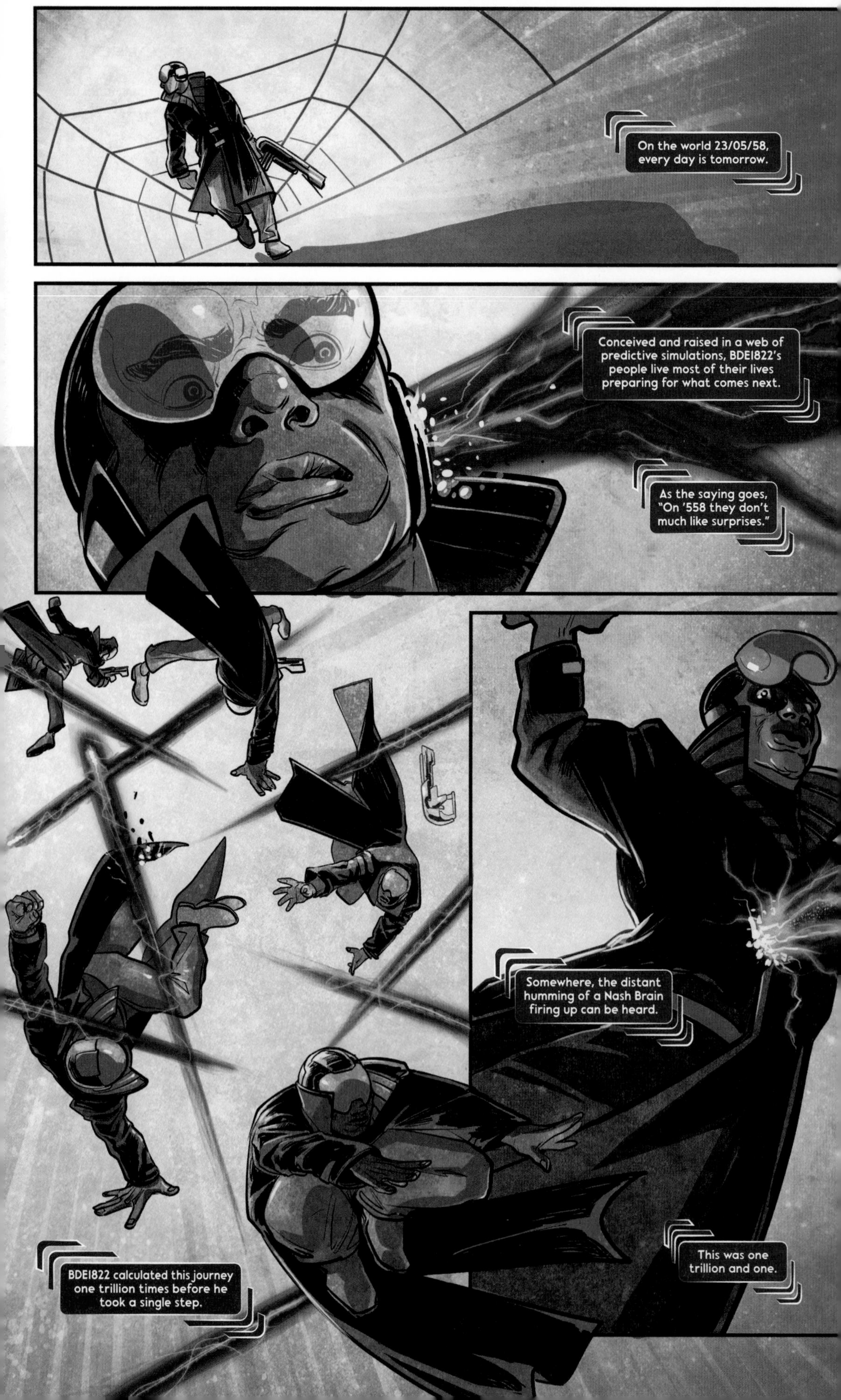
On the world 23/05/58, every day is tomorrow.
Conceived and raised in a web of predictive simulations, BDE1822's people live most of their lives preparing for what comes next.
As the saying goes, "On '558 they don't much like surprises."
Somewhere, the distant humming of a Nash Brain firing up can be heard.
BDE1822 calculated this journey one trillion times before he took a single step.
This was one trillion and one.

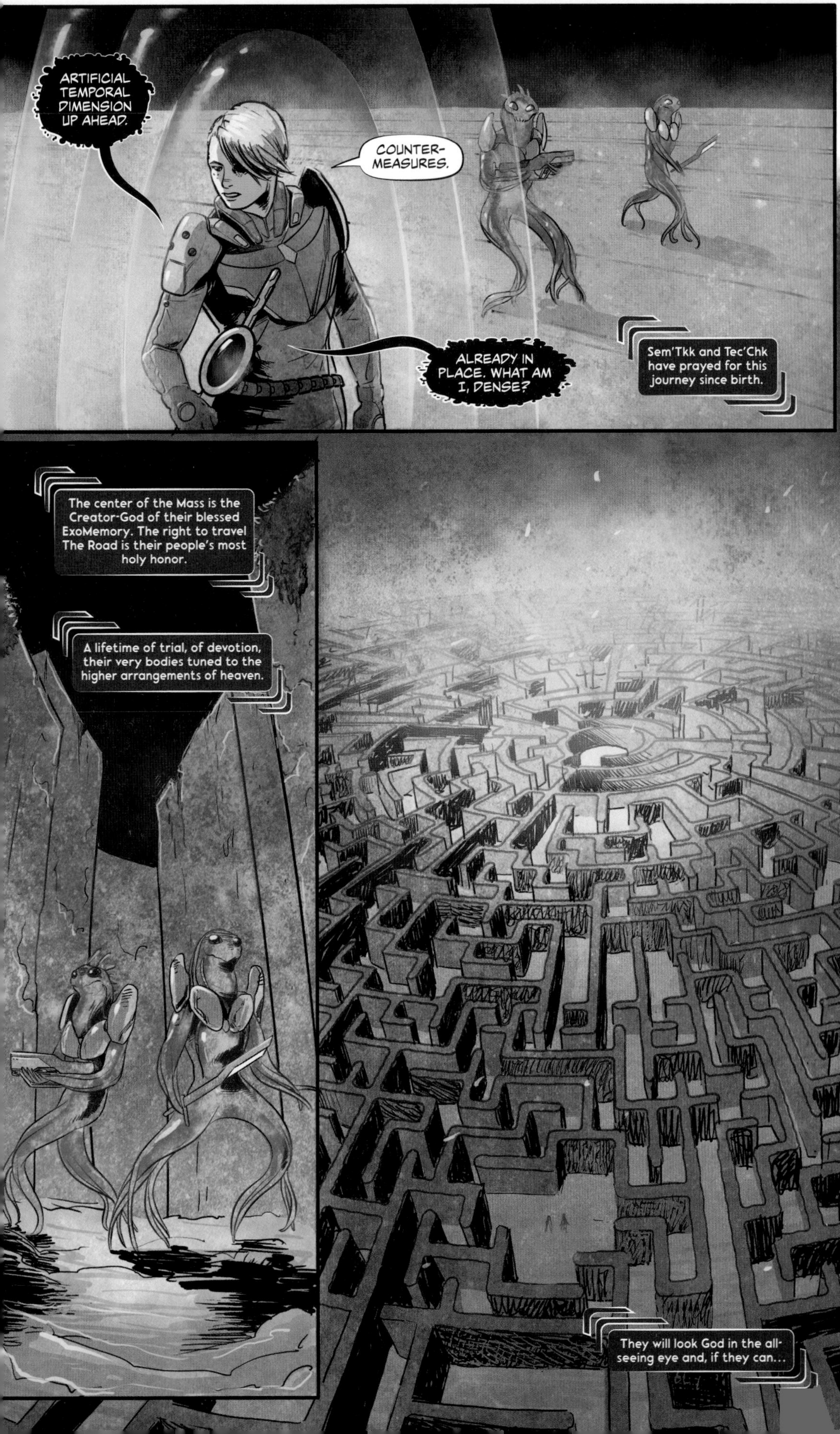

ARTIFICIAL TEMPORAL DIMENSION UP AHEAD.
COUNTER-MEASURES.
ALREADY IN PLACE. WHAT AM I, DENSE?
Sem'Tkk and Tec'Chk have prayed for this journey since birth.
The center of the Mass is the Creator-God of their blessed ExoMemory. The right to travel The Road is their people's most holy honor.
A lifetime of trial, of devotion, their very bodies tuned to the higher arrangements of heaven.
They will look God in the all-seeing eye and, if they can...

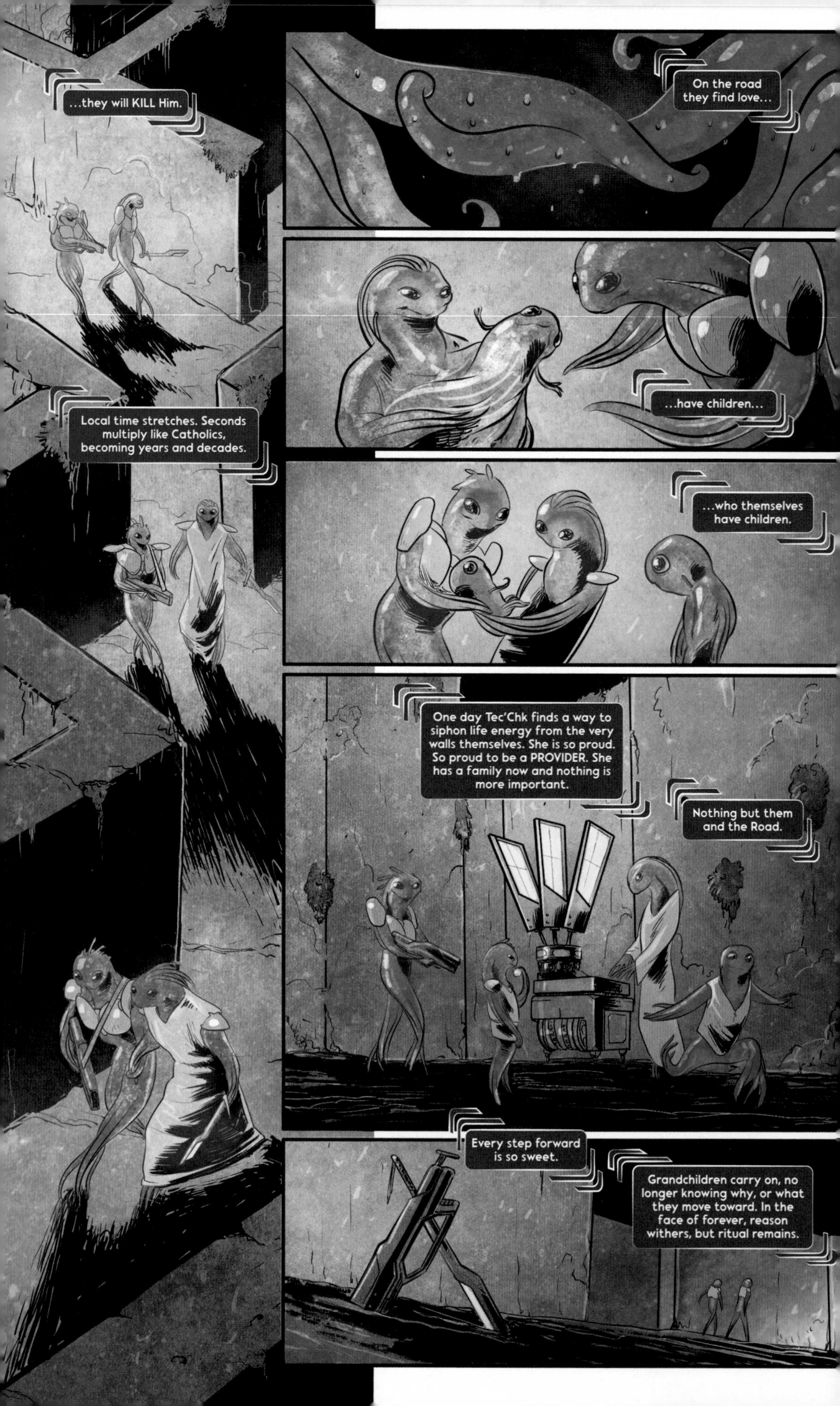
...they will KILL Him.
Local time stretches. Seconds multiply like Catholics, becoming years and decades.
On the road they find love...
...have children...
...who themselves have children.
One day Tec'Chk finds a way to siphon life energy from the very walls themselves. She is so proud. So proud to be a PROVIDER. She has a family now and nothing is more important.
Nothing but them and the Road.
Every step forward is so sweet.
Grandchildren carry on, no longer knowing why, or what they move toward. In the face of forever, reason withers, but ritual remains.

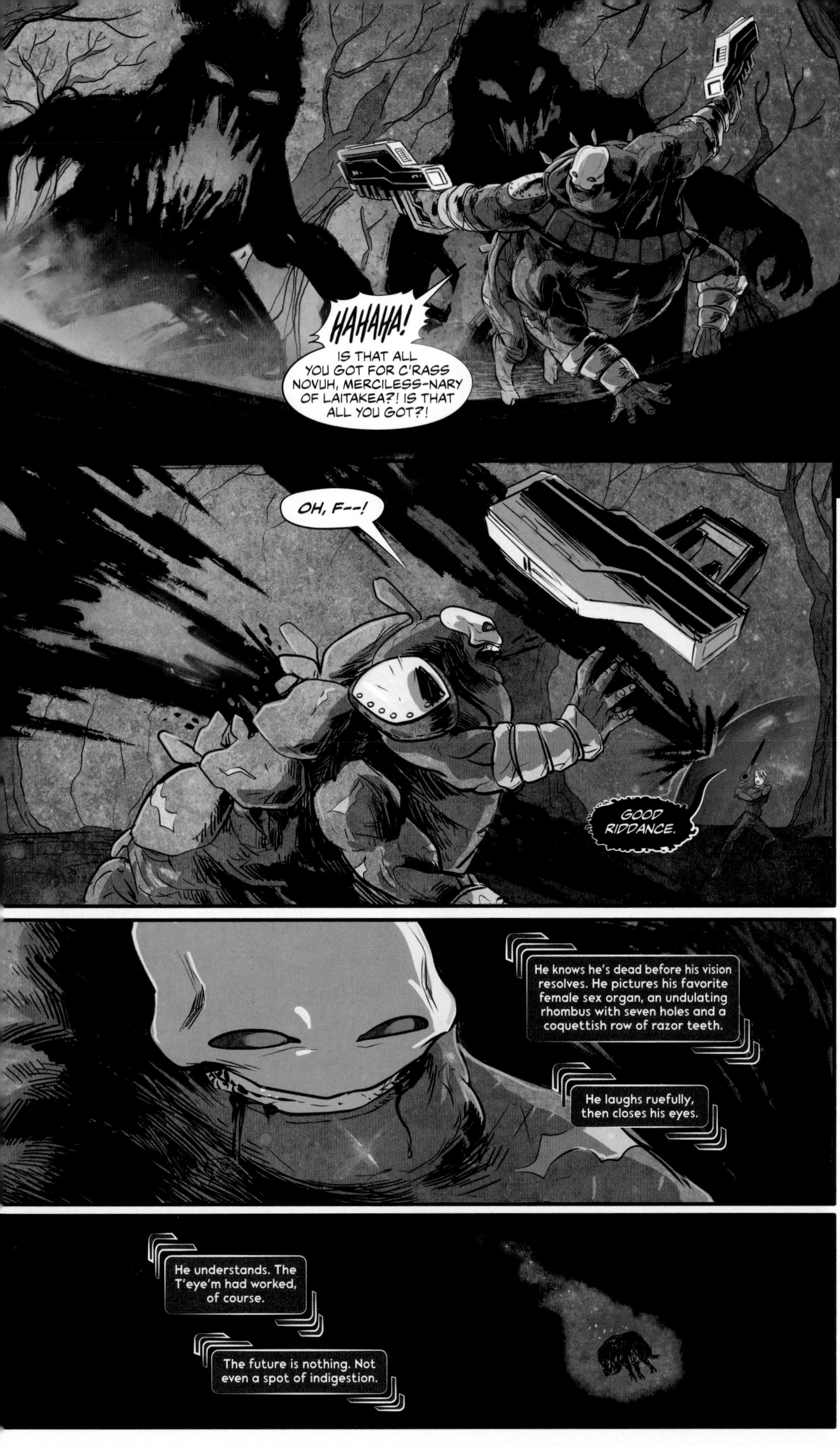
HAHAHA!
IS THAT ALL YOU GOT FOR C'RASS NOVUH, MERCILESS-NARY OF LAITAKEA?! IS THAT ALL YOU GOT?!
OH, F--!
GOOD RIDDANCE.
He knows he's dead before his vision resolves. He pictures his favorite female sex organ, an undulating rhombus with seven holes and a coquettish row of razor teeth.
He laughs ruefully, then closes his eyes.
He understands. The T'eye'm had worked, of course.
The future is nothing. Not even a spot of indigestion.

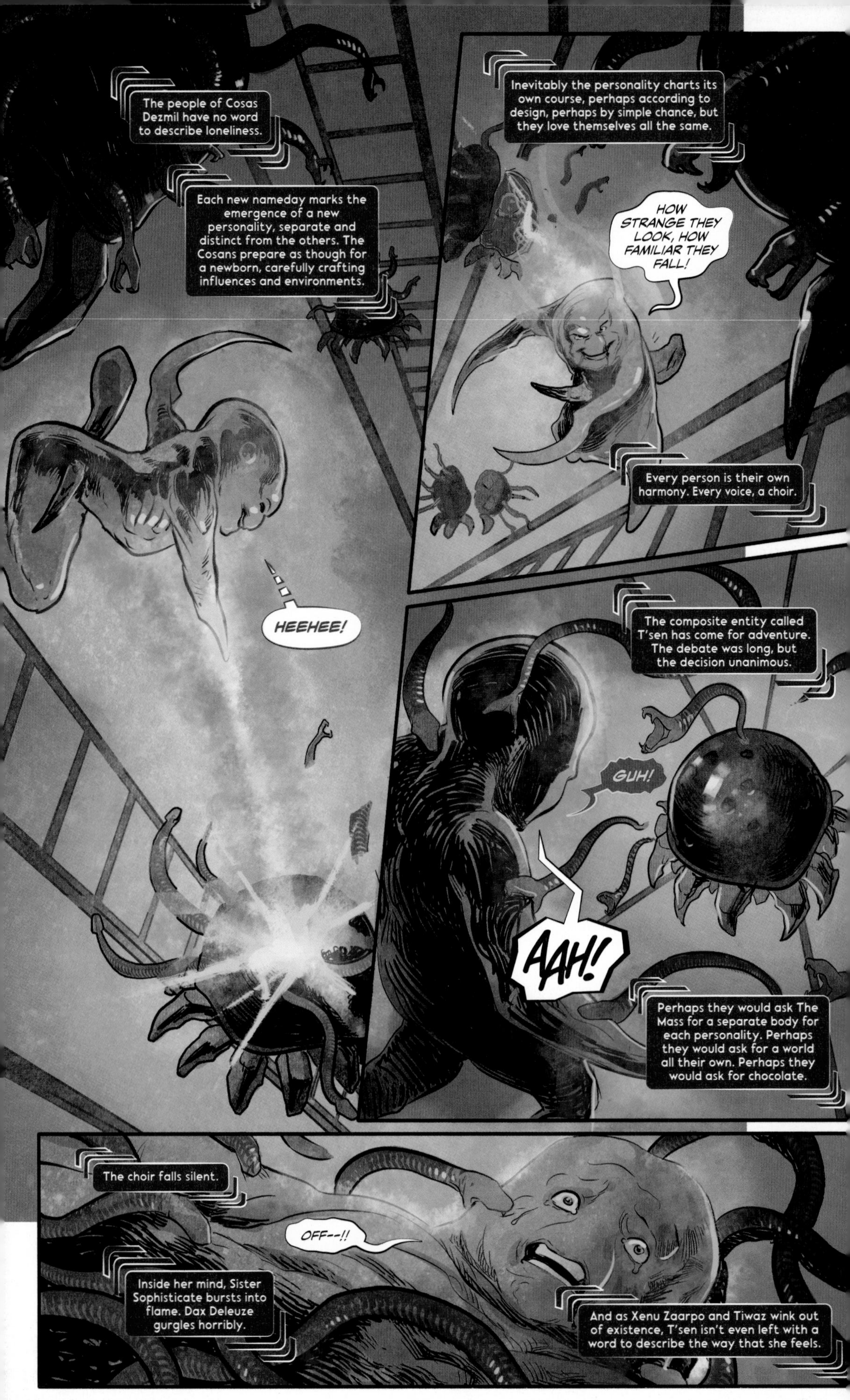

The people of Cosas Dezmil have no word to describe loneliness.
Each new nameday marks the emergence of a new personality, separate and distinct from the others. The Cosans prepare as though for a newborn, carefully crafting influences and environments.
Inevitably the personality charts its own course, perhaps according to design, perhaps by simple chance, but they love themselves all the same.
HOW STRANGE THEY LOOK, HOW FAMILIAR THEY FALL!
Every person is their own harmony. Every voice, a choir.
HEEHEE!
The composite entity called T'sen has come for adventure. The debate was long, but the decision unanimous.
GUH!
AAH!
Perhaps they would ask The Mass for a separate body for each personality. Perhaps they would ask for a world all their own. Perhaps they would ask for chocolate.
The choir falls silent.
OFF--!!
Inside her mind, Sister Sophisticate bursts into flame. Dax Deleuze gurgles horribly.
And as Xenu Zaarpo and Tiwaz wink out of existence, T'sen isn't even left with a word to describe the way that she feels.

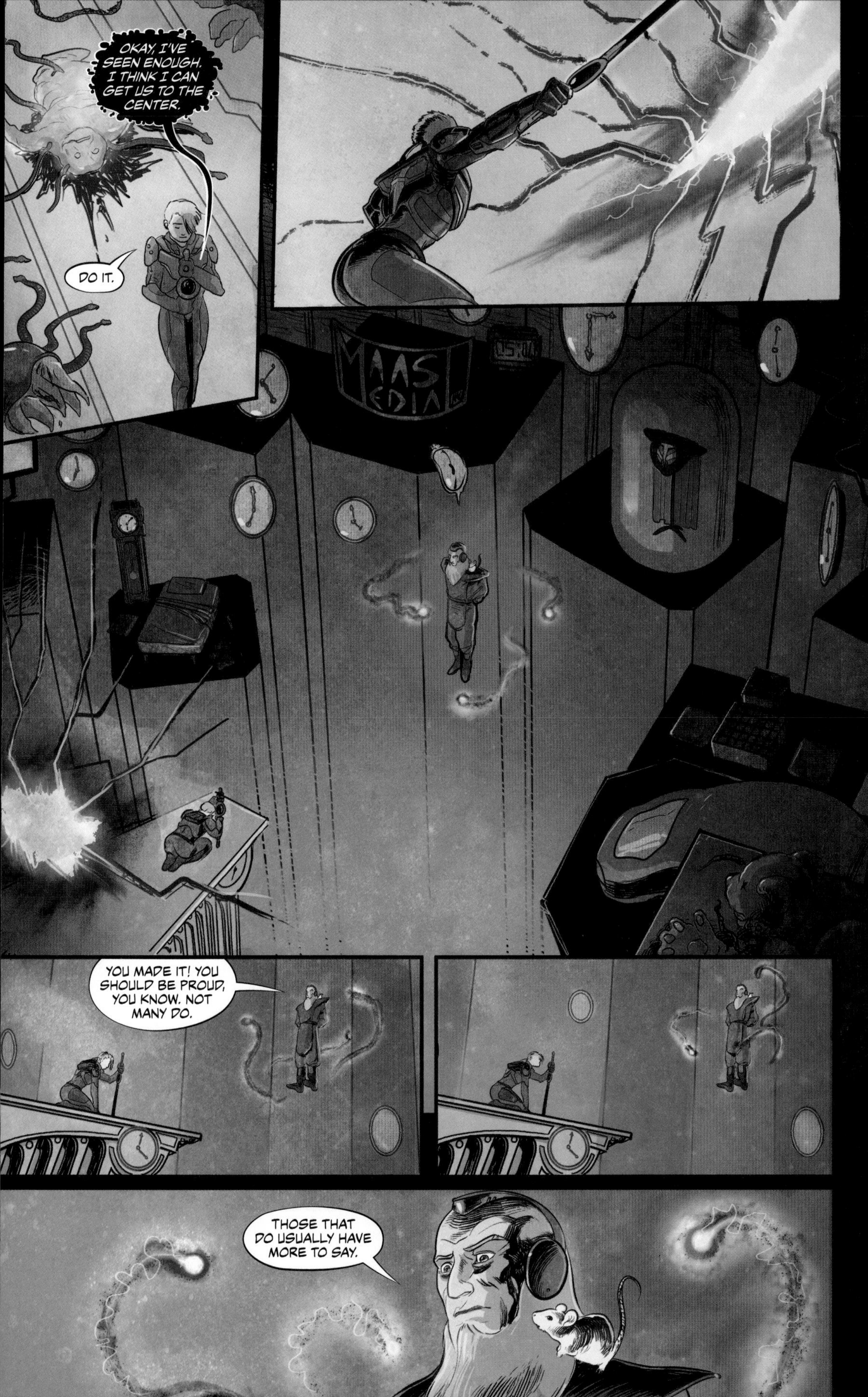
OKAY, I'VE SEEN ENOUGH. I THINK I CAN GET US TO THE CENTER.
DO IT.
YOU MADE IT! YOU SHOULD BE PROUD, YOU KNOW. NOT MANY DO.
THOSE THAT DO USUALLY HAVE MORE TO SAY.

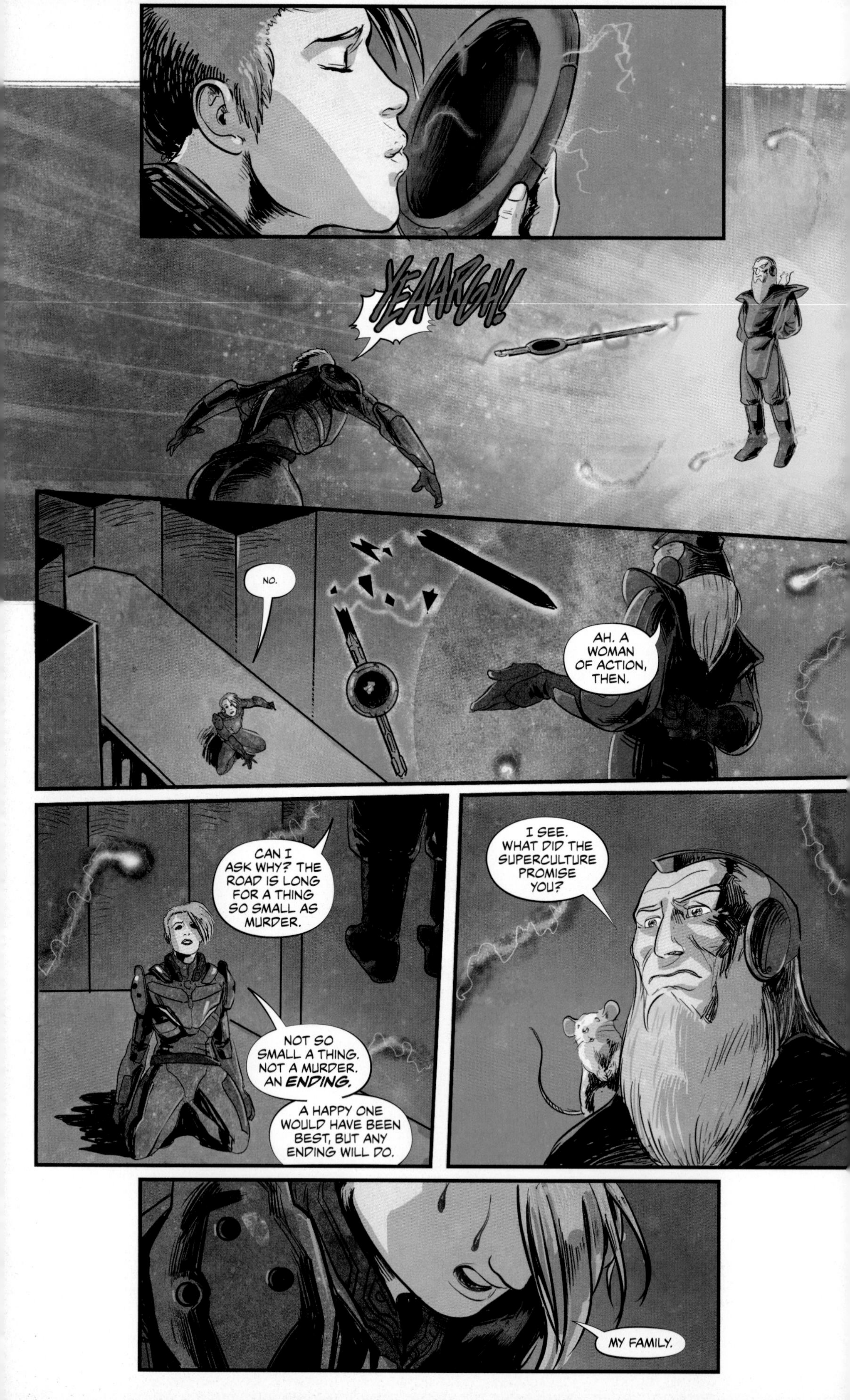
YEAARGH!
NO.
AH. A WOMAN OF ACTION, THEN.
CAN I ASK WHY? THE ROAD IS LONG FOR A THING SO SMALL AS MURDER.
NOT SO SMALL A THING. NOT A MURDER. AN ENDING.
A HAPPY ONE WOULD HAVE BEEN BEST, BUT ANY ENDING WILL DO.
I SEE. WHAT DID THE SUPERCULTURE PROMISE YOU?
MY FAMILY.

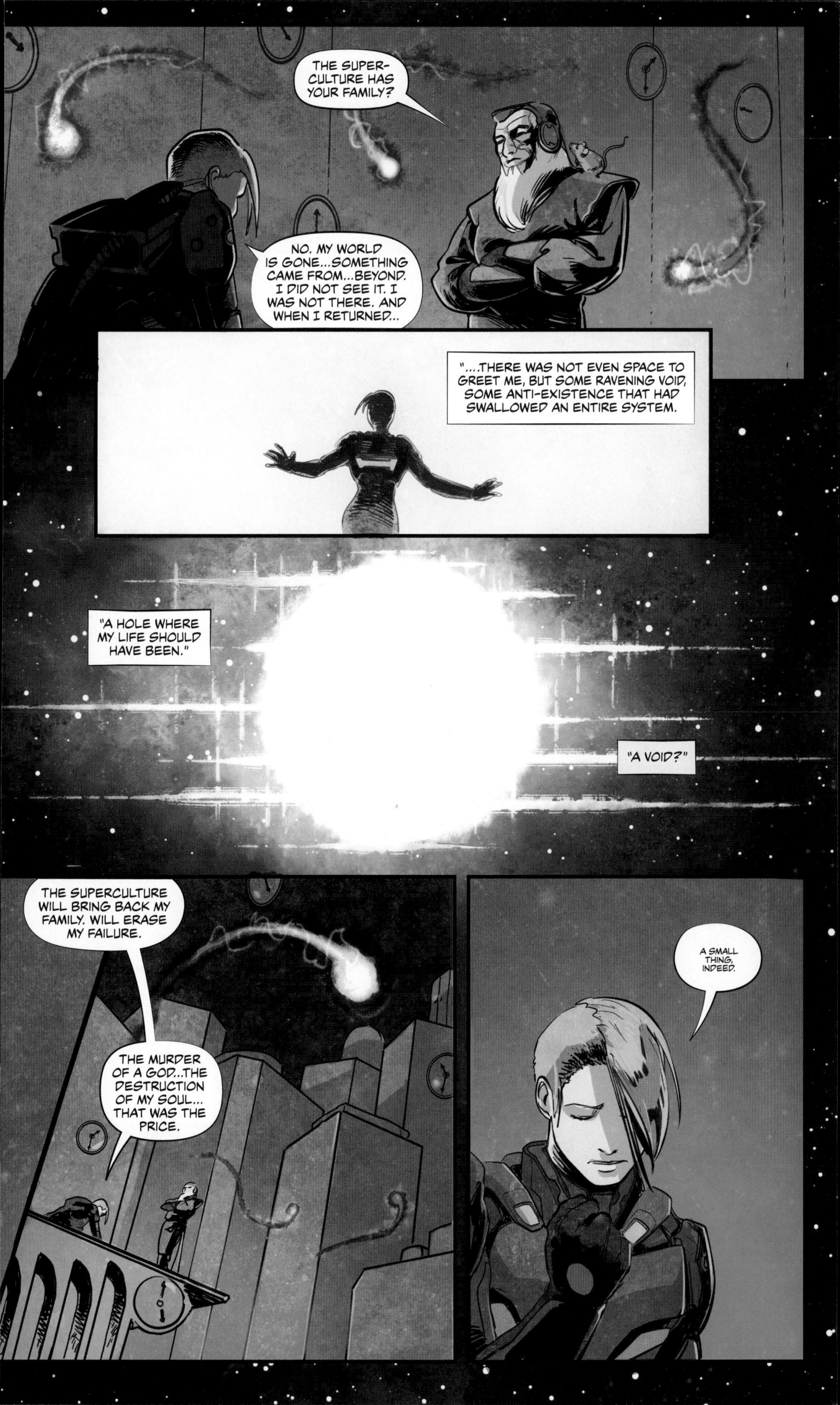
THE SUPER-CULTURE HAS YOUR FAMILY?
NO. MY WORLD IS GONE...SOMETHING CAME FROM...BEYOND. I DID NOT SEE IT. I WAS NOT THERE. AND WHEN I RETURNED...
"....THERE WAS NOT EVEN SPACE TO GREET ME, BUT SOME RAVENING VOID, SOME ANTI-EXISTENCE THAT HAD SWALLOWED AN ENTIRE SYSTEM.
"A HOLE WHERE MY LIFE SHOULD HAVE BEEN."
"A VOID?"
THE SUPERCULTURE WILL BRING BACK MY FAMILY. WILL ERASE MY FAILURE.
THE MURDER OF A GOD...THE DESTRUCTION OF MY SOUL... THAT WAS THE PRICE.
A SMALL THING, INDEED.

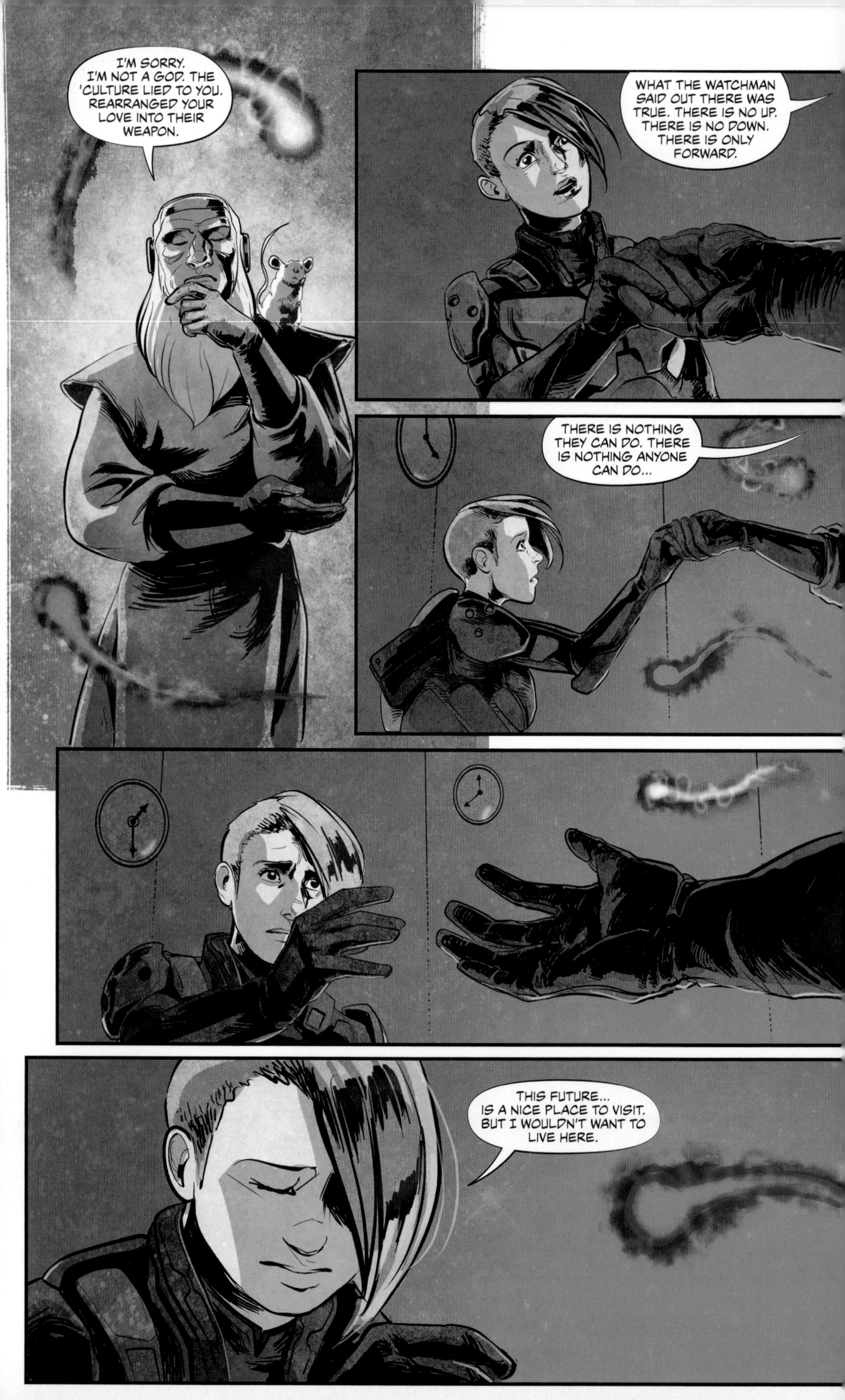

I'M SORRY. I'M NOT A GOD. THE 'CULTURE LIED TO YOU. REARRANGED YOUR LOVE INTO THEIR WEAPON.
WHAT THE WATCHMAN SAID OUT THERE WAS TRUE. THERE IS NO UP. THERE IS NO DOWN. THERE IS ONLY FORWARD.
THERE IS NOTHING THEY CAN DO. THERE IS NOTHING ANYONE CAN DO...
THIS FUTURE... IS A NICE PLACE TO VISIT. BUT I WOULDN'T WANT TO LIVE HERE.

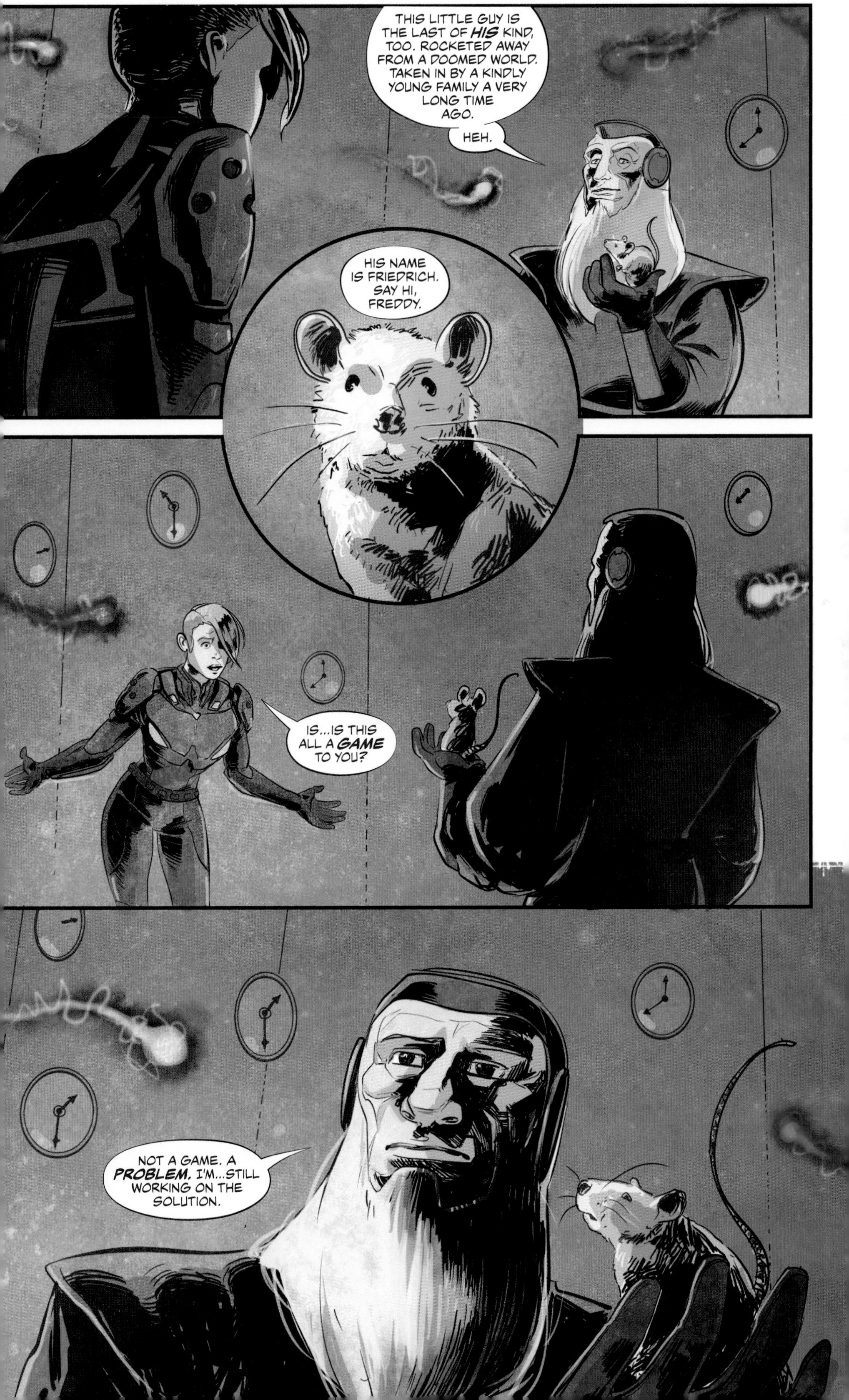
THIS LITTLE GUY IS THE LAST OF HIS KIND, TOO. ROCKETED AWAY FROM A DOOMED WORLD. TAKEN IN BY A KINDLY YOUNG FAMILY A VERY LONG TIME AGO.
HEH.
HIS NAME IS FRIEDRICH. SAY HI, FREDDY.
IS...IS THIS ALL A GAME TO YOU?
NOT A GAME. A PROBLEM. I'M...STILL WORKING ON THE SOLUTION.

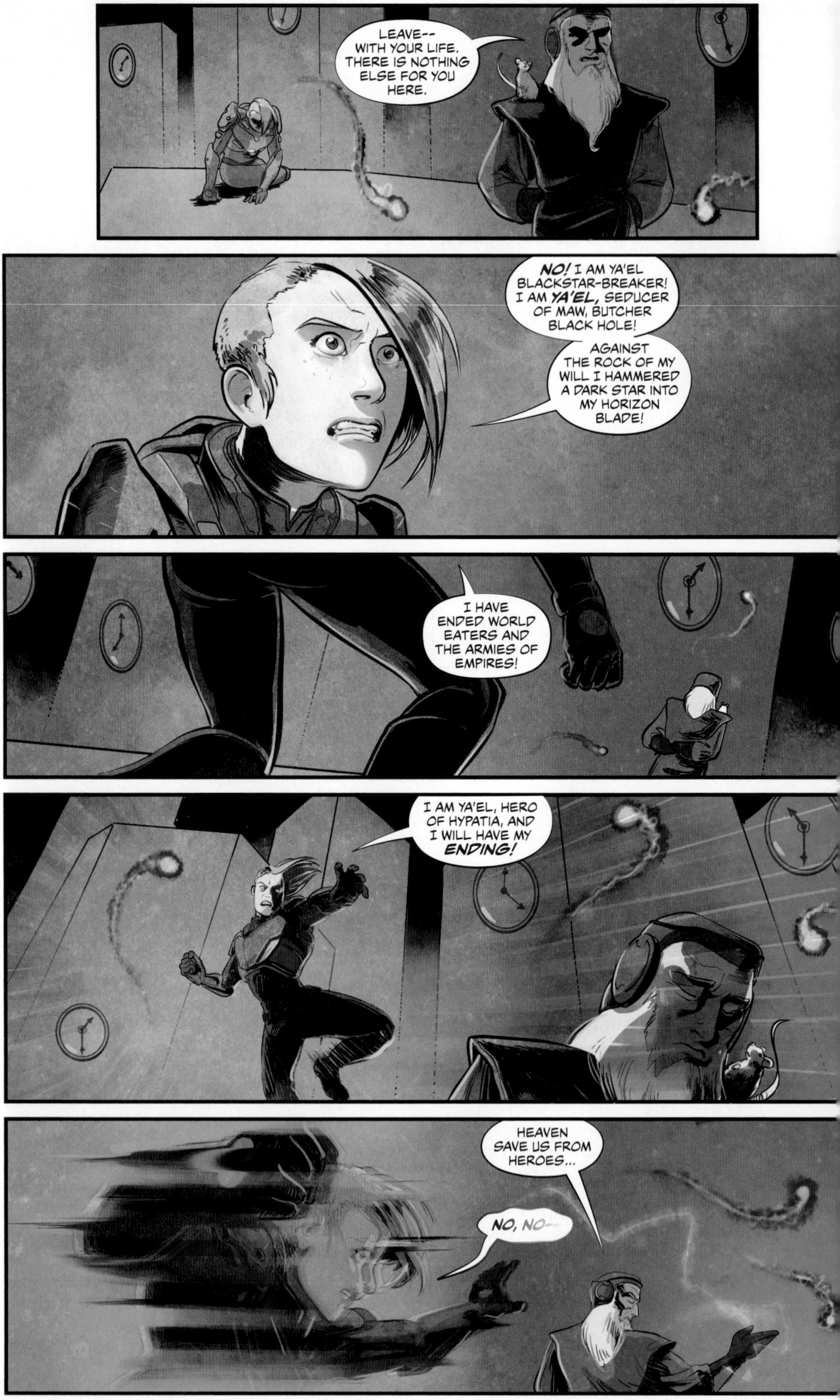
LEAVE-- WITH YOUR LIFE. THERE IS NOTHING ELSE FOR YOU HERE.
NO! I AM YA'EL BLACKSTAR-BREAKER! I AM YA'EL, SEDUCER OF MAW, BUTCHER BLACK HOLE!
AGAINST THE ROCK OF MY WILL I HAMMERED A DARK STAR INTO MY HORIZON BLADE!
I HAVE ENDED WORLD EATERS AND THE ARMIES OF EMPIRES!
I AM YA'EL, HERO OF HYPATIA, AND I WILL HAVE MY ENDING!
HEAVEN SAVE US FROM HEROES...
NO, NO--

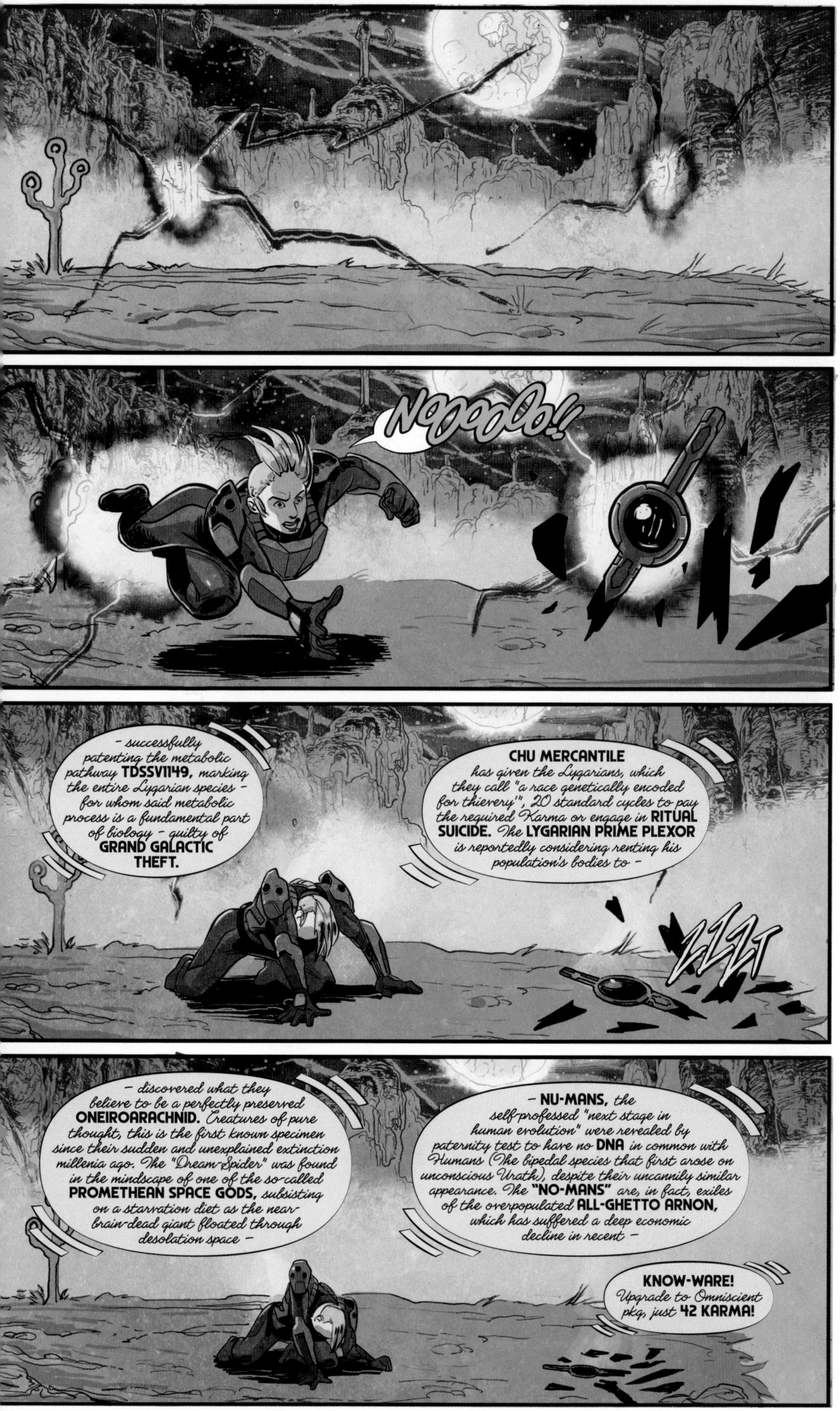

NOOOOOO!!
– successfully patenting the metabolic pathway TDSSV1149, marking the entire Lygarian species – for whom said metabolic process is a fundamental part of biology – guilty of GRAND GALACTIC THEFT.
CHU MERCANTILE has given the Lygarians, which they call "a race genetically encoded for thievery", 20 standard cycles to pay the required Karma or engage in RITUAL SUICIDE. The LYGARIAN PRIME PLEXOR is reportedly considering renting his population's bodies to –
ZZZT
– discovered what they believe to be a perfectly preserved ONEIROARACHNID. Creatures of pure thought, this is the first known specimen since their sudden and unexplained extinction millenia ago. The "Dream-Spider" was found in the mindscape of one of the so-called PROMETHEAN SPACE GODS, subsisting on a starvation diet as the near-brain-dead giant floated through desolation space –
– NU-MANS, the self-professed "next stage in human evolution" were revealed by paternity test to have no DNA in common with Humans (The bipedal species that first arose on unconscious Urath), despite their uncannily similar appearance. The "NO-MANS" are, in fact, exiles of the overpopulated ALL-GHETTO ARNON, which has suffered a deep economic decline in recent –
KNOW-WARE! Upgrade to Omniscient pkg, just 42 KARMA!

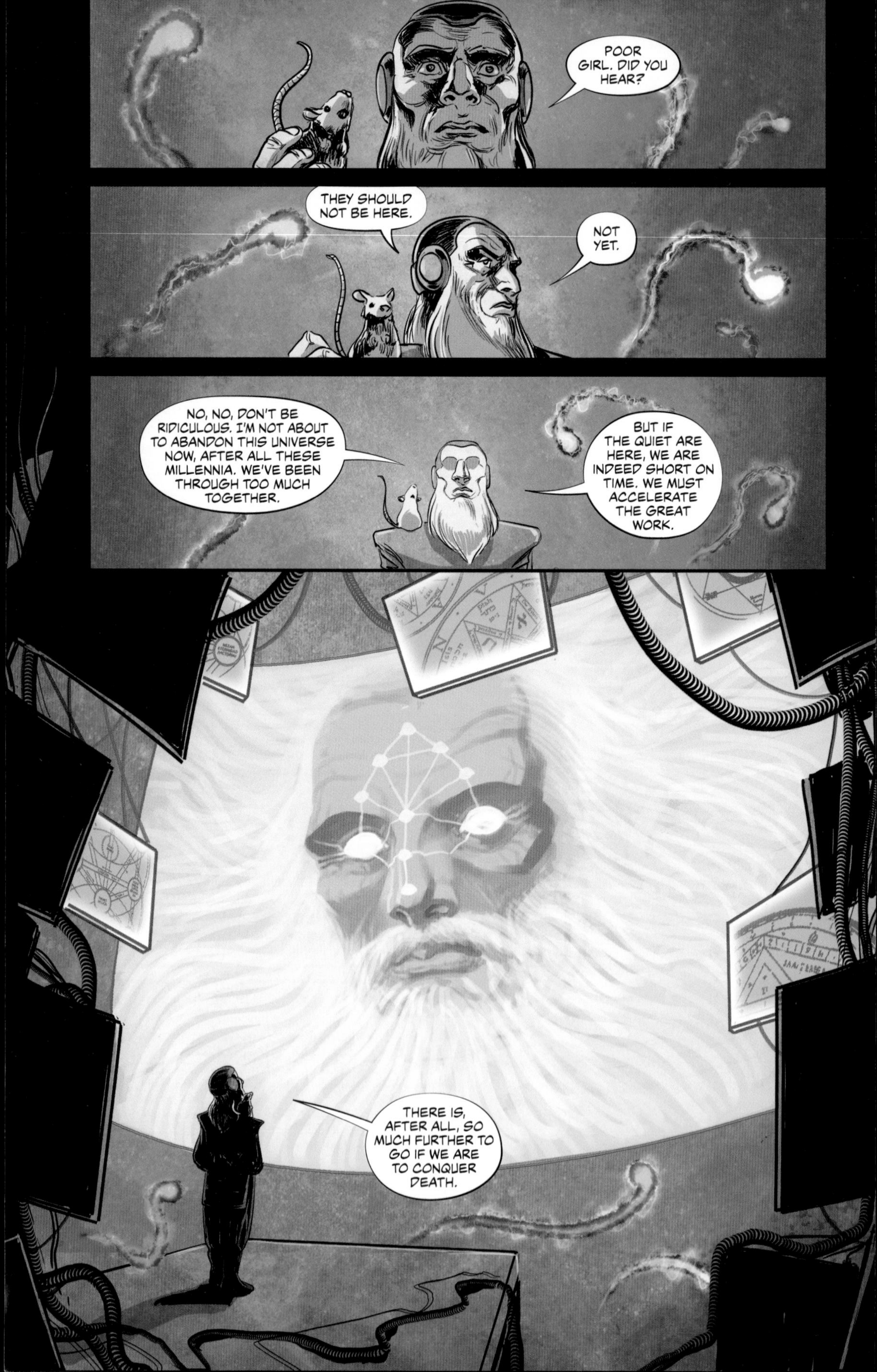
POOR GIRL. DID YOU HEAR?
THEY SHOULD NOT BE HERE.
NOT YET.
NO, NO, DON'T BE RIDICULOUS. I'M NOT ABOUT TO ABANDON THIS UNIVERSE NOW, AFTER ALL THESE MILLENNIA. WE'VE BEEN THROUGH TOO MUCH TOGETHER.
BUT IF THE QUIET ARE HERE, WE ARE INDEED SHORT ON TIME. WE MUST ACCELERATE THE GREAT WORK.
THERE IS, AFTER ALL, SO MUCH FURTHER TO GO IF WE ARE TO CONQUER DEATH.

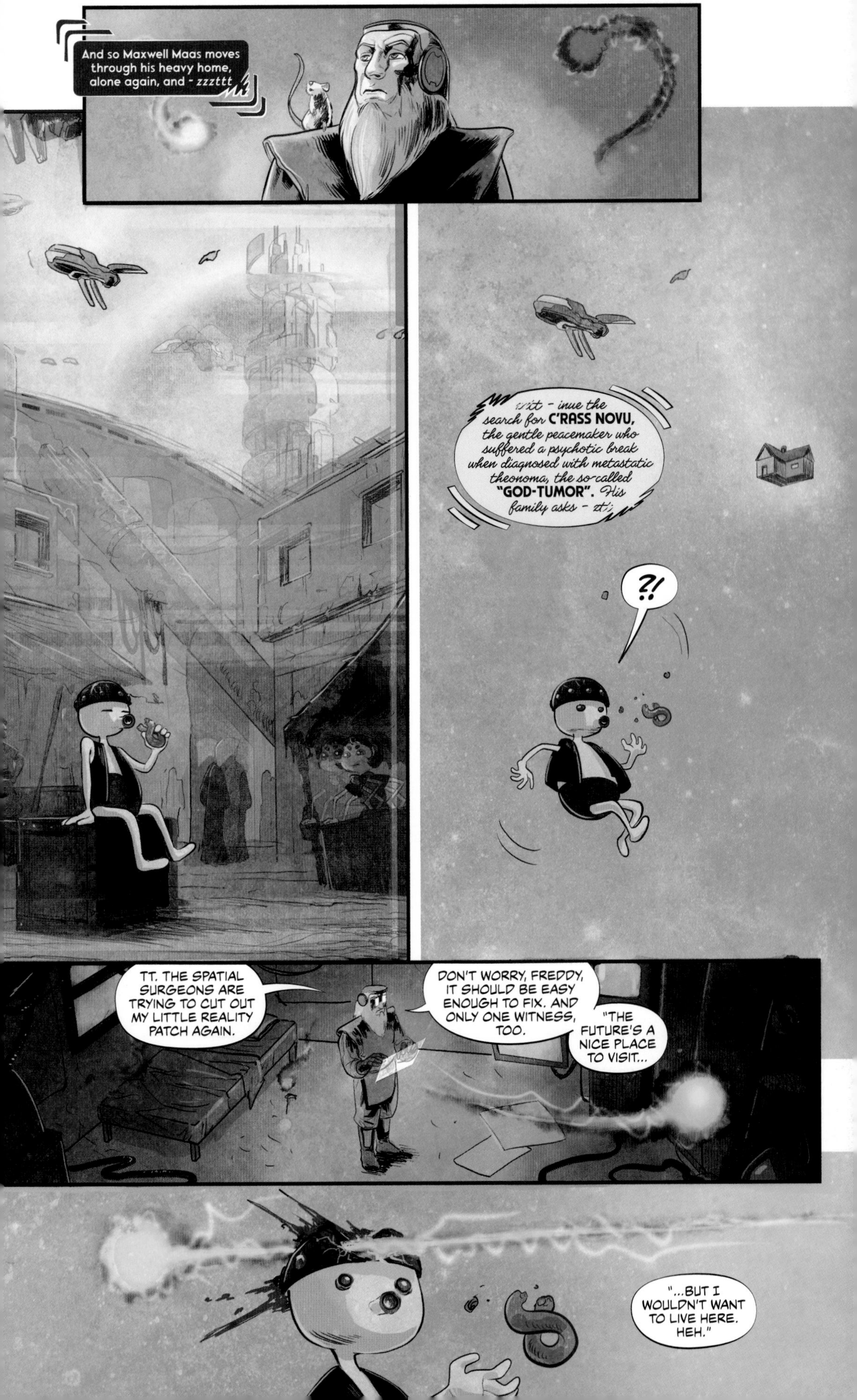
And so Maxwell Maas moves through his heavy home, alone again, and - zzzttt
-zzt - inue the search for C'RASS NOVU, the gentle peacemaker who suffered a psychotic break when diagnosed with metastatic theonoma, the so-called "GOD-TUMOR". His family asks - zt;
?!
TT. THE SPATIAL SURGEONS ARE TRYING TO CUT OUT MY LITTLE REALITY PATCH AGAIN.
DON'T WORRY, FREDDY, IT SHOULD BE EASY ENOUGH TO FIX. AND ONLY ONE WITNESS, TOO.
"THE FUTURE'S A NICE PLACE TO VISIT...
"...BUT I WOULDN'T WANT TO LIVE HERE. HEH."

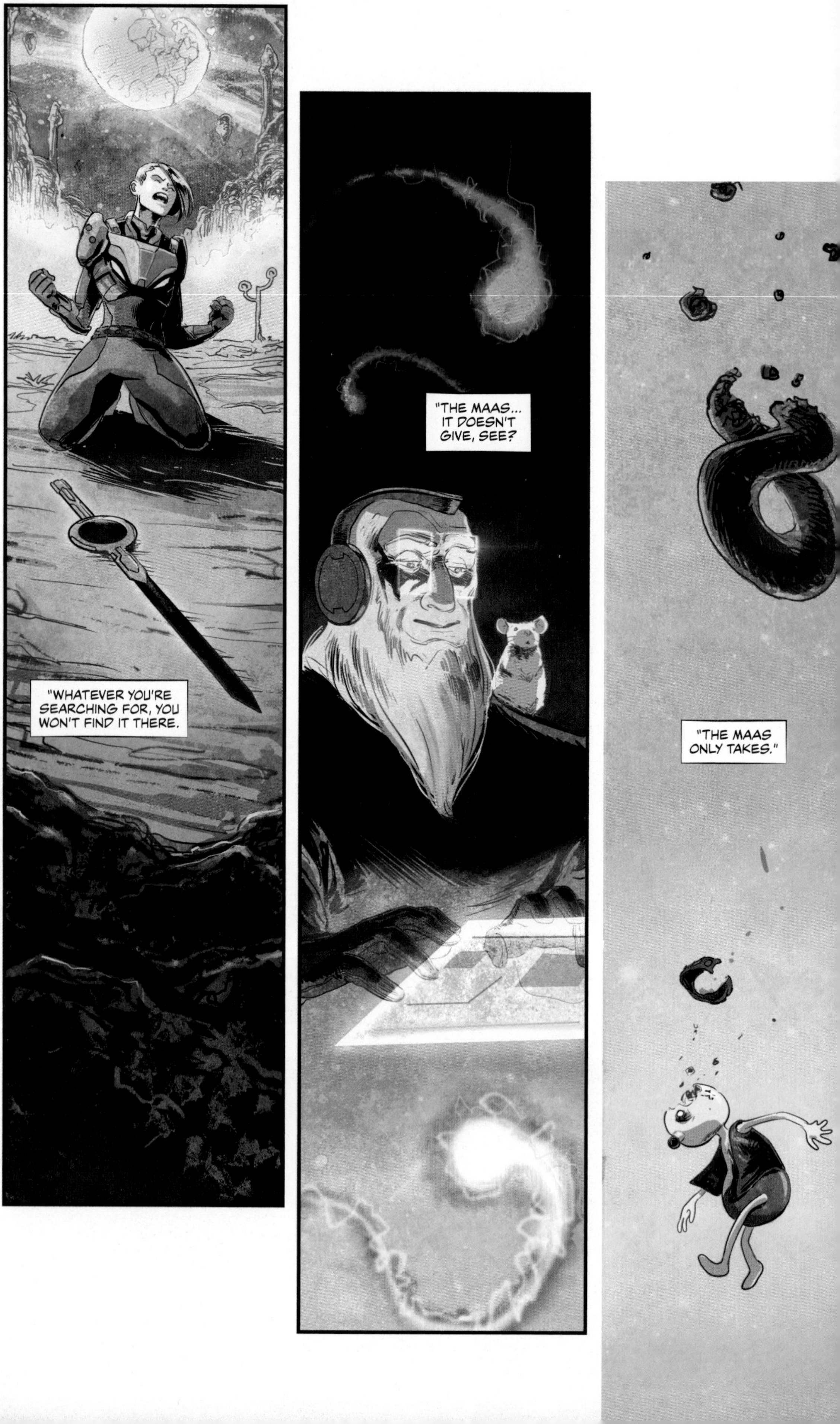

"WHATEVER YOU'RE SEARCHING FOR, YOU WON'T FIND IT THERE.
"THE MAAS... IT DOESN'T GIVE, SEE?
"THE MAAS ONLY TAKES."

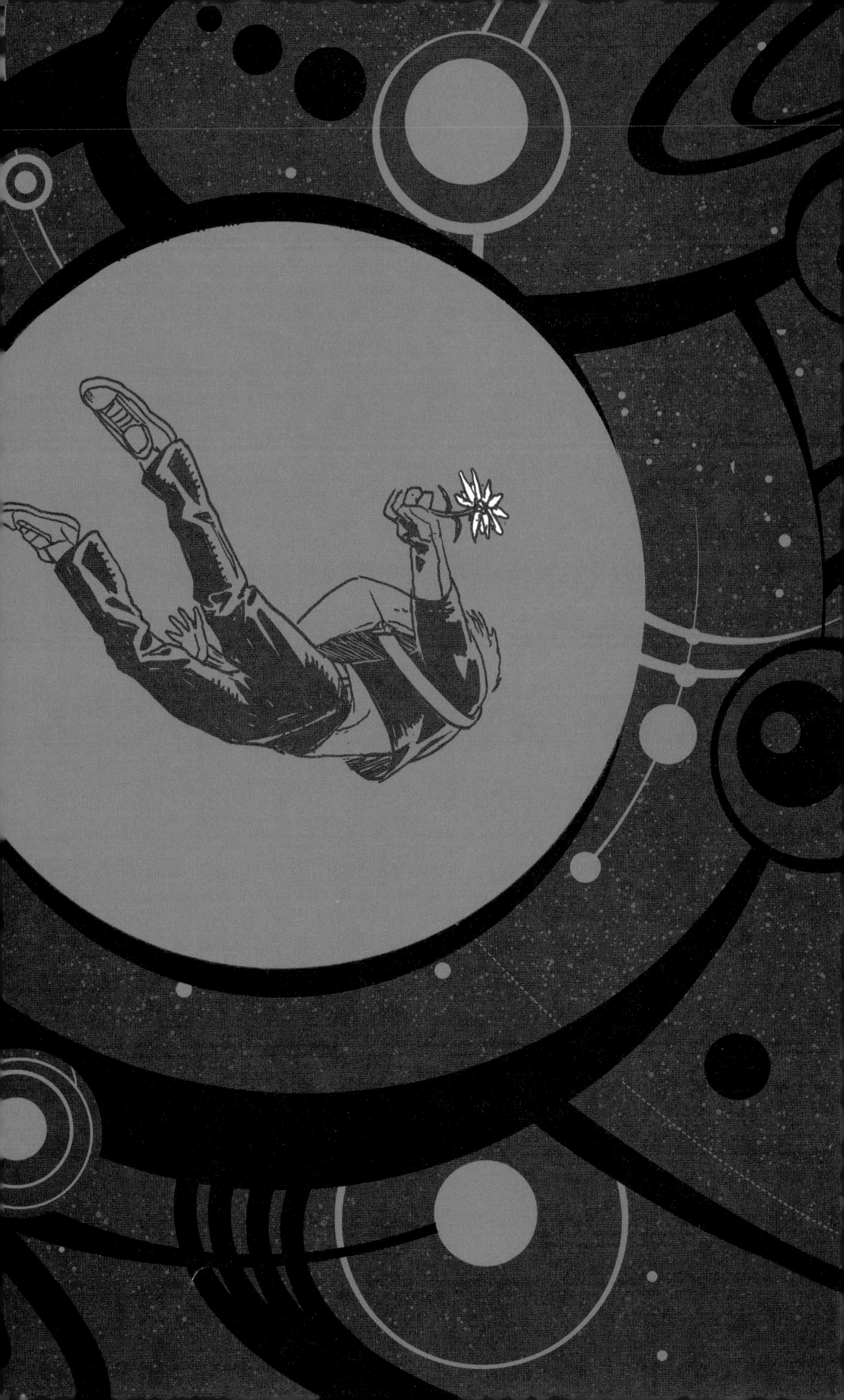

THREE

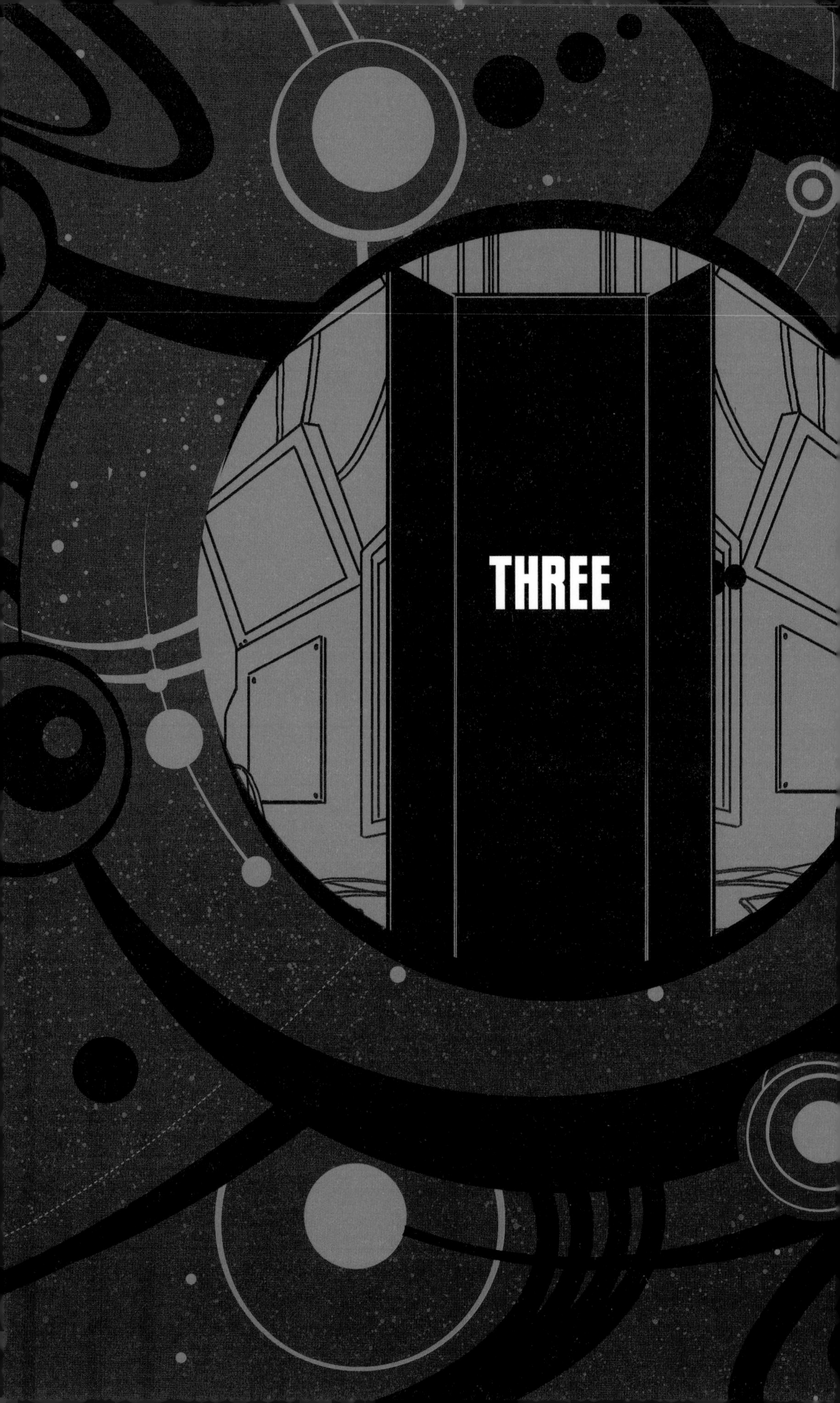

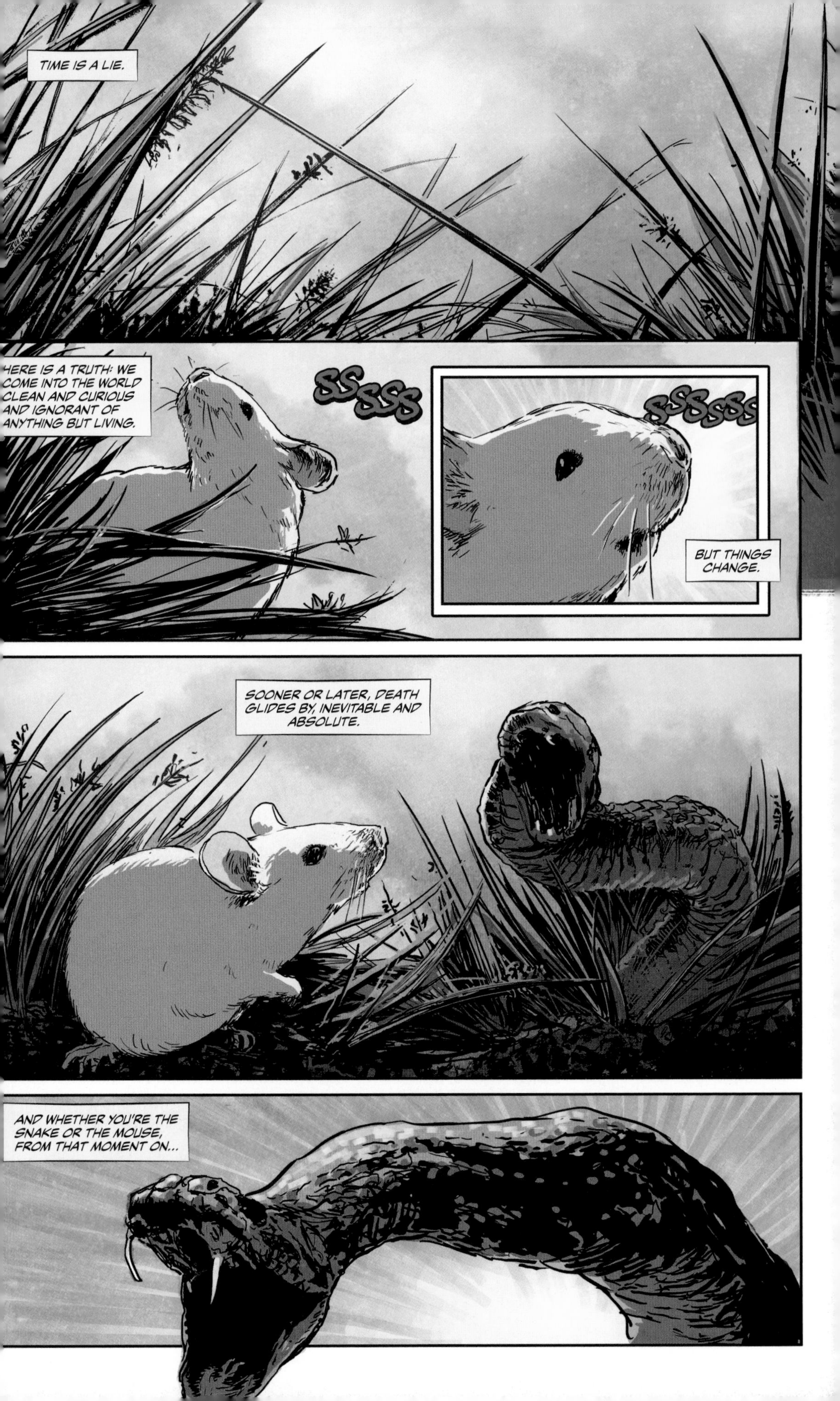
TIME IS A LIE.
HERE IS A TRUTH: WE COME INTO THE WORLD CLEAN AND CURIOUS AND IGNORANT OF ANYTHING BUT LIVING.
SSSSS
SSSSSS
BUT THINGS CHANGE.
SOONER OR LATER, DEATH GLIDES BY, INEVITABLE AND ABSOLUTE.
AND WHETHER YOU'RE THE SNAKE OR THE MOUSE, FROM THAT MOMENT ON...

...YOU STEP IN ITS SHADOW.

FRIEDRICH! YOU HAVE TO STOP GETTING OUT OF YOUR CAGE!

I WON'T ALWAYS BE AROUND TO SAVE YOU. YOU'LL HAVE TO LEARN TO SAVE YOURSELF.

MAX. YOU BETTER GET YOURSELF READY. WE'RE LEAVING IN AN HOUR.

IS THAT THE ROYAL "WE"?

DON'T START.

TIME IS A LIE.

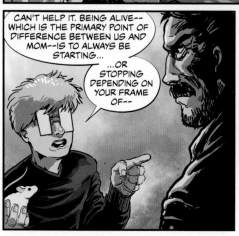

CAN'T HELP IT. BEING ALIVE-- WHICH IS THE PRIMARY POINT OF DIFFERENCE BETWEEN US AND MOM--IS TO ALWAYS BE STARTING...

...OR STOPPING DEPENDING ON YOUR FRAME OF--

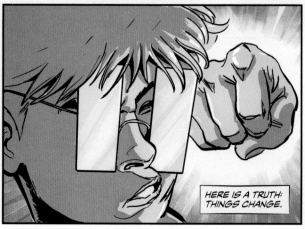

HERE IS A TRUTH: THINGS CHANGE.

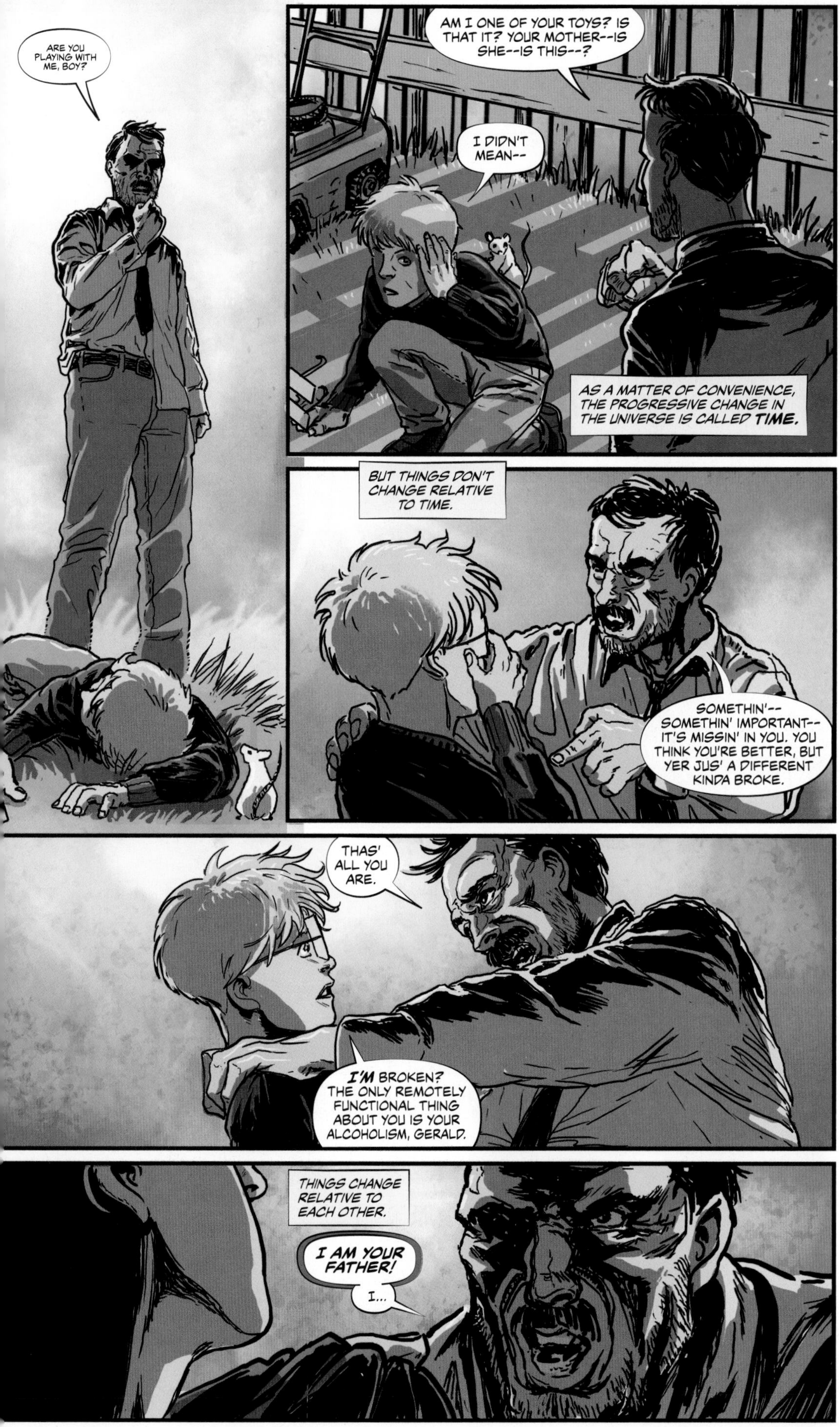
ARE YOU PLAYING WITH ME, BOY?
AM I ONE OF YOUR TOYS? IS THAT IT? YOUR MOTHER--IS SHE--IS THIS--?
I DIDN'T MEAN--
AS A MATTER OF CONVENIENCE, THE PROGRESSIVE CHANGE IN THE UNIVERSE IS CALLED TIME.
BUT THINGS DON'T CHANGE RELATIVE TO TIME.
SOMETHIN'-- SOMETHIN' IMPORTANT-- IT'S MISSIN' IN YOU. YOU THINK YOU'RE BETTER, BUT YER JUS' A DIFFERENT KINDA BROKE.
THAS' ALL YOU ARE.
I'M BROKEN? THE ONLY REMOTELY FUNCTIONAL THING ABOUT YOU IS YOUR ALCOHOLISM, GERALD.
THINGS CHANGE RELATIVE TO EACH OTHER.
I AM YOUR FATHER!
I...

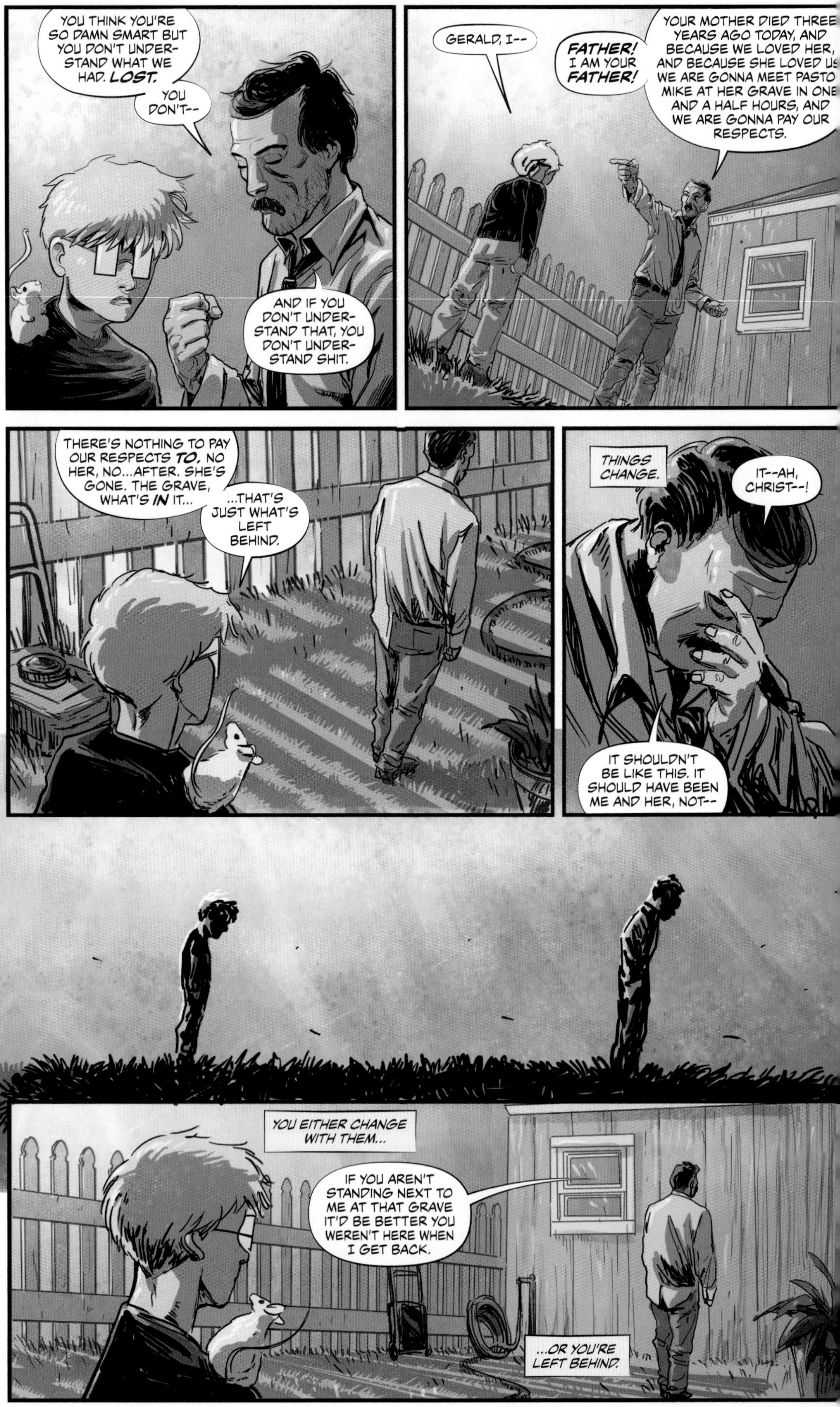
YOU THINK YOU'RE SO DAMN SMART BUT YOU DON'T UNDERSTAND WHAT WE HAD. LOST.
YOU DON'T--
AND IF YOU DON'T UNDERSTAND THAT, YOU DON'T UNDERSTAND SHIT.
GERALD, I--
FATHER! I AM YOUR FATHER!
YOUR MOTHER DIED THREE YEARS AGO TODAY, AND BECAUSE WE LOVED HER, AND BECAUSE SHE LOVED US WE ARE GONNA MEET PASTO MIKE AT HER GRAVE IN ONE AND A HALF HOURS, AND WE ARE GONNA PAY OUR RESPECTS.
THERE'S NOTHING TO PAY OUR RESPECTS TO. NO HER, NO...AFTER. SHE'S GONE. THE GRAVE, WHAT'S IN IT...
...THAT'S JUST WHAT'S LEFT BEHIND.
THINGS CHANGE.
IT--AH, CHRIST--!
IT SHOULDN'T BE LIKE THIS. IT SHOULD HAVE BEEN ME AND HER, NOT--
YOU EITHER CHANGE WITH THEM...
IF YOU AREN'T STANDING NEXT TO ME AT THAT GRAVE IT'D BE BETTER YOU WEREN'T HERE WHEN I GET BACK.
...OR YOU'RE LEFT BEHIND.

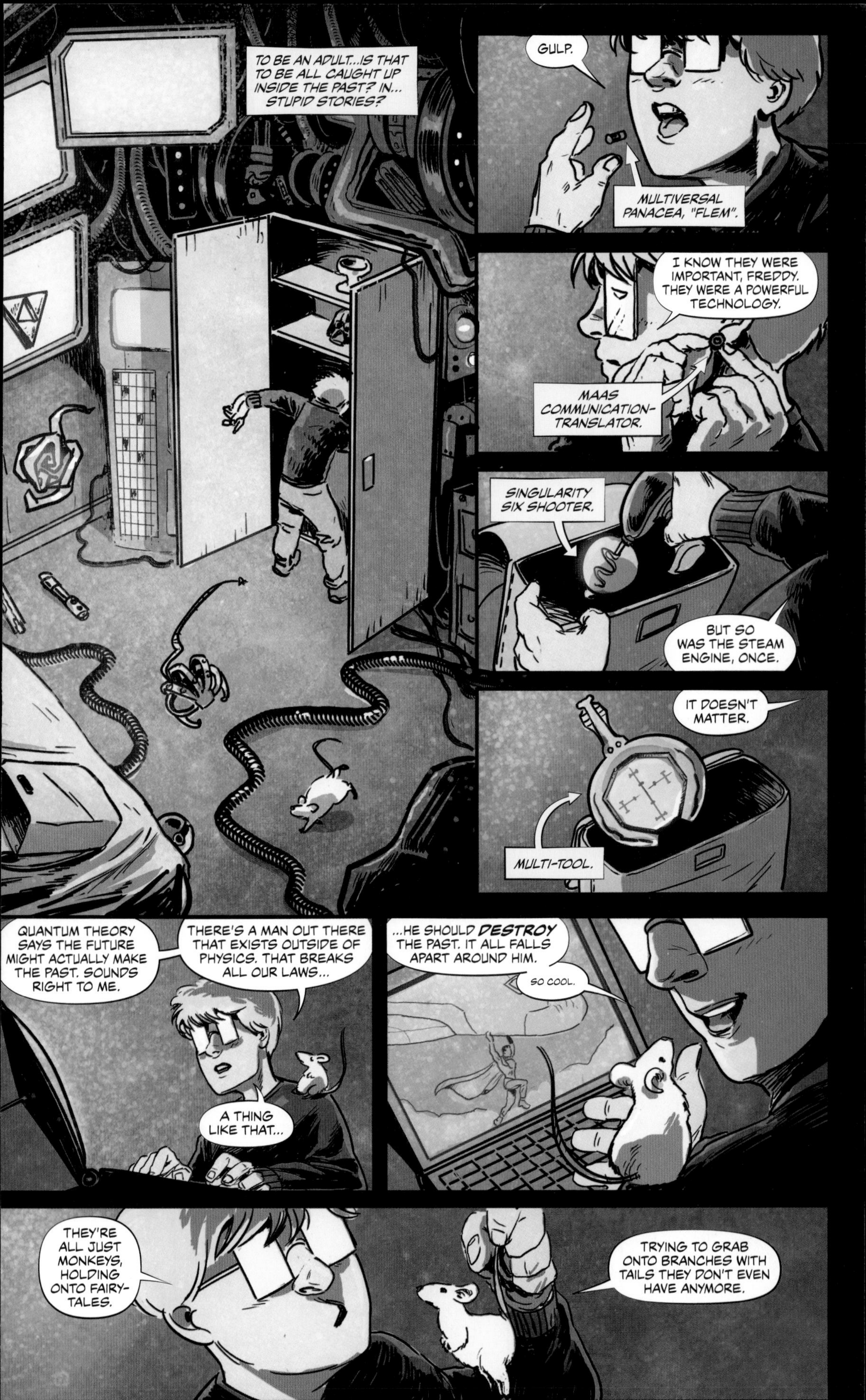
TO BE AN ADULT...IS THAT TO BE ALL CAUGHT UP INSIDE THE PAST? IN... STUPID STORIES?
GULP.
MULTIVERSAL PANACEA, "FLEM".
I KNOW THEY WERE IMPORTANT, FREDDY. THEY WERE A POWERFUL TECHNOLOGY.
MAAS COMMUNICATION-TRANSLATOR.
SINGULARITY SIX SHOOTER.
BUT SO WAS THE STEAM ENGINE, ONCE.
IT DOESN'T MATTER.
MULTI-TOOL.
QUANTUM THEORY SAYS THE FUTURE MIGHT ACTUALLY MAKE THE PAST. SOUNDS RIGHT TO ME.
THERE'S A MAN OUT THERE THAT EXISTS OUTSIDE OF PHYSICS. THAT BREAKS ALL OUR LAWS...
A THING LIKE THAT...
...HE SHOULD DESTROY THE PAST. IT ALL FALLS APART AROUND HIM.
SO COOL.
THEY'RE ALL JUST MONKEYS, HOLDING ONTO FAIRY-TALES.
TRYING TO GRAB ONTO BRANCHES WITH TAILS THEY DON'T EVEN HAVE ANYMORE.

I KNOW IT'S MY FAULT, FREDDY. I KNOW THAT. I...

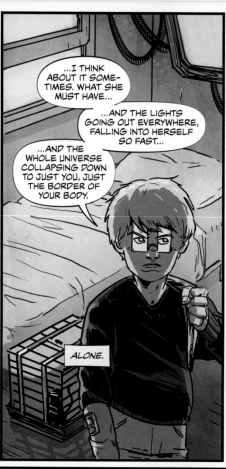

...I THINK ABOUT IT SOME- TIMES. WHAT SHE MUST HAVE...

...AND THE LIGHTS GOING OUT EVERYWHERE, FALLING INTO HERSELF SO FAST...

...AND THE WHOLE UNIVERSE COLLAPSING DOWN TO JUST YOU, JUST THE BORDER OF YOUR BODY.

ALONE.

EVERYBODY DIES ALONE.

BEEP

I'M NOT...I'M NOT GONNA LET MY UNIVERSE KEEP GETTING SMALLER. I'LL FIND NEW ONES...

AND I GOTTA DO IT ALONE.

EEP?

THE FUTURE MAKES THE PAST. OR AT LEAST IT *SHOULD.* MAYBE...

...MAYBE IT CAN EVEN MAKE THE PAST WORTH SOMETHING.

≈SIGH≈

FINE, I GUESS YOU CAN COME TOO.

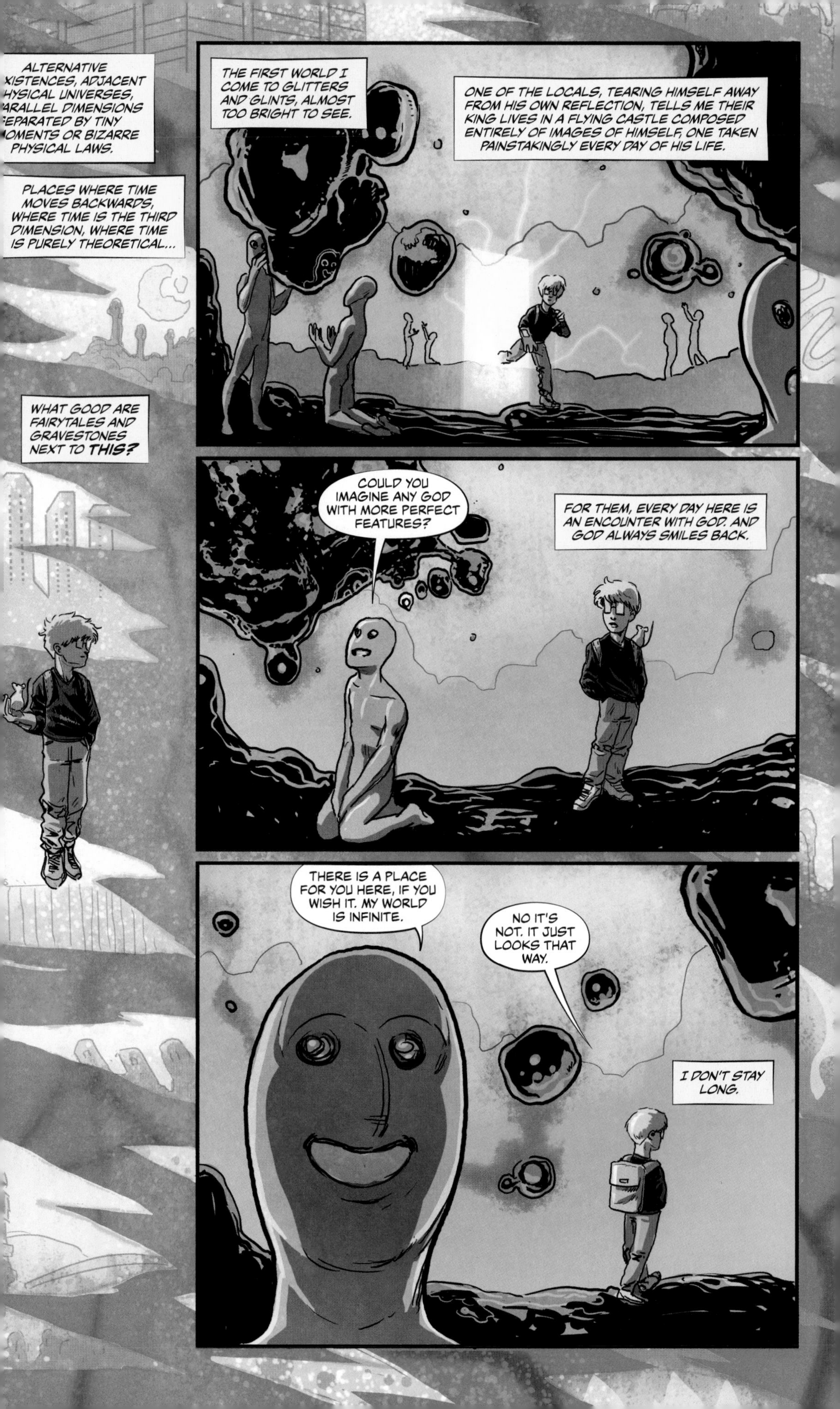
ALTERNATIVE
XISTENCES, ADJACENT
HYSICAL UNIVERSES,
ARALLEL DIMENSIONS
EPARATED BY TINY
OMENTS OR BIZARRE
PHYSICAL LAWS.
PLACES WHERE TIME MOVES BACKWARDS, WHERE TIME IS THE THIRD DIMENSION, WHERE TIME IS PURELY THEORETICAL...
WHAT GOOD ARE FAIRYTALES AND GRAVESTONES NEXT TO **THIS?**
THE FIRST WORLD I COME TO GLITTERS AND GLINTS, ALMOST TOO BRIGHT TO SEE.
ONE OF THE LOCALS, TEARING HIMSELF AWAY FROM HIS OWN REFLECTION, TELLS ME THEIR KING LIVES IN A FLYING CASTLE COMPOSED ENTIRELY OF IMAGES OF HIMSELF, ONE TAKEN PAINSTAKINGLY EVERY DAY OF HIS LIFE.
COULD YOU IMAGINE ANY GOD WITH MORE PERFECT FEATURES?
FOR THEM, EVERY DAY HERE IS AN ENCOUNTER WITH GOD. AND GOD ALWAYS SMILES BACK.
THERE IS A PLACE FOR YOU HERE, IF YOU WISH IT. MY WORLD IS INFINITE.
NO IT'S NOT. IT JUST LOOKS THAT WAY.
I DON'T STAY LONG.

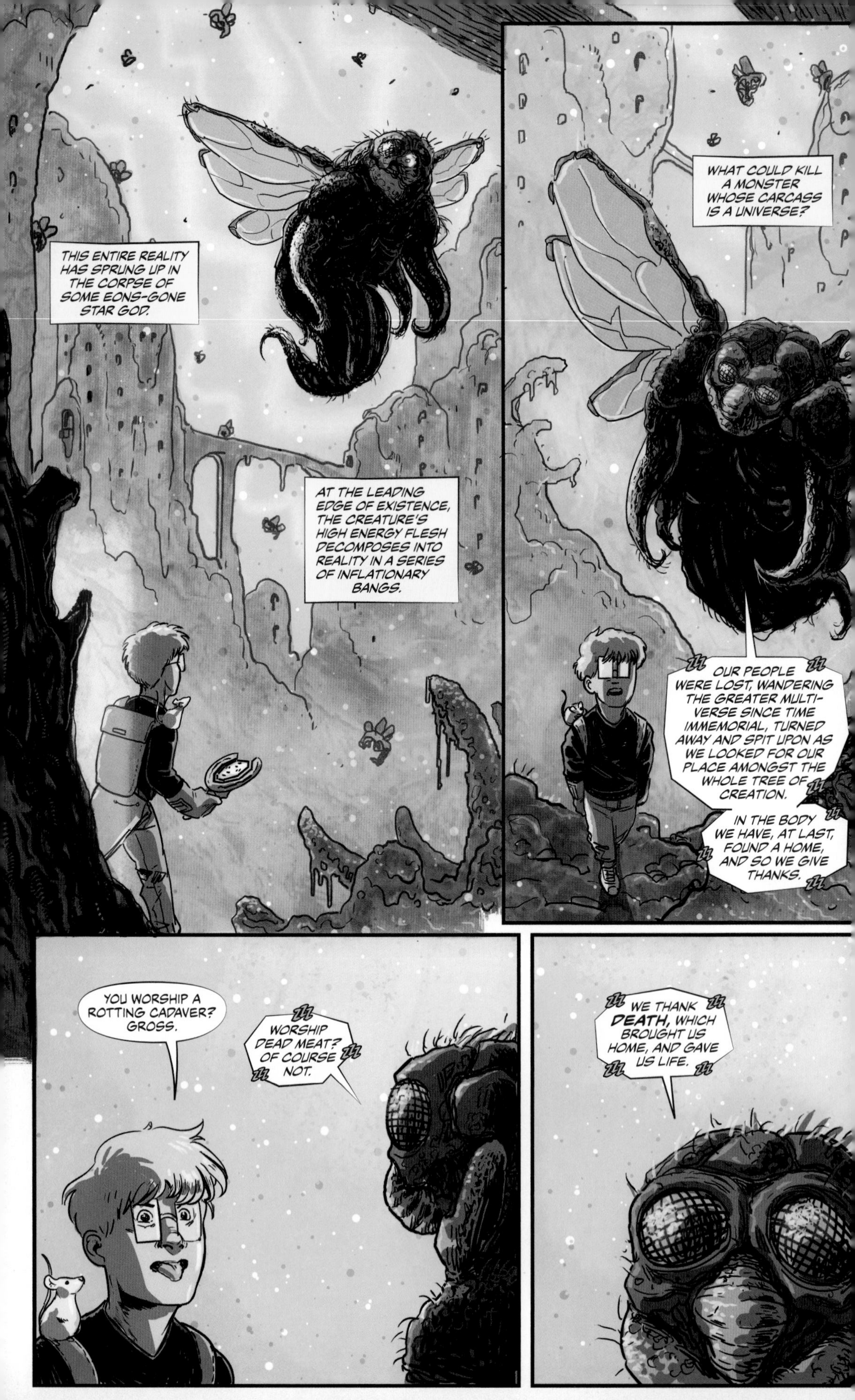

THIS ENTIRE REALITY HAS SPRUNG UP IN THE CORPSE OF SOME EONS-GONE STAR GOD.
AT THE LEADING EDGE OF EXISTENCE, THE CREATURE'S HIGH ENERGY FLESH DECOMPOSES INTO REALITY IN A SERIES OF INFLATIONARY BANGS.
WHAT COULD KILL A MONSTER WHOSE CARCASS IS A UNIVERSE?
OUR PEOPLE WERE LOST, WANDERING THE GREATER MULTI-VERSE SINCE TIME IMMEMORIAL, TURNED AWAY AND SPIT UPON AS WE LOOKED FOR OUR PLACE AMONGST THE WHOLE TREE OF CREATION.
IN THE BODY WE HAVE, AT LAST, FOUND A HOME, AND SO WE GIVE THANKS.
YOU WORSHIP A ROTTING CADAVER? GROSS.
WORSHIP DEAD MEAT? OF COURSE NOT.
WE THANK DEATH, WHICH BROUGHT US HOME, AND GAVE US LIFE.

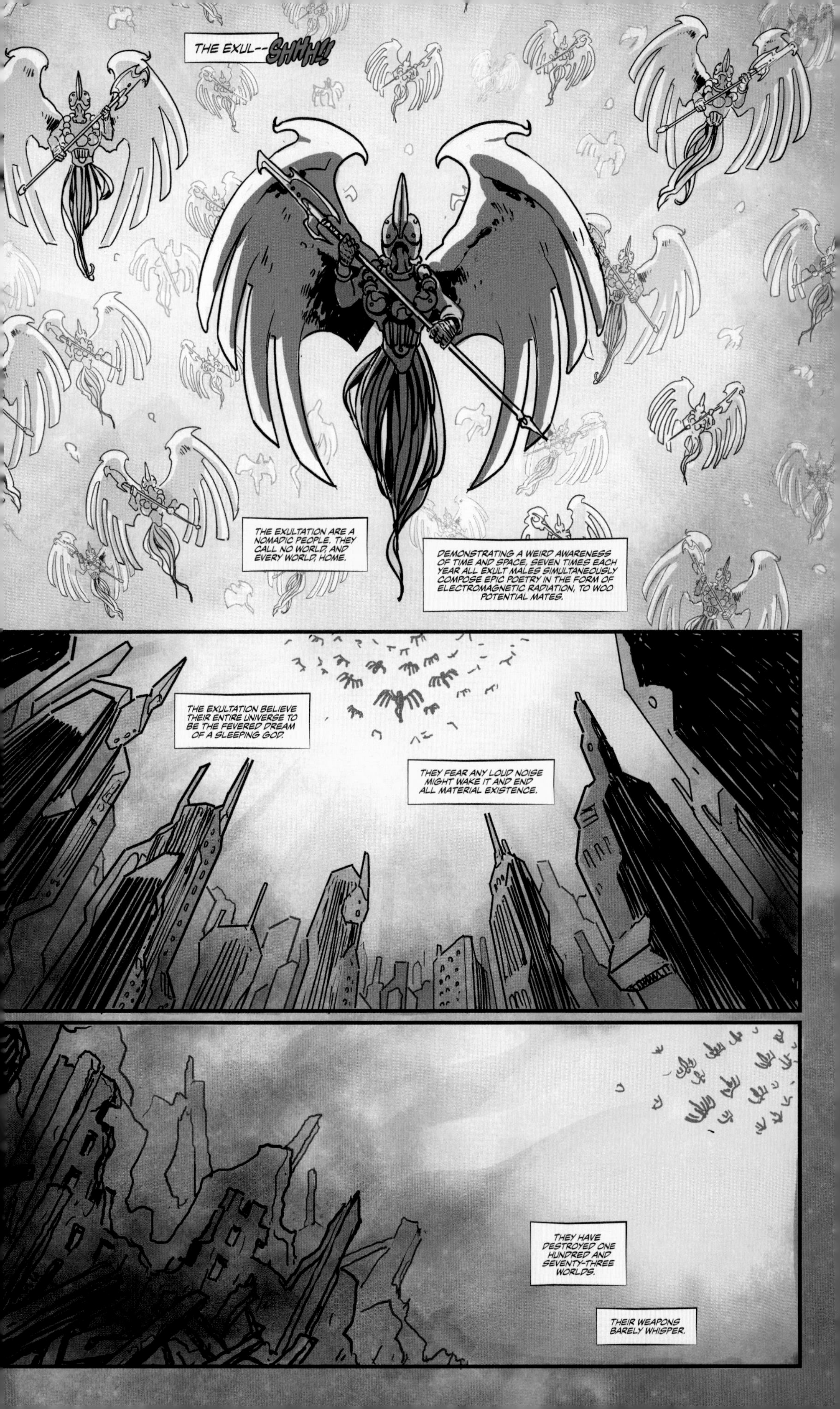
THE EXUL--SHHH!!
THE EXULTATION ARE A NOMADIC PEOPLE. THEY CALL NO WORLD, AND EVERY WORLD, HOME.
DEMONSTRATING A WEIRD AWARENESS OF TIME AND SPACE, SEVEN TIMES EACH YEAR ALL EXULT MALES SIMULTANEOUSLY COMPOSE EPIC POETRY IN THE FORM OF ELECTROMAGNETIC RADIATION, TO WOO POTENTIAL MATES.
THE EXULTATION BELIEVE THEIR ENTIRE UNIVERSE TO BE THE FEVERED DREAM OF A SLEEPING GOD.
THEY FEAR ANY LOUD NOISE MIGHT WAKE IT AND END ALL MATERIAL EXISTENCE.
THEY HAVE DESTROYED ONE HUNDRED AND SEVENTY-THREE WORLDS.
THEIR WEAPONS BARELY WHISPER.

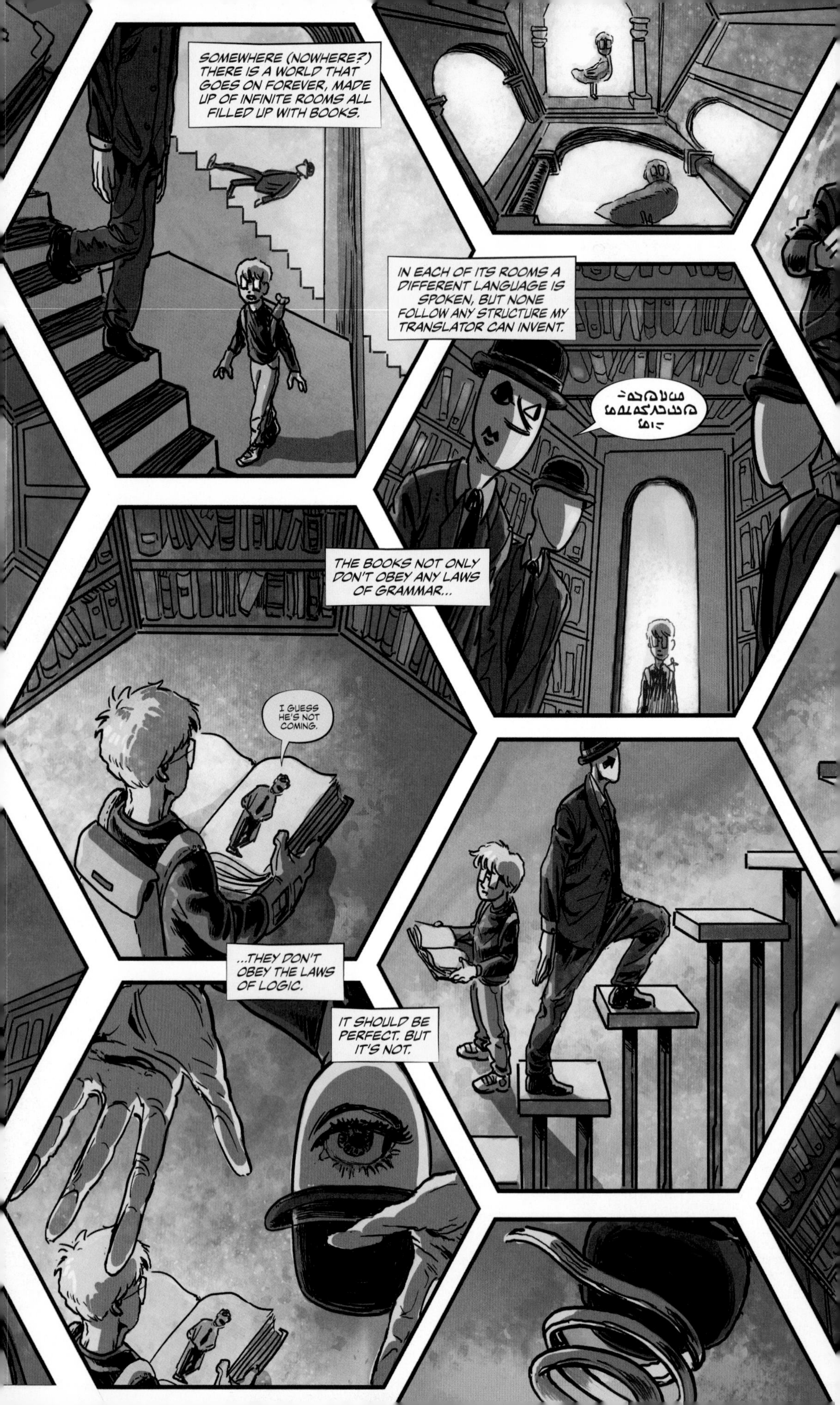

SOMEWHERE (NOWHERE?) THERE IS A WORLD THAT GOES ON FOREVER, MADE UP OF INFINITE ROOMS ALL FILLED UP WITH BOOKS.
IN EACH OF ITS ROOMS A DIFFERENT LANGUAGE IS SPOKEN, BUT NONE FOLLOW ANY STRUCTURE MY TRANSLATOR CAN INVENT.
THE BOOKS NOT ONLY DON'T OBEY ANY LAWS OF GRAMMAR...
I GUESS HE'S NOT COMING.
...THEY DON'T OBEY THE LAWS OF LOGIC.
IT SHOULD BE PERFECT. BUT IT'S NOT.

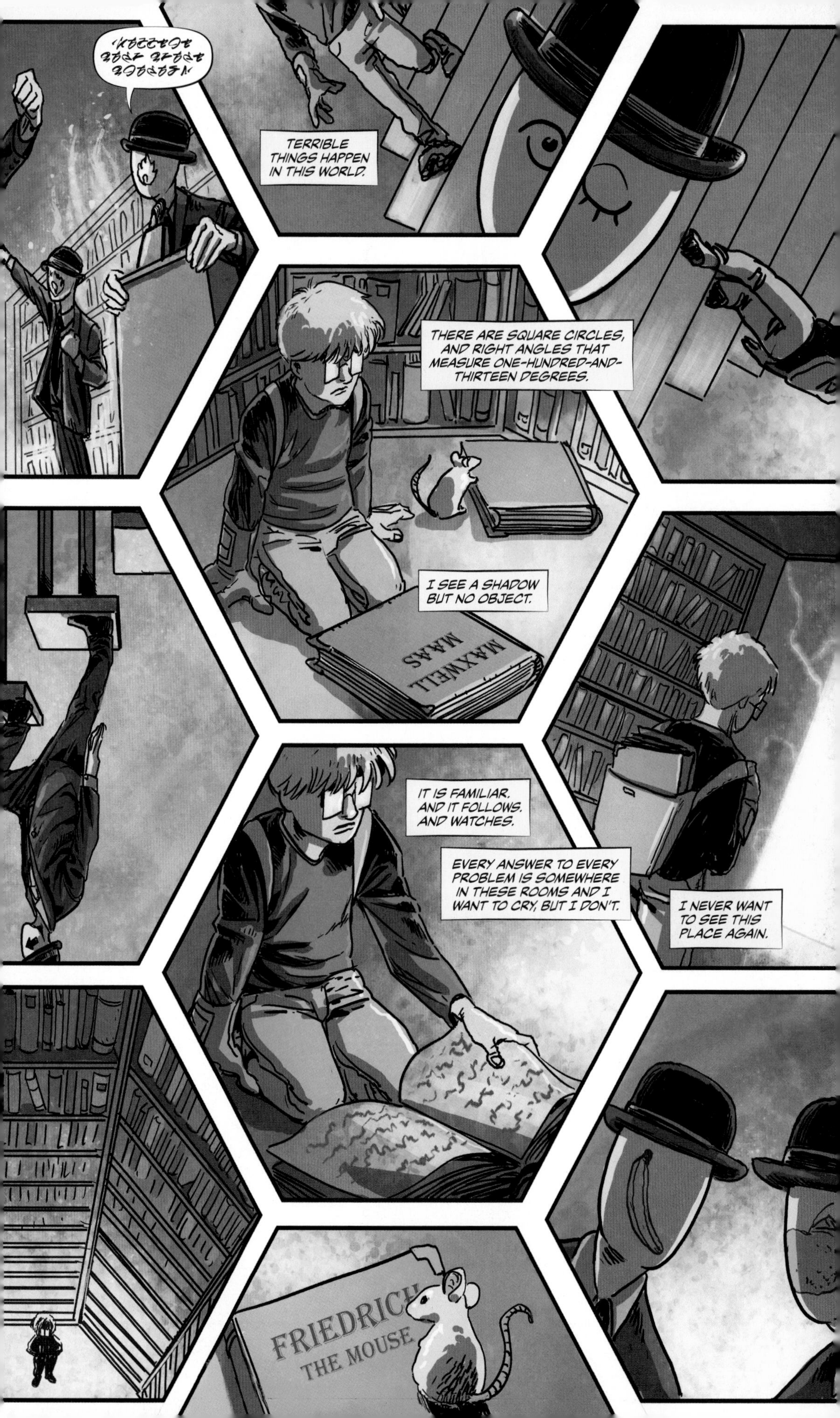
TERRIBLE THINGS HAPPEN IN THIS WORLD.
THERE ARE SQUARE CIRCLES, AND RIGHT ANGLES THAT MEASURE ONE-HUNDRED-AND-THIRTEEN DEGREES.
I SEE A SHADOW BUT NO OBJECT.
MAXWELL MAAS
IT IS FAMILIAR. AND IT FOLLOWS. AND WATCHES.
EVERY ANSWER TO EVERY PROBLEM IS SOMEWHERE IN THESE ROOMS AND I WANT TO CRY, BUT I DON'T.
I NEVER WANT TO SEE THIS PLACE AGAIN.
FRIEDRICH THE MOUSE

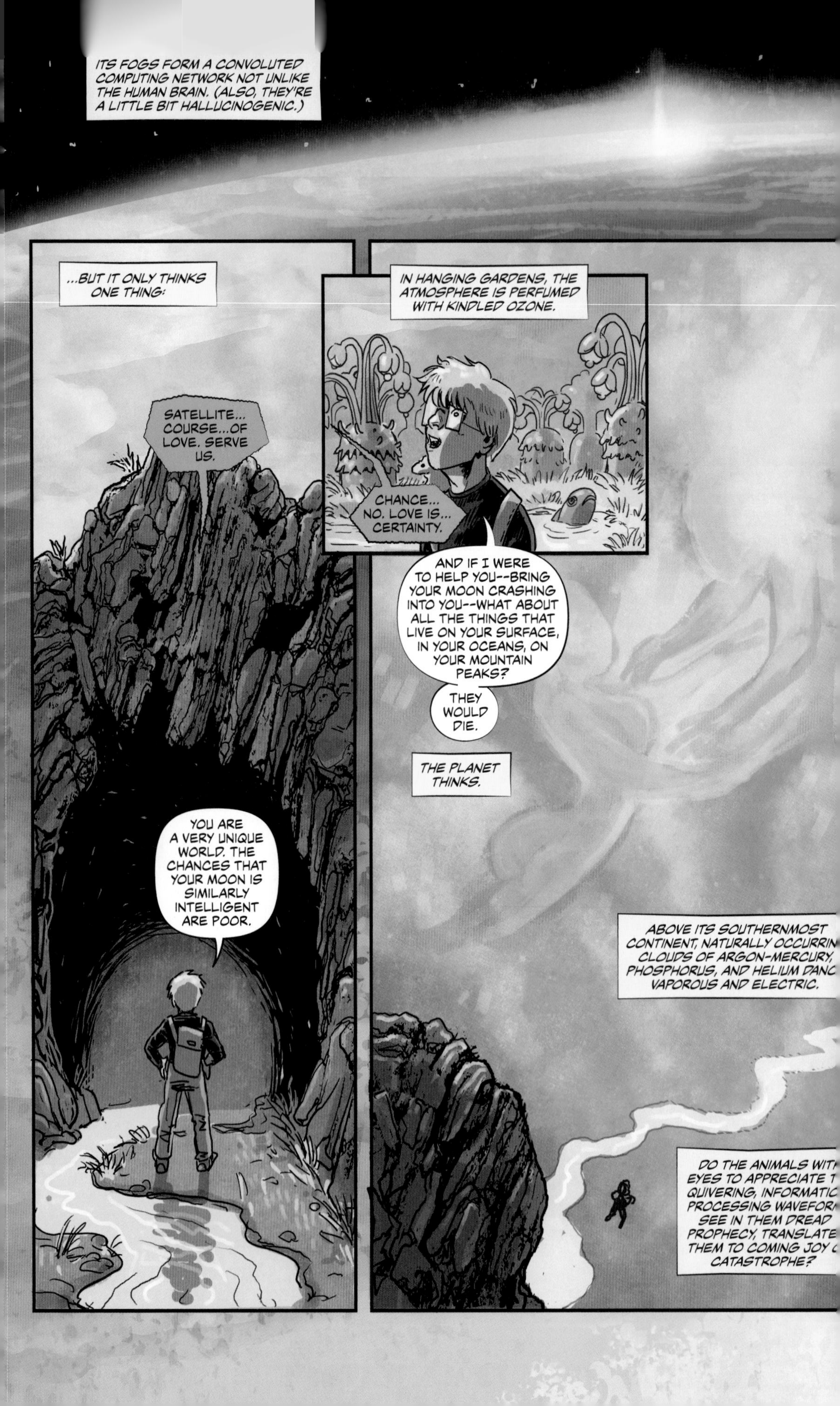
ITS FOGS FORM A CONVOLUTED COMPUTING NETWORK NOT UNLIKE THE HUMAN BRAIN. (ALSO, THEY'RE A LITTLE BIT HALLUCINOGENIC.)
...BUT IT ONLY THINKS ONE THING:
SATELLITE... COURSE...OF LOVE. SERVE US.
YOU ARE A VERY UNIQUE WORLD. THE CHANCES THAT YOUR MOON IS SIMILARLY INTELLIGENT ARE POOR.
IN HANGING GARDENS, THE ATMOSPHERE IS PERFUMED WITH KINDLED OZONE.
CHANCE... NO. LOVE IS... CERTAINTY.
AND IF I WERE TO HELP YOU--BRING YOUR MOON CRASHING INTO YOU--WHAT ABOUT ALL THE THINGS THAT LIVE ON YOUR SURFACE, IN YOUR OCEANS, ON YOUR MOUNTAIN PEAKS?
THEY WOULD DIE.
THE PLANET THINKS.
ABOVE ITS SOUTHERNMOST CONTINENT, NATURALLY OCCURRIN CLOUDS OF ARGON-MERCURY, PHOSPHORUS, AND HELIUM DANC VAPOROUS AND ELECTRIC.
DO THE ANIMALS WIT EYES TO APPRECIATE T QUIVERING, INFORMATIC PROCESSING WAVEFOR SEE IN THEM DREAD PROPHECY, TRANSLATE THEM TO COMING JOY CATASTROPHE?

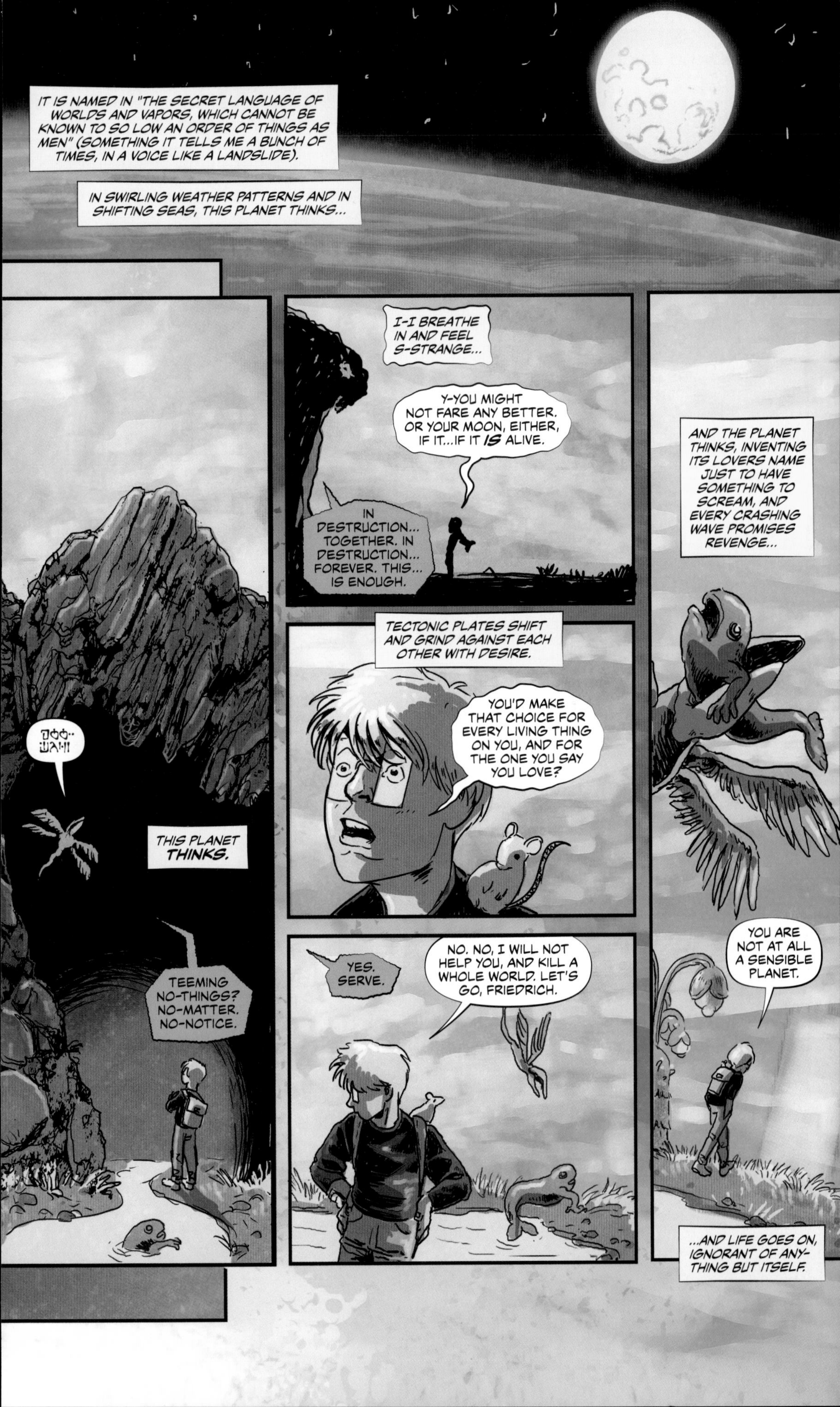

IT IS NAMED IN "THE SECRET LANGUAGE OF WORLDS AND VAPORS, WHICH CANNOT BE KNOWN TO SO LOW AN ORDER OF THINGS AS MEN" (SOMETHING IT TELLS ME A BUNCH OF TIMES, IN A VOICE LIKE A LANDSLIDE).
IN SWIRLING WEATHER PATTERNS AND IN SHIFTING SEAS, THIS PLANET THINKS...
THIS PLANET THINKS.
TEEMING NO-THINGS? NO-MATTER. NO-NOTICE.
I-I BREATHE IN AND FEEL S-STRANGE...
Y-YOU MIGHT NOT FARE ANY BETTER. OR YOUR MOON, EITHER, IF IT...IF IT IS ALIVE.
IN DESTRUCTION... TOGETHER. IN DESTRUCTION... FOREVER. THIS... IS ENOUGH.
TECTONIC PLATES SHIFT AND GRIND AGAINST EACH OTHER WITH DESIRE.
YOU'D MAKE THAT CHOICE FOR EVERY LIVING THING ON YOU, AND FOR THE ONE YOU SAY YOU LOVE?
YES. SERVE.
NO. NO, I WILL NOT HELP YOU, AND KILL A WHOLE WORLD. LET'S GO, FRIEDRICH.
AND THE PLANET THINKS, INVENTING ITS LOVERS NAME JUST TO HAVE SOMETHING TO SCREAM, AND EVERY CRASHING WAVE PROMISES REVENGE...
YOU ARE NOT AT ALL A SENSIBLE PLANET.
...AND LIFE GOES ON, IGNORANT OF ANYTHING BUT ITSELF.

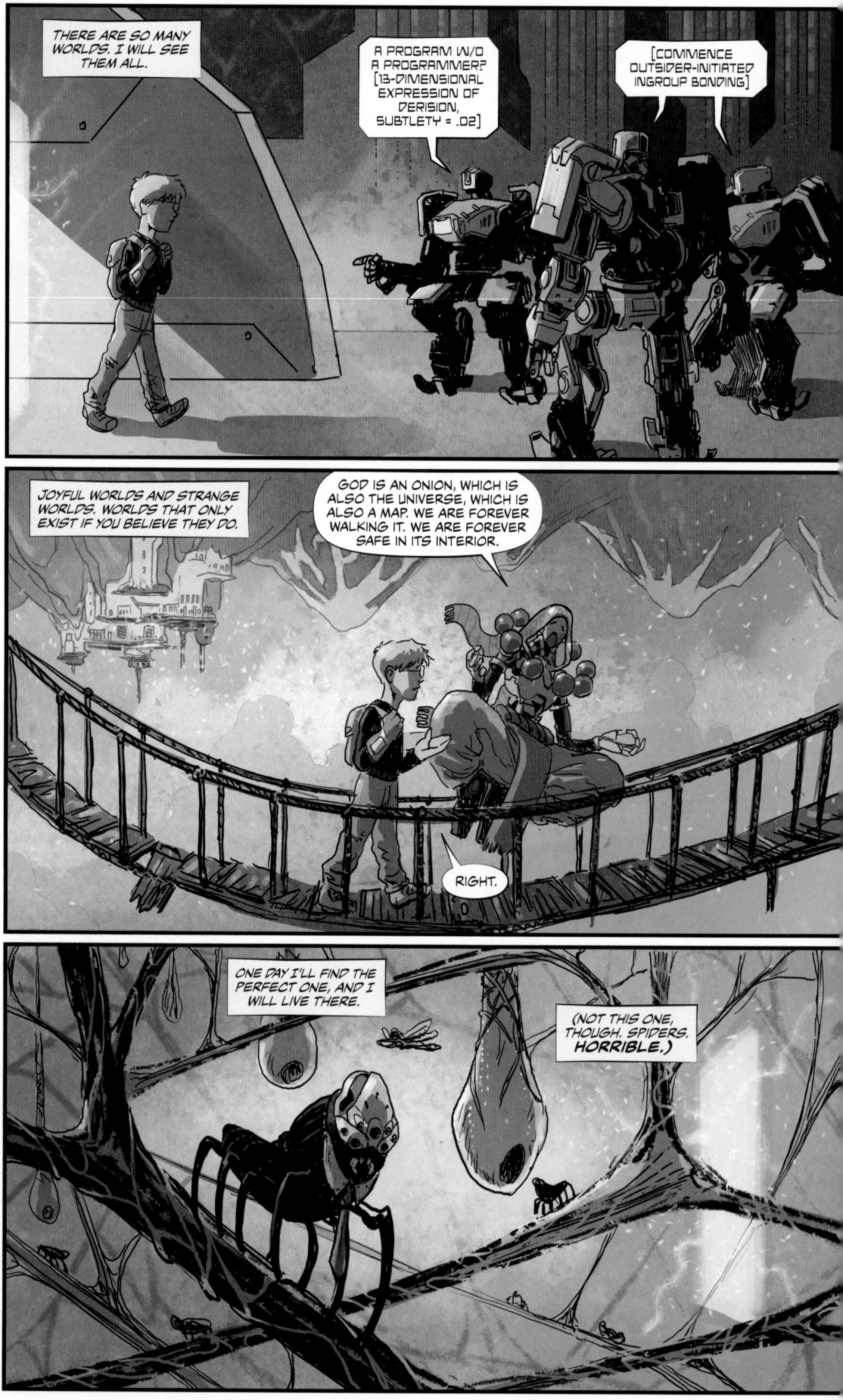
THERE ARE SO MANY WORLDS. I WILL SEE THEM ALL.
A PROGRAM W/O A PROGRAMMER? [13-DIMENSIONAL EXPRESSION OF DERISION, SUBTLETY = .02]
[COMMENCE OUTSIDER-INITIATED INGROUP BONDING]
JOYFUL WORLDS AND STRANGE WORLDS. WORLDS THAT ONLY EXIST IF YOU BELIEVE THEY DO.
GOD IS AN ONION, WHICH IS ALSO THE UNIVERSE, WHICH IS ALSO A MAP. WE ARE FOREVER WALKING IT. WE ARE FOREVER SAFE IN ITS INTERIOR.
RIGHT.
ONE DAY I'LL FIND THE PERFECT ONE, AND I WILL LIVE THERE.
(NOT THIS ONE, THOUGH. SPIDERS. HORRIBLE.)

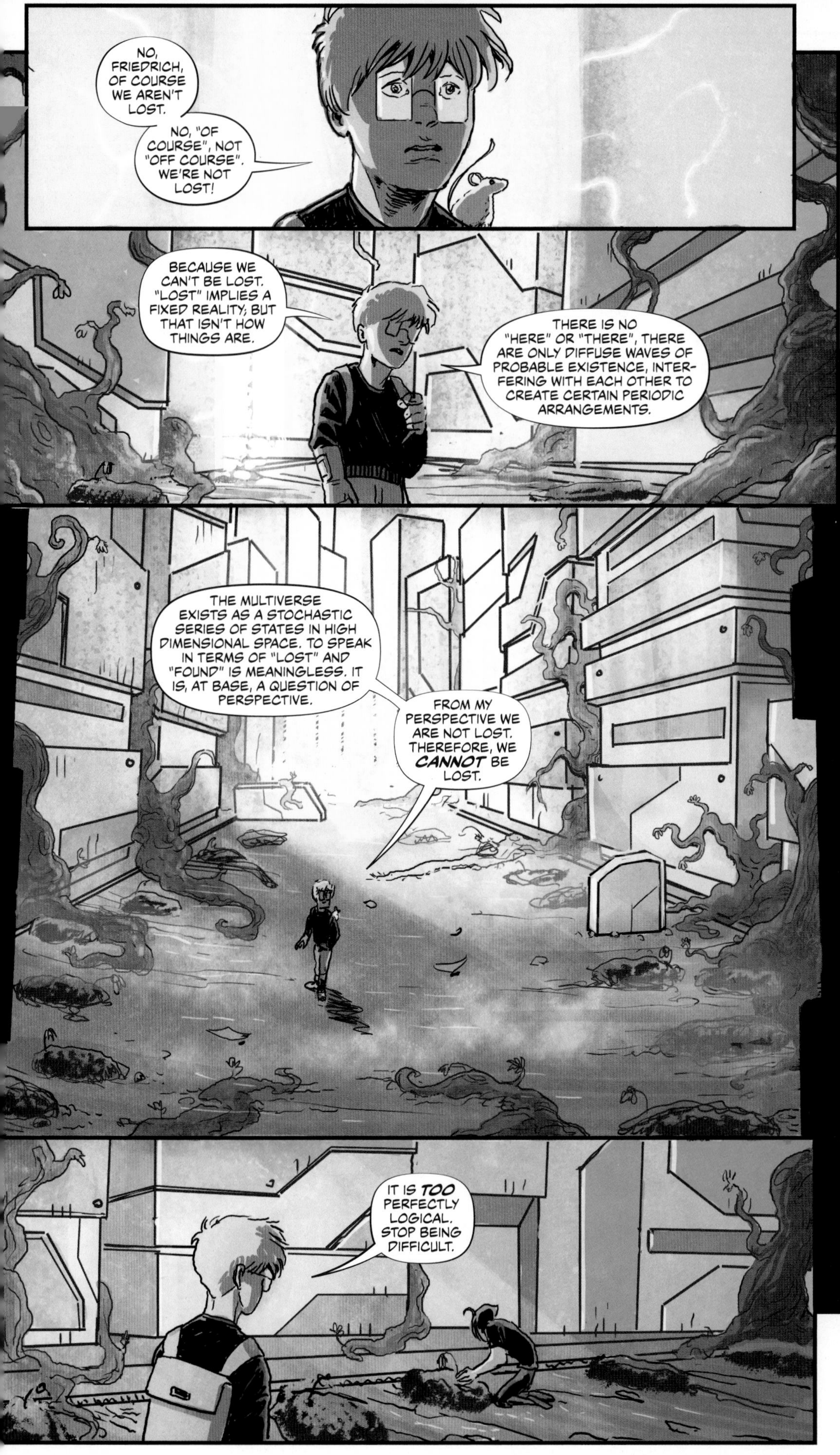
NO, FRIEDRICH, OF COURSE WE AREN'T LOST.
NO, "OF COURSE", NOT "OFF COURSE". WE'RE NOT LOST!
BECAUSE WE CAN'T BE LOST. "LOST" IMPLIES A FIXED REALITY; BUT THAT ISN'T HOW THINGS ARE.
THERE IS NO "HERE" OR "THERE", THERE ARE ONLY DIFFUSE WAVES OF PROBABLE EXISTENCE, INTERFERING WITH EACH OTHER TO CREATE CERTAIN PERIODIC ARRANGEMENTS.
THE MULTIVERSE EXISTS AS A STOCHASTIC SERIES OF STATES IN HIGH DIMENSIONAL SPACE. TO SPEAK IN TERMS OF "LOST" AND "FOUND" IS MEANINGLESS. IT IS, AT BASE, A QUESTION OF PERSPECTIVE.
FROM MY PERSPECTIVE WE ARE NOT LOST. THEREFORE, WE ***CANNOT*** BE LOST.
IT IS ***TOO*** PERFECTLY LOGICAL. STOP BEING DIFFICULT.

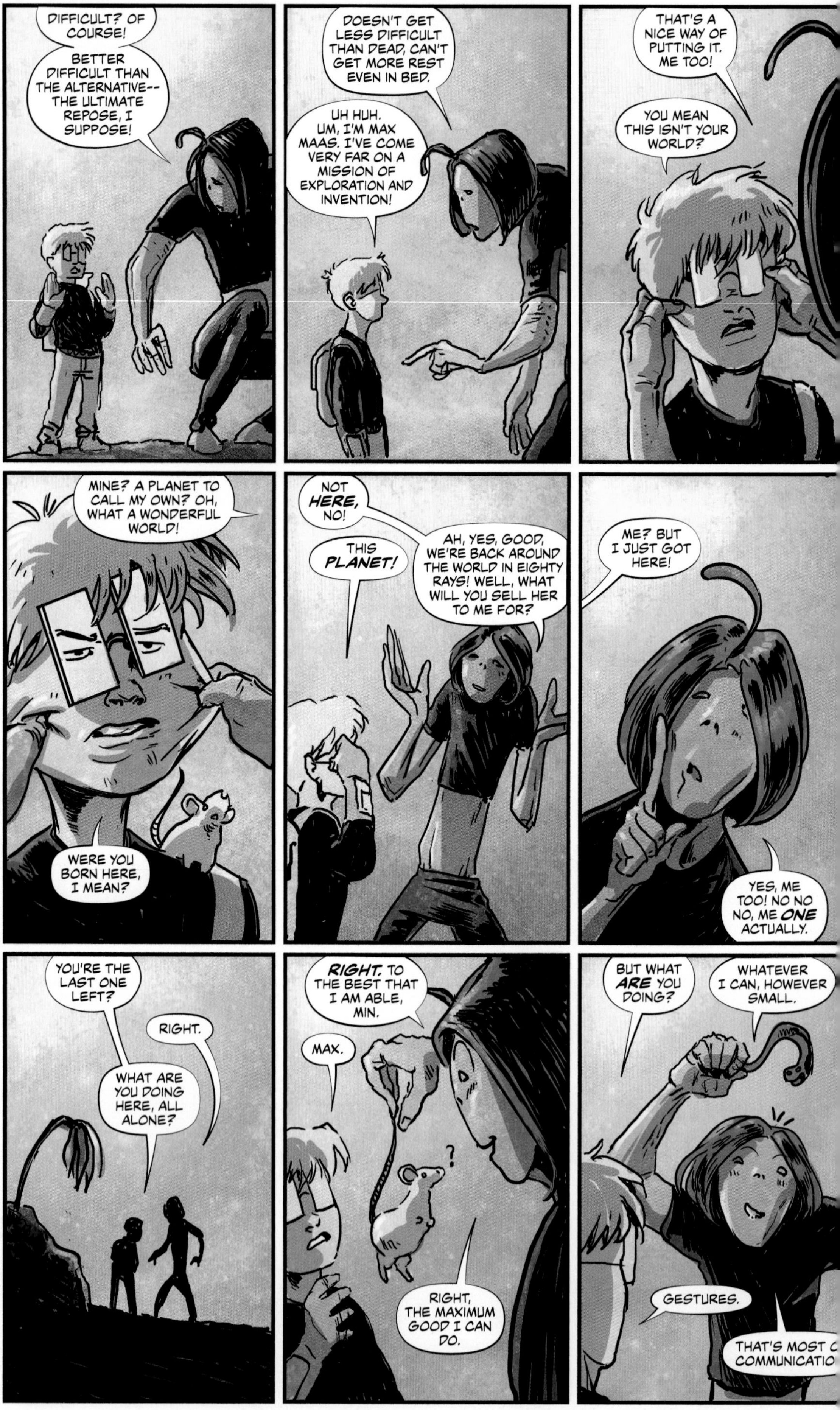
DIFFICULT? OF COURSE!
BETTER DIFFICULT THAN THE ALTERNATIVE-- THE ULTIMATE REPOSE, I SUPPOSE!
DOESN'T GET LESS DIFFICULT THAN DEAD, CAN'T GET MORE REST EVEN IN BED.
UH HUH. UM, I'M MAX MAAS. I'VE COME VERY FAR ON A MISSION OF EXPLORATION AND INVENTION!
THAT'S A NICE WAY OF PUTTING IT. ME TOO!
YOU MEAN THIS ISN'T YOUR WORLD?
MINE? A PLANET TO CALL MY OWN? OH, WHAT A WONDERFUL WORLD!
WERE YOU BORN HERE, I MEAN?
NOT HERE, NO!
THIS PLANET!
AH, YES, GOOD, WE'RE BACK AROUND THE WORLD IN EIGHTY RAYS! WELL, WHAT WILL YOU SELL HER TO ME FOR?
ME? BUT I JUST GOT HERE!
YES, ME TOO! NO NO NO, ME ONE ACTUALLY.
YOU'RE THE LAST ONE LEFT?
RIGHT.
WHAT ARE YOU DOING HERE, ALL ALONE?
RIGHT. TO THE BEST THAT I AM ABLE, MIN.
MAX.
?
RIGHT, THE MAXIMUM GOOD I CAN DO.
BUT WHAT ARE YOU DOING?
WHATEVER I CAN, HOWEVER SMALL.
GESTURES.
THAT'S MOST C
COMMUNICATIO

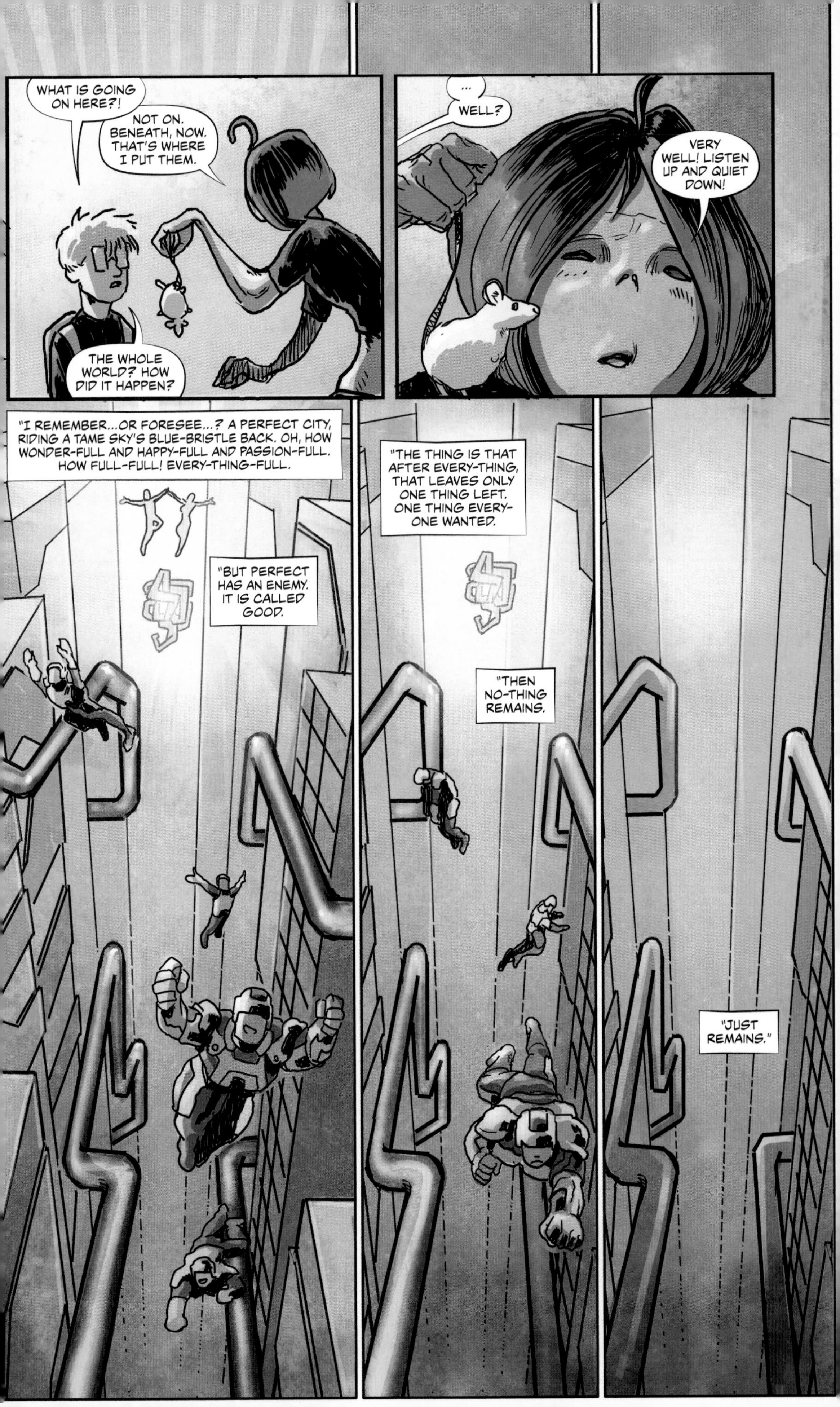
WHAT IS GOING ON HERE?!
NOT ON. BENEATH, NOW. THAT'S WHERE I PUT THEM.
THE WHOLE WORLD? HOW DID IT HAPPEN?
...
WELL?
VERY WELL! LISTEN UP AND QUIET DOWN!
"I REMEMBER...OR FORESEE...? A PERFECT CITY, RIDING A TAME SKY'S BLUE-BRISTLE BACK. OH, HOW WONDER-FULL AND HAPPY-FULL AND PASSION-FULL. HOW FULL-FULL! EVERY-THING-FULL.
"BUT PERFECT HAS AN ENEMY. IT IS CALLED GOOD.
"THE THING IS THAT AFTER EVERY-THING, THAT LEAVES ONLY ONE THING LEFT. ONE THING EVERY-ONE WANTED.
"THEN NO-THING REMAINS.
"JUST REMAINS."

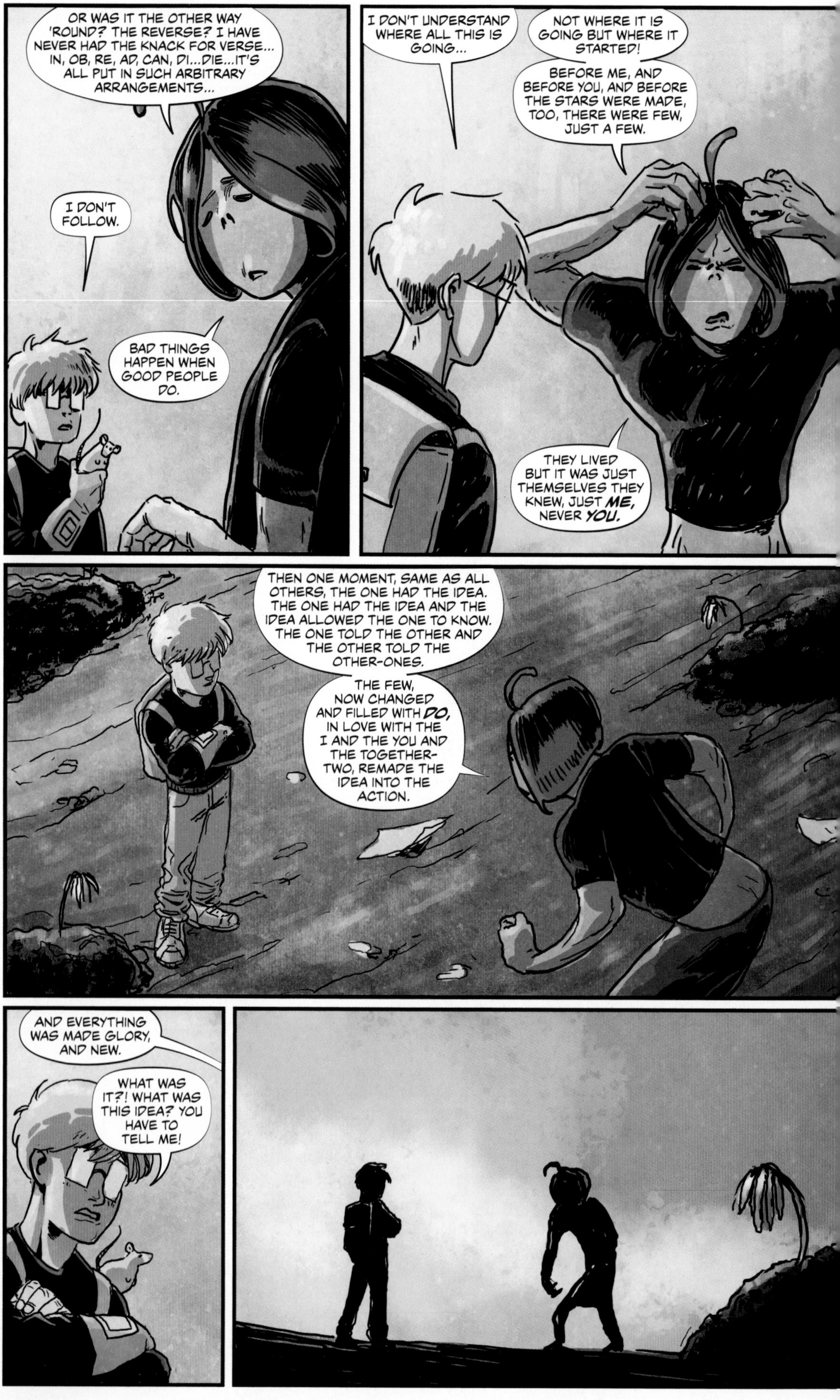
OR WAS IT THE OTHER WAY 'ROUND? THE REVERSE? I HAVE NEVER HAD THE KNACK FOR VERSE... IN, OB, RE, AD, CAN, DI...DIE...IT'S ALL PUT IN SUCH ARBITRARY ARRANGEMENTS...
I DON'T FOLLOW.
BAD THINGS HAPPEN WHEN GOOD PEOPLE DO.
I DON'T UNDERSTAND WHERE ALL THIS IS GOING...
NOT WHERE IT IS GOING BUT WHERE IT STARTED!
BEFORE ME, AND BEFORE YOU, AND BEFORE THE STARS WERE MADE, TOO, THERE WERE FEW, JUST A FEW.
THEY LIVED BUT IT WAS JUST THEMSELVES THEY KNEW, JUST ME, NEVER YOU.
THEN ONE MOMENT, SAME AS ALL OTHERS, THE ONE HAD THE IDEA. THE ONE HAD THE IDEA AND THE IDEA ALLOWED THE ONE TO KNOW. THE ONE TOLD THE OTHER AND THE OTHER TOLD THE OTHER-ONES.
THE FEW, NOW CHANGED AND FILLED WITH DO, IN LOVE WITH THE I AND THE YOU AND THE TOGETHER-TWO, REMADE THE IDEA INTO THE ACTION.
AND EVERYTHING WAS MADE GLORY, AND NEW.
WHAT WAS IT?! WHAT WAS THIS IDEA? YOU HAVE TO TELL ME!

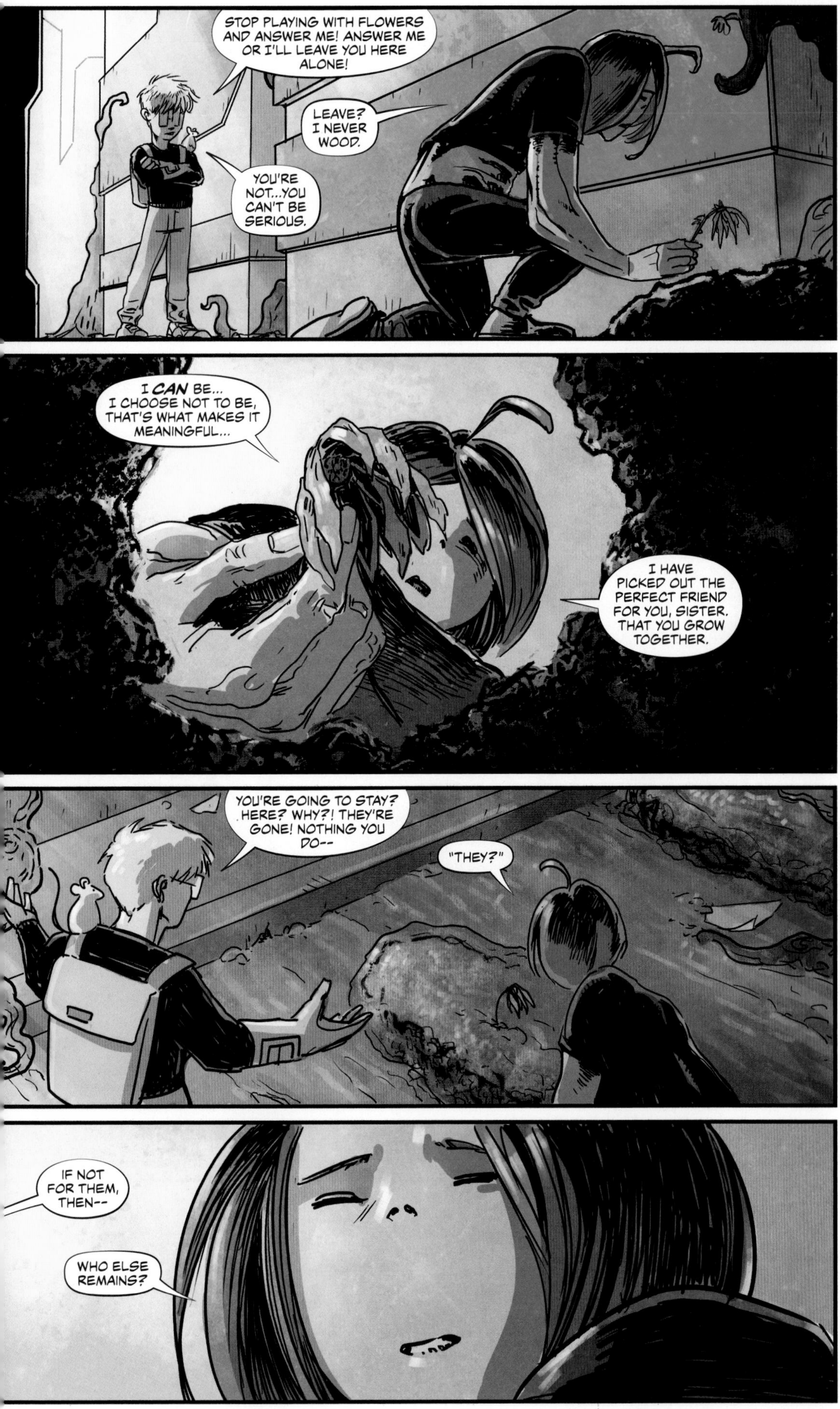

STOP PLAYING WITH FLOWERS AND ANSWER ME! ANSWER ME OR I'LL LEAVE YOU HERE ALONE!
LEAVE? I NEVER WOOD.
YOU'RE NOT...YOU CAN'T BE SERIOUS.
I CAN BE... I CHOOSE NOT TO BE, THAT'S WHAT MAKES IT MEANINGFUL...
I HAVE PICKED OUT THE PERFECT FRIEND FOR YOU, SISTER. THAT YOU GROW TOGETHER.
YOU'RE GOING TO STAY? HERE? WHY?! THEY'RE GONE! NOTHING YOU DO--
"THEY?"
IF NOT FOR THEM, THEN--
WHO ELSE REMAINS?

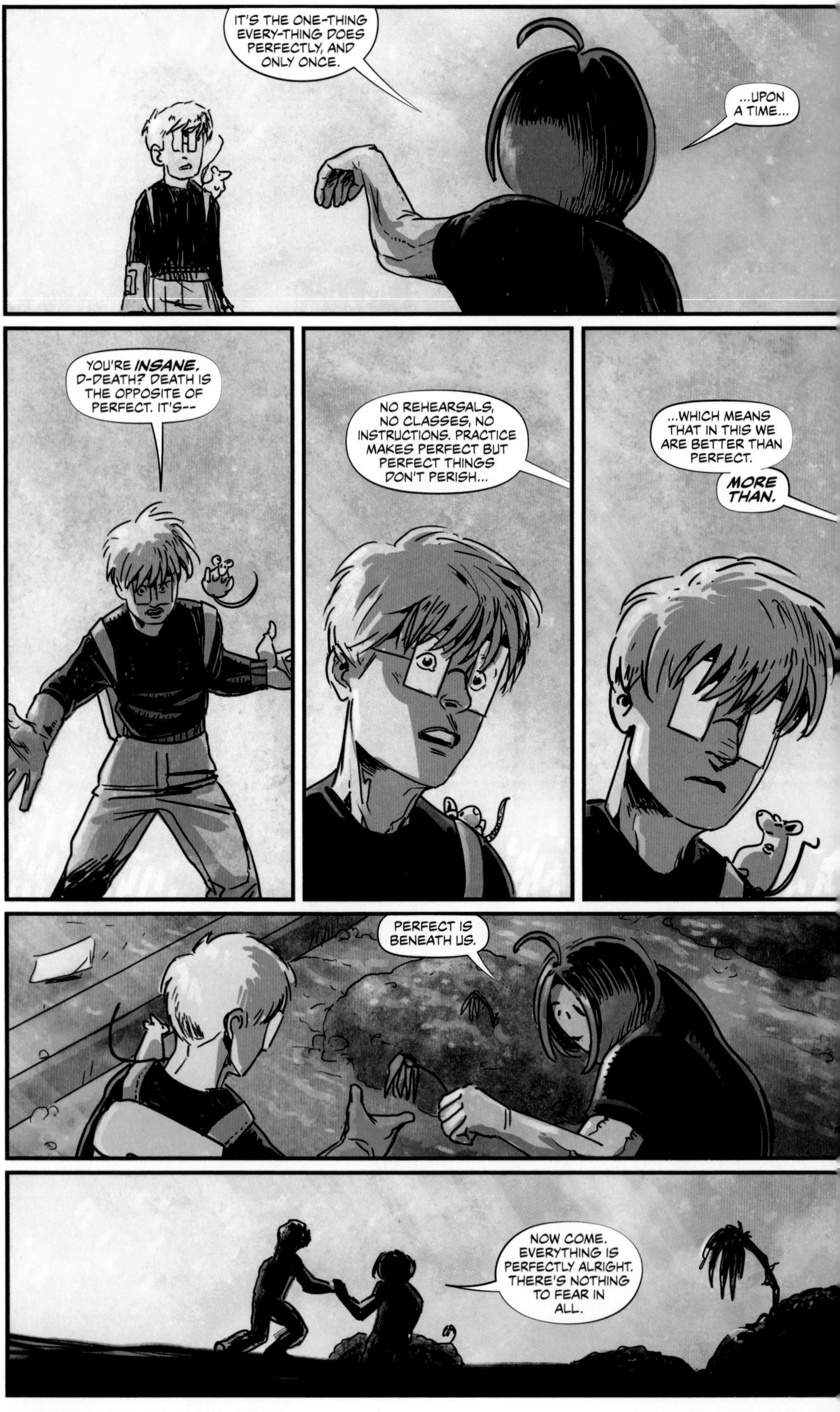
IT'S THE ONE-THING EVERY-THING DOES PERFECTLY, AND ONLY ONCE.
...UPON A TIME...
YOU'RE INSANE. D-DEATH? DEATH IS THE OPPOSITE OF PERFECT. IT'S--
NO REHEARSALS, NO CLASSES, NO INSTRUCTIONS. PRACTICE MAKES PERFECT BUT PERFECT THINGS DON'T PERISH...
...WHICH MEANS THAT IN THIS WE ARE BETTER THAN PERFECT.
MORE THAN.
PERFECT IS BENEATH US.
NOW COME. EVERYTHING IS PERFECTLY ALRIGHT. THERE'S NOTHING TO FEAR IN ALL.

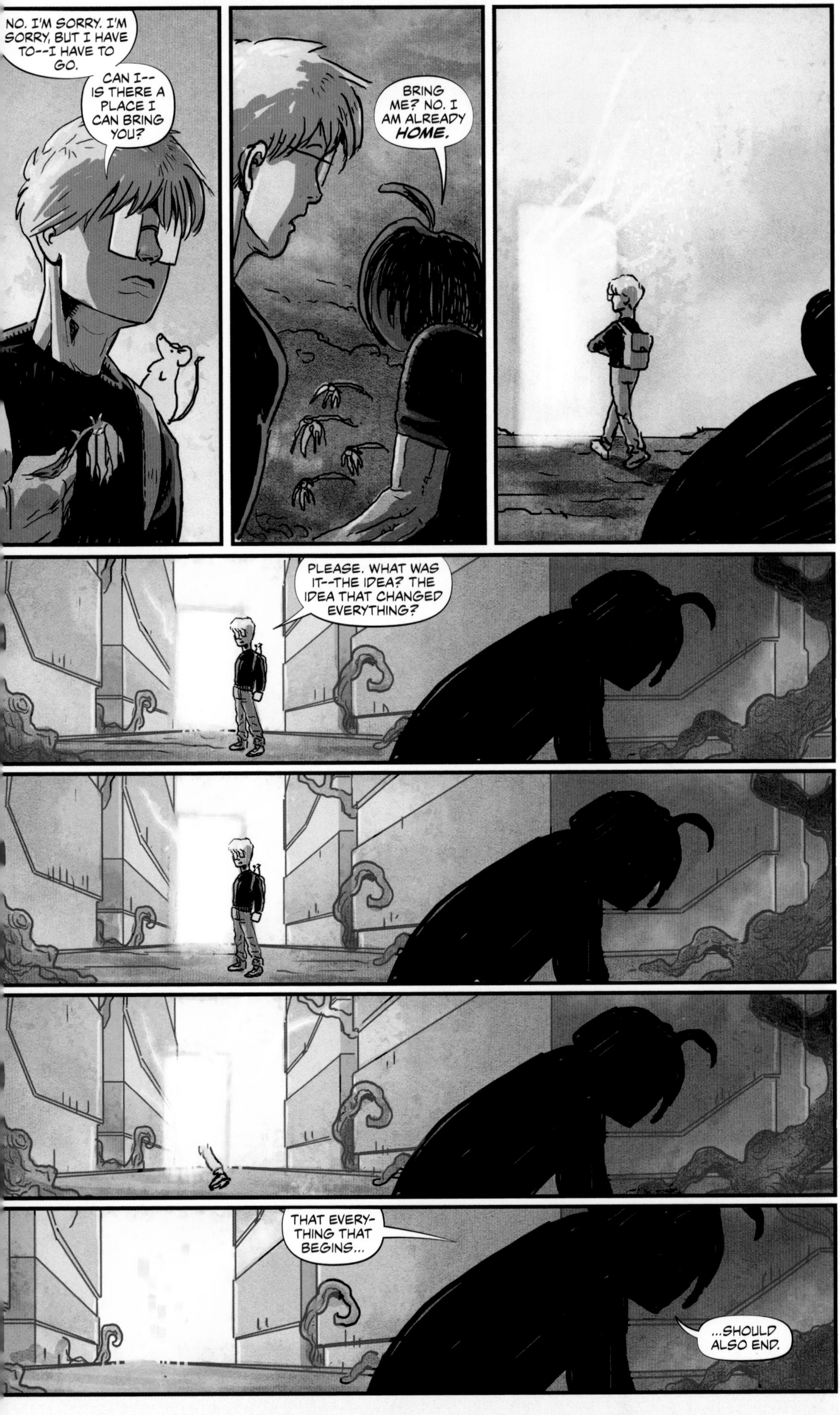
NO. I'M SORRY. I'M SORRY, BUT I HAVE TO--I HAVE TO GO.
CAN I-- IS THERE A PLACE I CAN BRING YOU?
BRING ME? NO. I AM ALREADY *HOME.*
PLEASE. WHAT WAS IT--THE IDEA? THE IDEA THAT CHANGED EVERYTHING?
THAT EVERYTHING THAT BEGINS...
...SHOULD ALSO END.

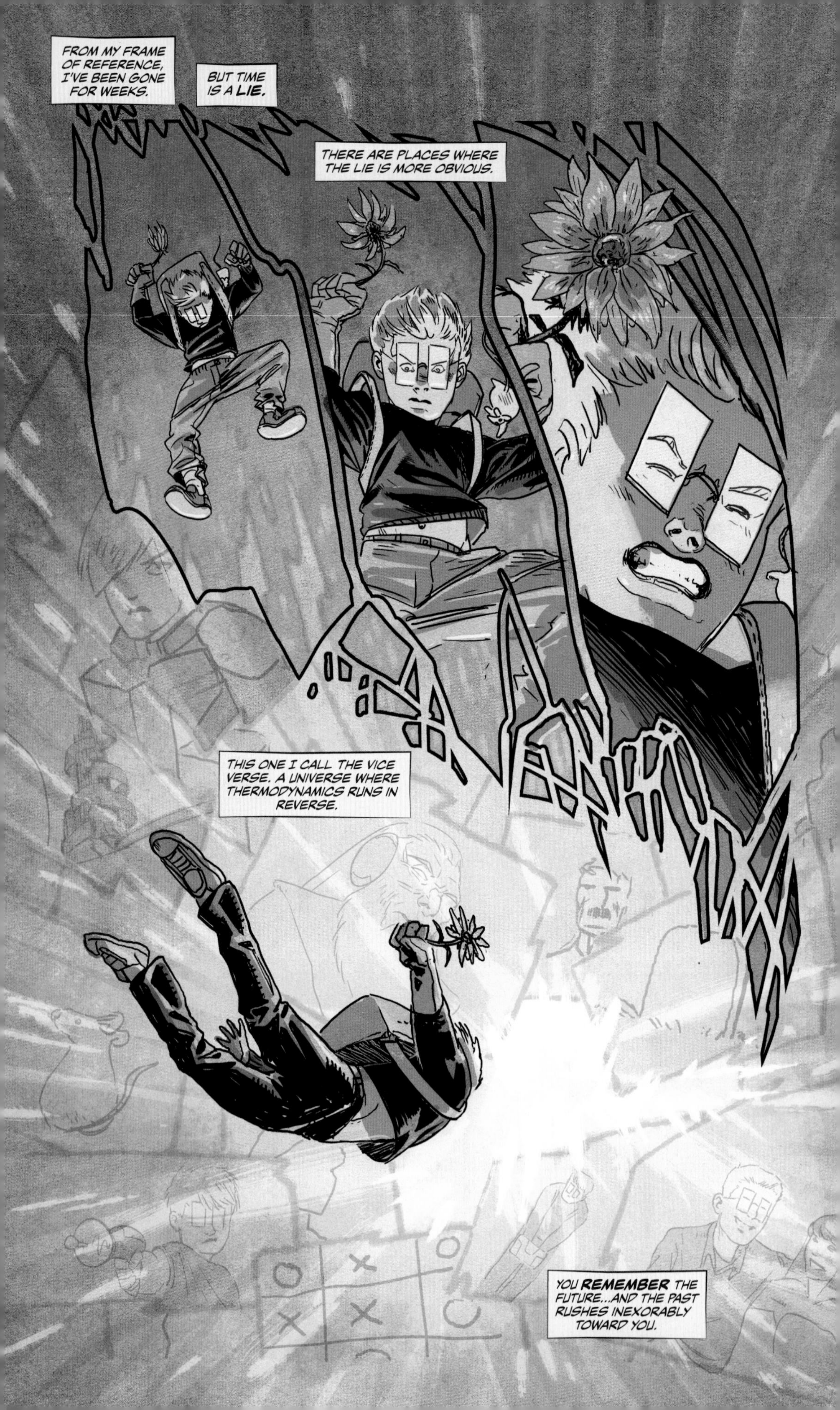
FROM MY FRAME OF REFERENCE, I'VE BEEN GONE FOR WEEKS.
BUT TIME IS A **LIE.**
THERE ARE PLACES WHERE THE LIE IS MORE OBVIOUS.
THIS ONE I CALL THE VICE VERSE. A UNIVERSE WHERE THERMODYNAMICS RUNS IN REVERSE.
YOU **REMEMBER** THE FUTURE...AND THE PAST RUSHES INEXORABLY TOWARD YOU.

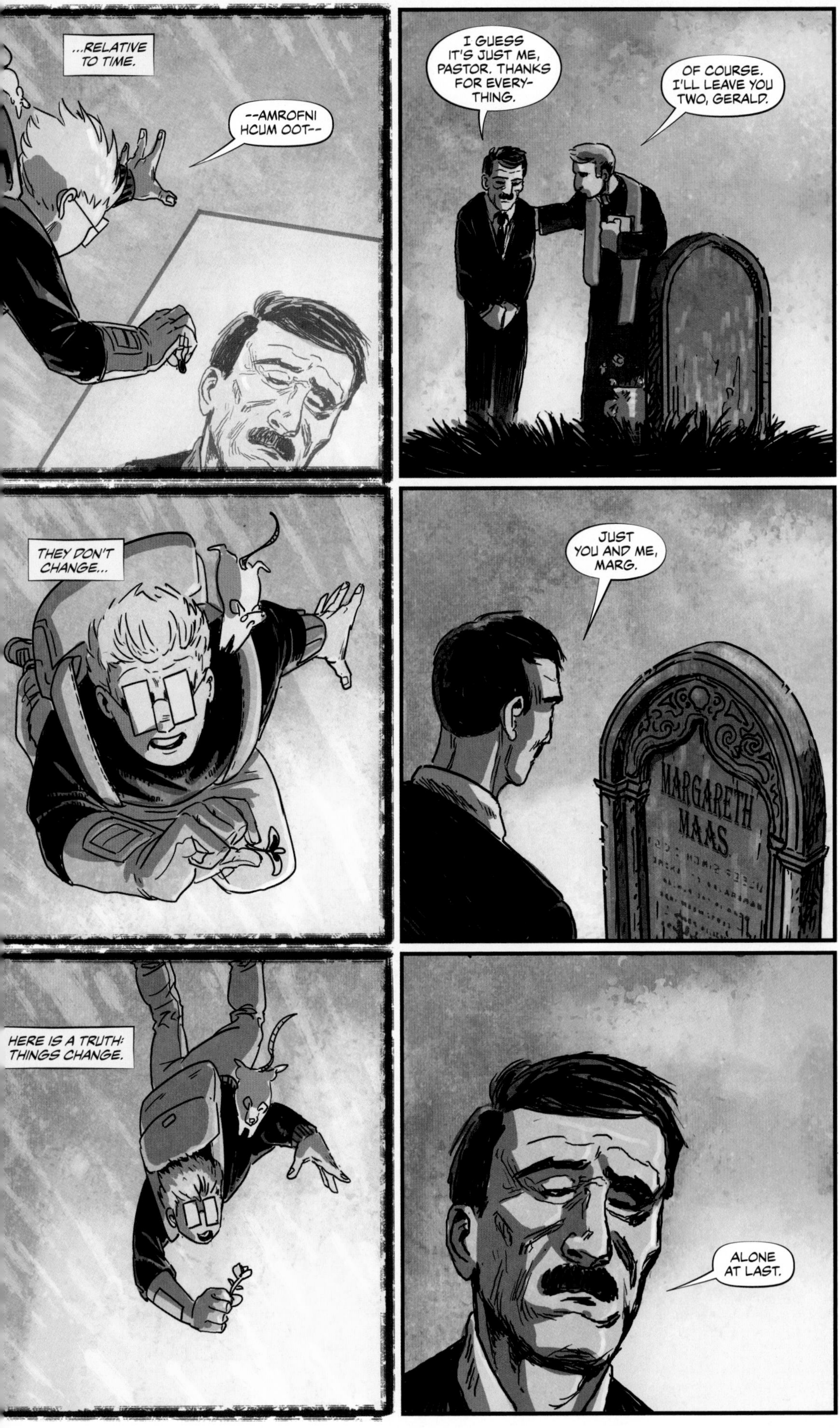
...RELATIVE TO TIME.
--AMROFNI HCUM OOT--
I GUESS IT'S JUST ME, PASTOR. THANKS FOR EVERY-THING.
OF COURSE. I'LL LEAVE YOU TWO, GERALD.
THEY DON'T CHANGE...
JUST YOU AND ME, MARG.
MARGARETH MAAS
HERE IS A TRUTH: THINGS CHANGE.
ALONE AT LAST.

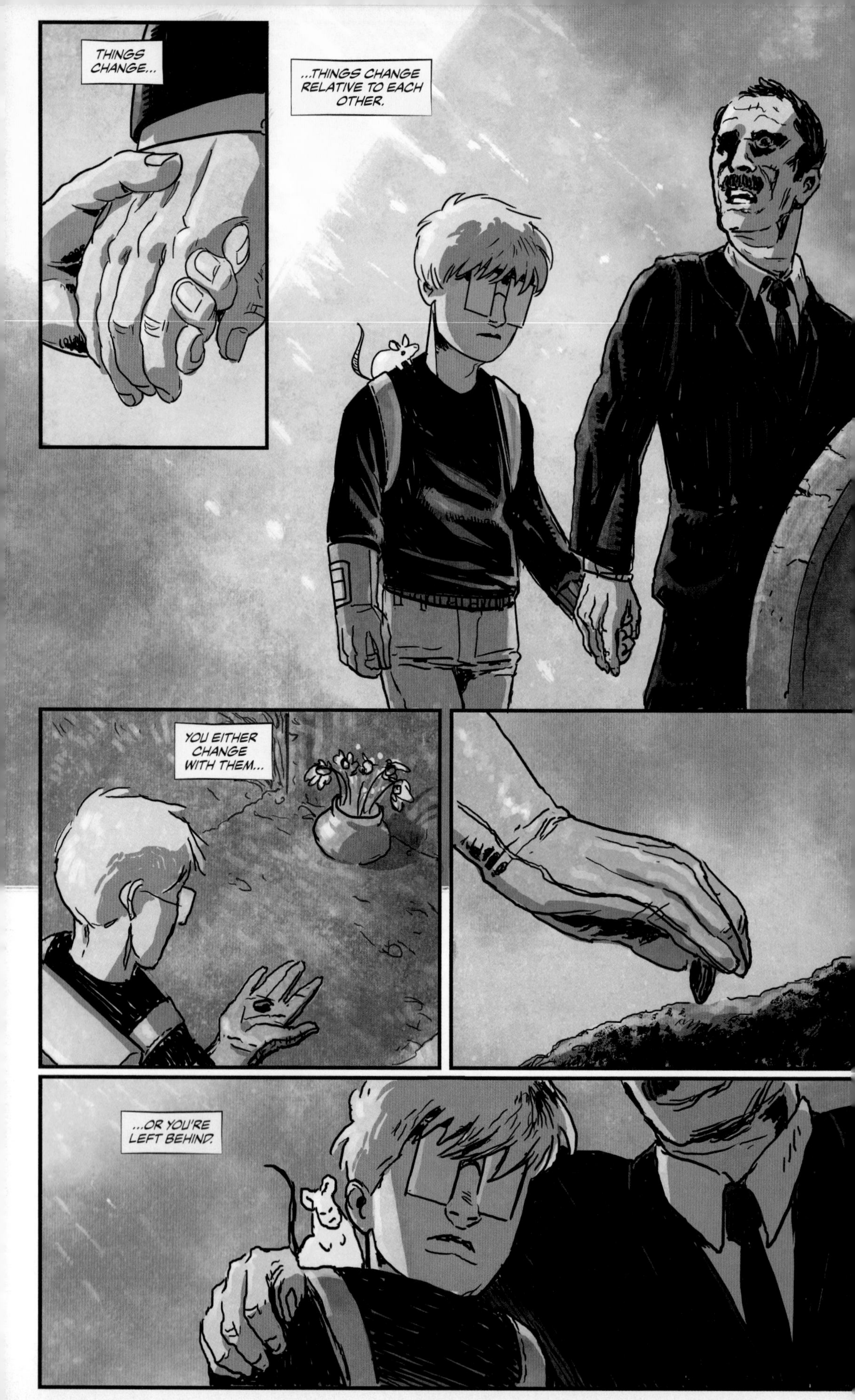
THINGS CHANGE...
...THINGS CHANGE RELATIVE TO EACH OTHER.
YOU EITHER CHANGE WITH THEM...
...OR YOU'RE LEFT BEHIND.

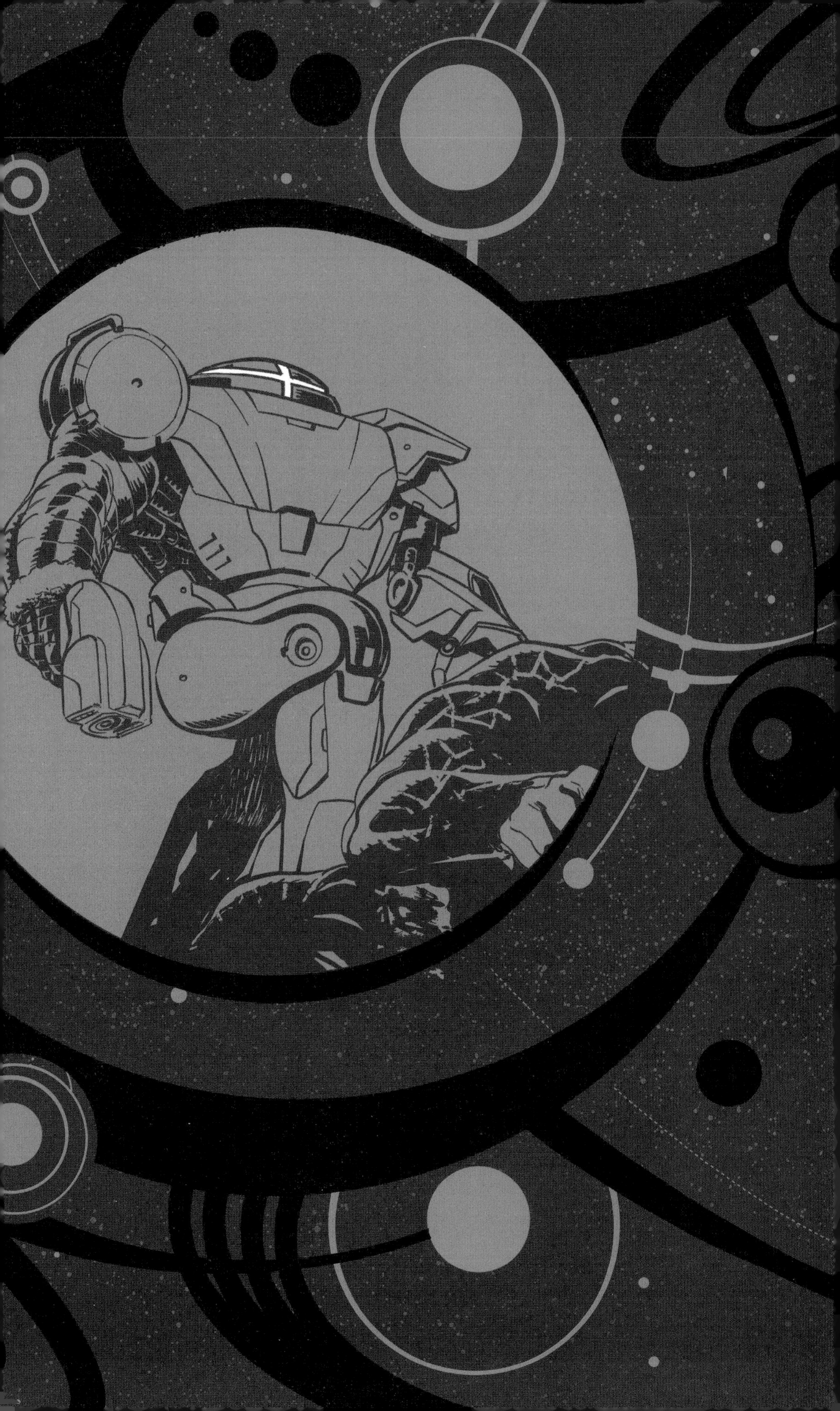

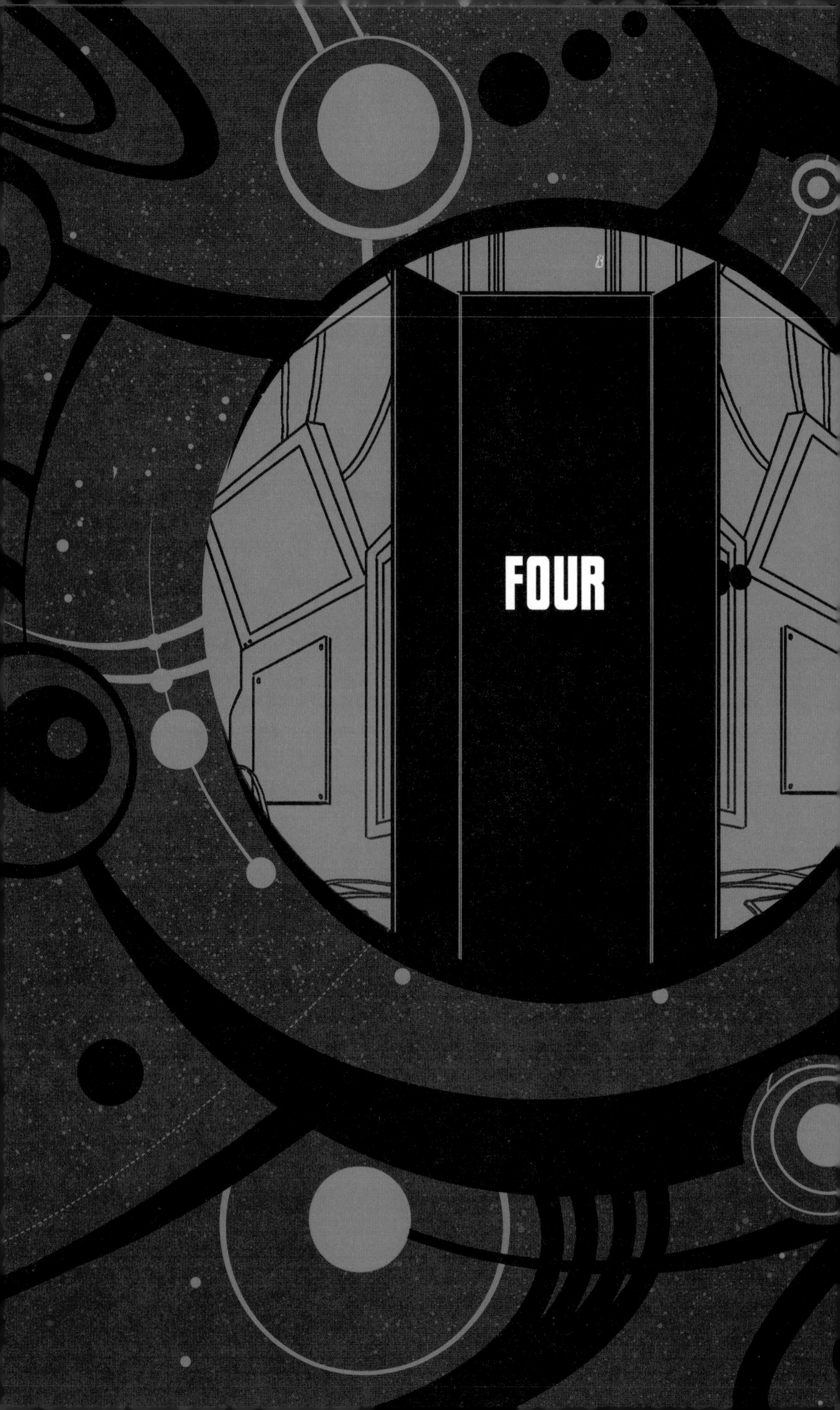

FOUR

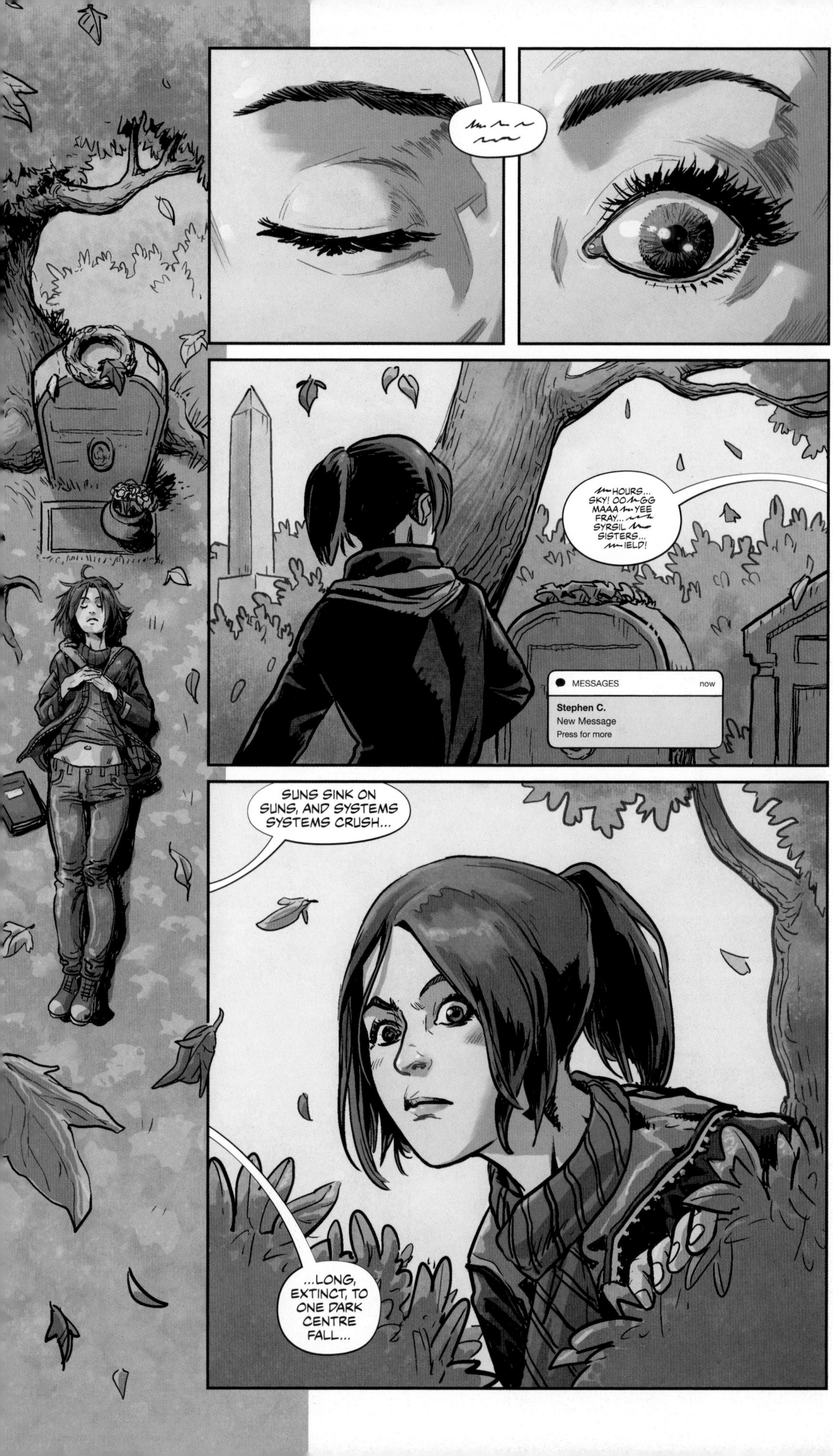

HOURS... SKY! OO GG MAAA YEE FRAY... SYRSIL SISTERS... IELD!
MESSAGES now
Stephen C.
New Message
Press for more
SUNS SINK ON SUNS, AND SYSTEMS SYSTEMS CRUSH...
...LONG, EXTINCT, TO ONE DARK CENTRE FALL...

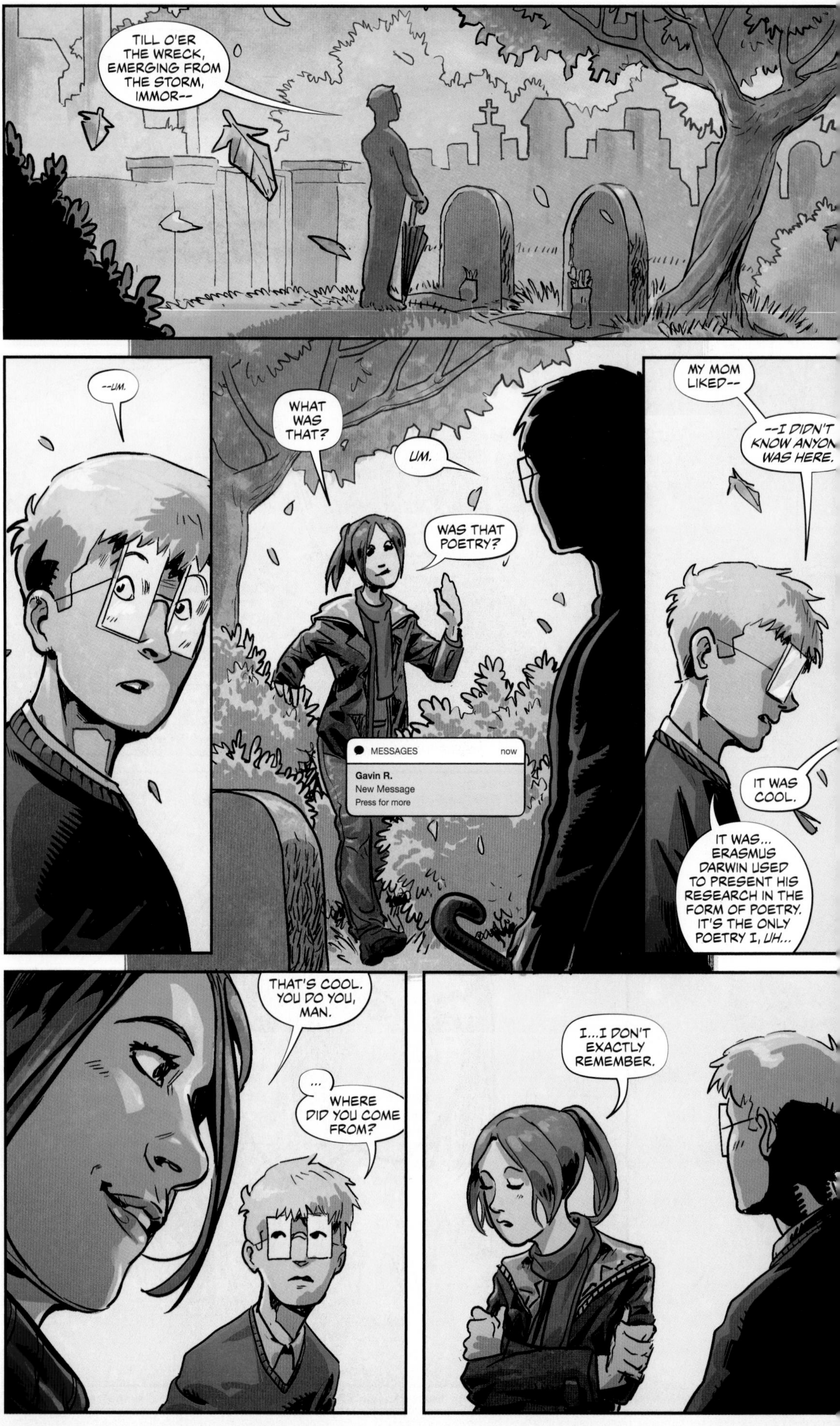
TILL O'ER THE WRECK, EMERGING FROM THE STORM, IMMOR--
--UM.
WHAT WAS THAT?
UM.
WAS THAT POETRY?
MESSAGES now
Gavin R.
New Message
Press for more
MY MOM LIKED--
--I DIDN'T KNOW ANYON WAS HERE.
IT WAS COOL.
IT WAS... ERASMUS DARWIN USED TO PRESENT HIS RESEARCH IN THE FORM OF POETRY. IT'S THE ONLY POETRY I, UH...
THAT'S COOL. YOU DO YOU, MAN.
...
WHERE DID YOU COME FROM?
I...I DON'T EXACTLY REMEMBER.

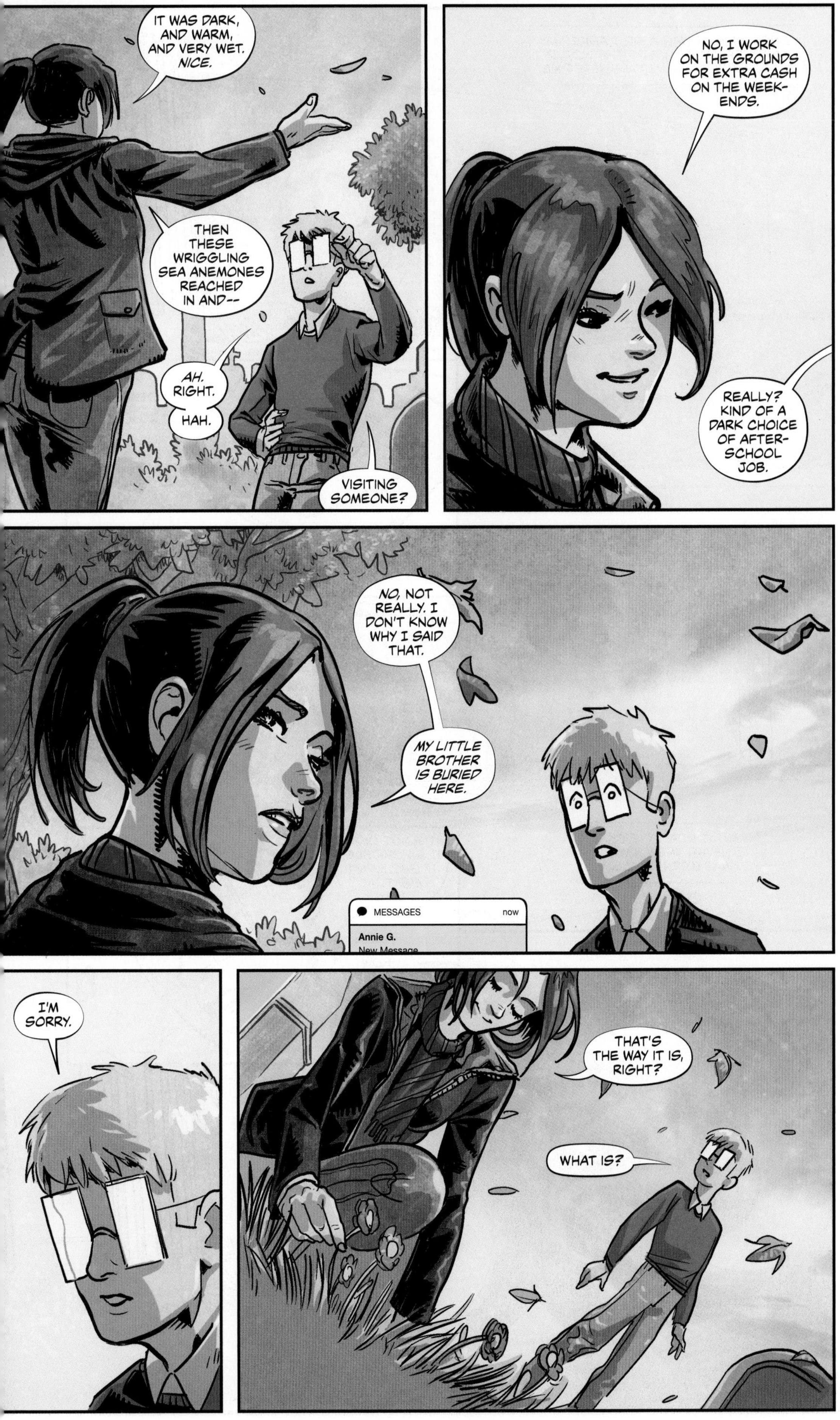
IT WAS DARK, AND WARM, AND VERY WET. *NICE.*
THEN THESE WRIGGLING SEA ANEMONES REACHED IN AND--
AH. RIGHT.
HAH.
VISITING SOMEONE?
NO, I WORK ON THE GROUNDS FOR EXTRA CASH ON THE WEEK-ENDS.
REALLY? KIND OF A DARK CHOICE OF AFTER-SCHOOL JOB.
NO, NOT REALLY. I DON'T KNOW WHY I SAID THAT.
MY LITTLE BROTHER IS BURIED HERE.
MESSAGES
now
Annie G.
I'M SORRY.
THAT'S THE WAY IT IS, RIGHT?
WHAT IS?

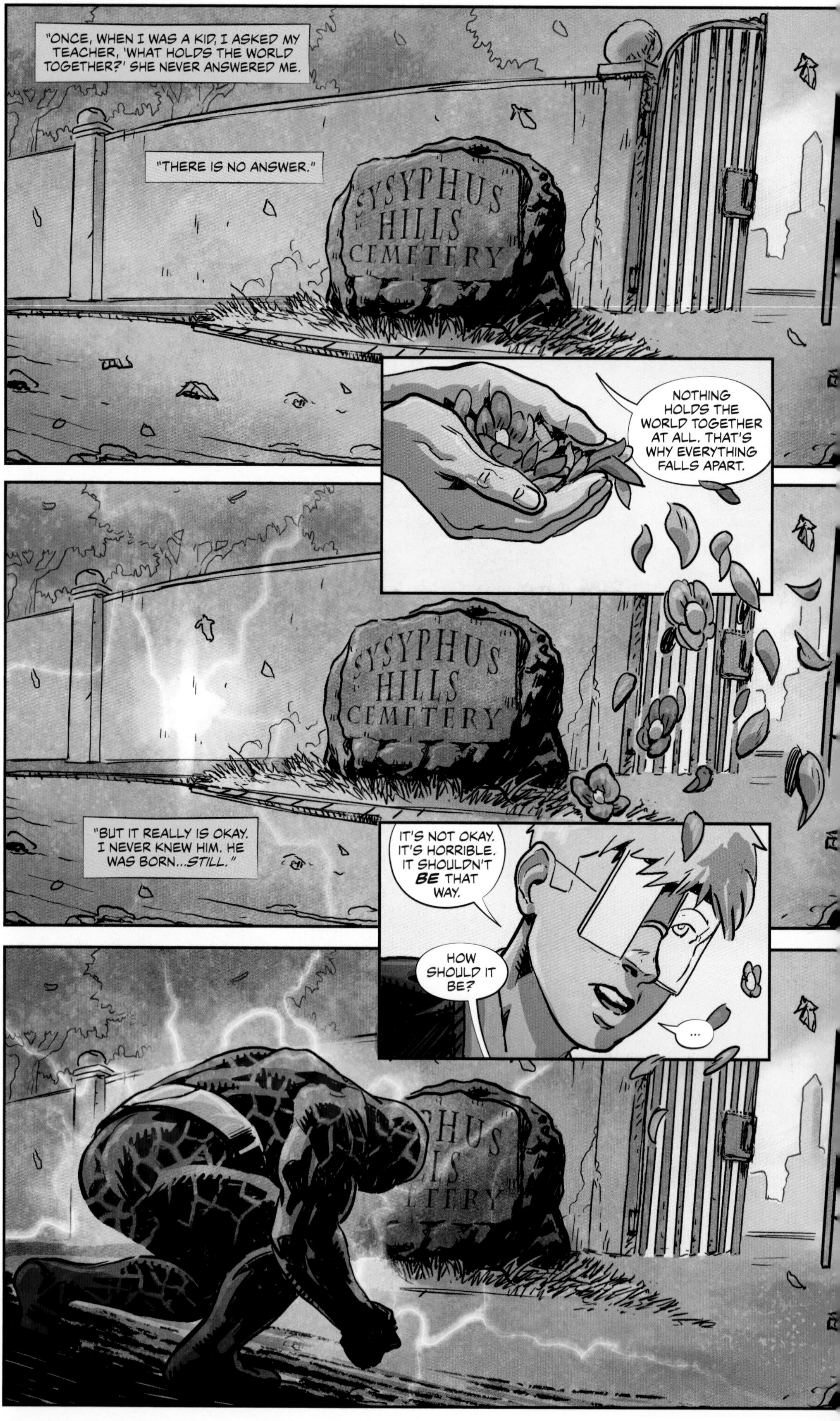
"ONCE, WHEN I WAS A KID, I ASKED MY TEACHER, 'WHAT HOLDS THE WORLD TOGETHER?' SHE NEVER ANSWERED ME.
"THERE IS NO ANSWER."
SYSYPHUS HILLS CEMETERY
NOTHING HOLDS THE WORLD TOGETHER AT ALL. THAT'S WHY EVERYTHING FALLS APART.
SYSYPHUS HILLS CEMETERY
"BUT IT REALLY IS OKAY. I NEVER KNEW HIM. HE WAS BORN...STILL."
IT'S NOT OKAY. IT'S HORRIBLE. IT SHOULDN'T BE THAT WAY.
HOW SHOULD IT BE?
...

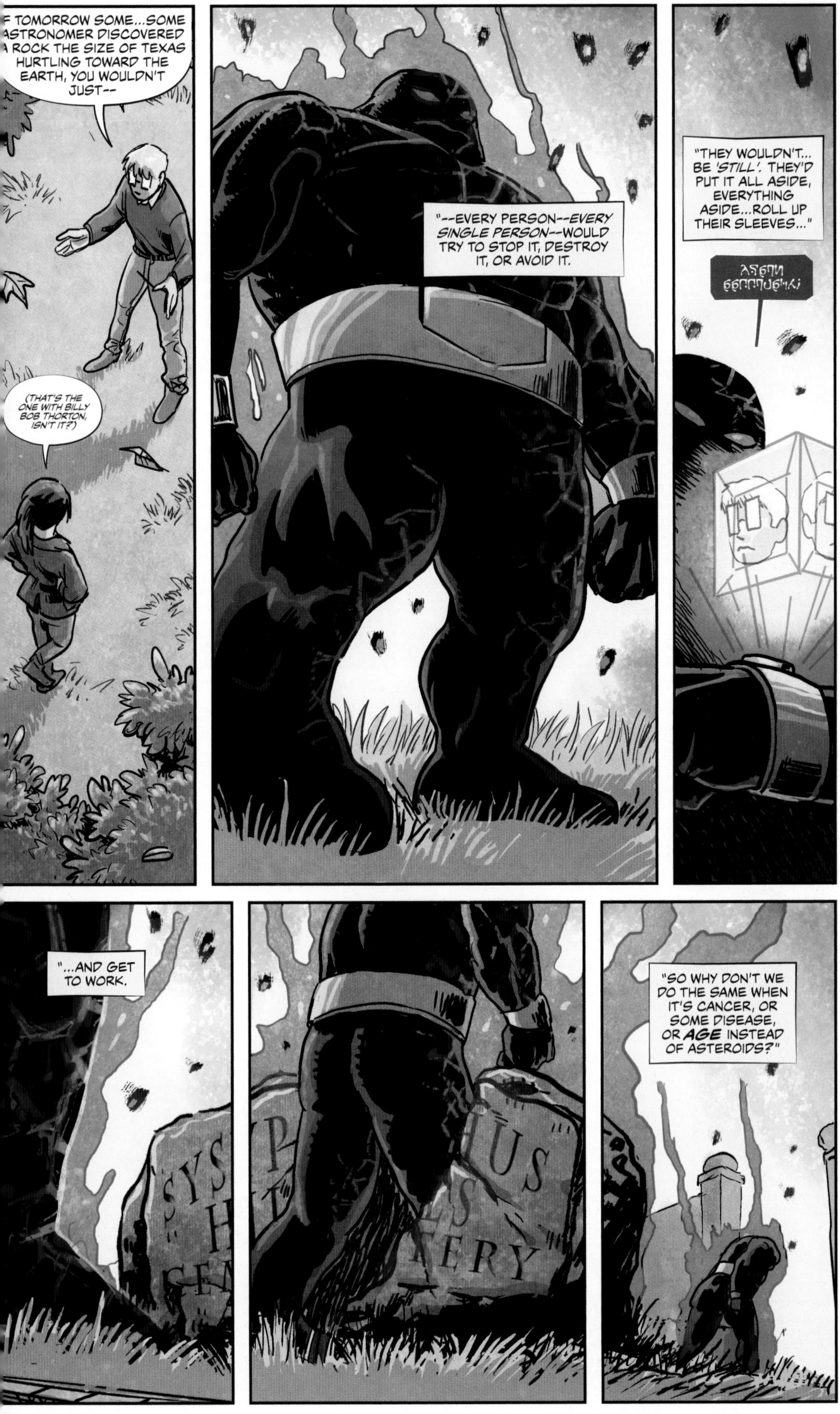
F TOMORROW SOME...SOME ASTRONOMER DISCOVERED A ROCK THE SIZE OF TEXAS HURTLING TOWARD THE EARTH, YOU WOULDN'T JUST--
(THAT'S THE ONE WITH BILLY BOB THORTON, ISN'T IT?)
"--EVERY PERSON--*EVERY SINGLE PERSON*--WOULD TRY TO STOP IT, DESTROY IT, OR AVOID IT.
"THEY WOULDN'T... BE *'STILL'*. THEY'D PUT IT ALL ASIDE, EVERYTHING ASIDE...ROLL UP THEIR SLEEVES..."
"...AND GET TO WORK.
"SO WHY DON'T WE DO THE SAME WHEN IT'S CANCER, OR SOME DISEASE, OR ***AGE*** INSTEAD OF ASTEROIDS?"

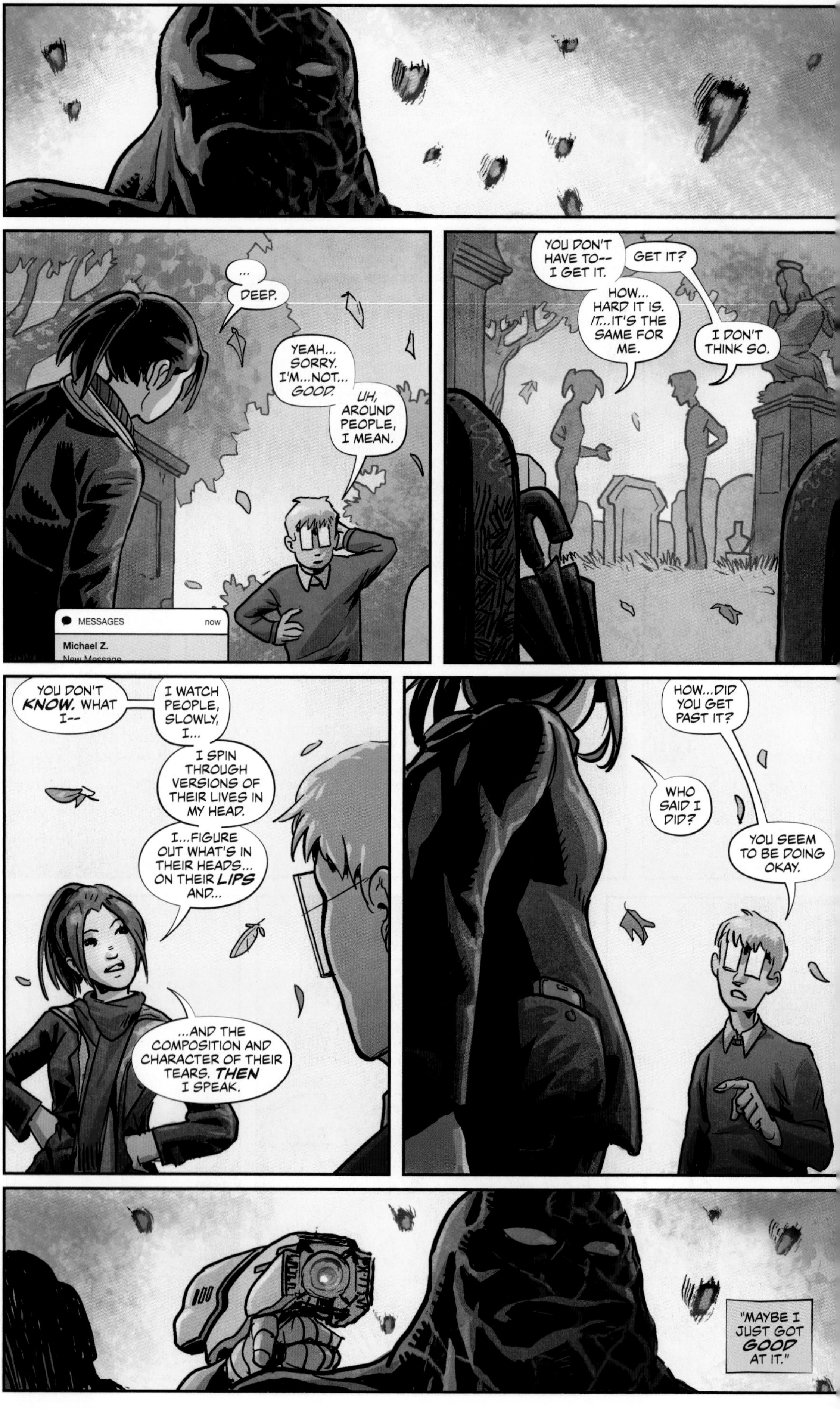
...
DEEP.
YEAH... SORRY. I'M...NOT... GOOD.
UH, AROUND PEOPLE, I MEAN.
MESSAGES now
Michael Z.
YOU DON'T HAVE TO-- I GET IT.
GET IT?
HOW... HARD IT IS. IT...IT'S THE SAME FOR ME.
I DON'T THINK SO.
YOU DON'T KNOW. WHAT I--
I WATCH PEOPLE, SLOWLY, I...
I SPIN THROUGH VERSIONS OF THEIR LIVES IN MY HEAD.
I...FIGURE OUT WHAT'S IN THEIR HEADS... ON THEIR LIPS AND...
...AND THE COMPOSITION AND CHARACTER OF THEIR TEARS. THEN I SPEAK.
HOW...DID YOU GET PAST IT?
WHO SAID I DID?
YOU SEEM TO BE DOING OKAY.
"MAYBE I JUST GOT GOOD AT IT."

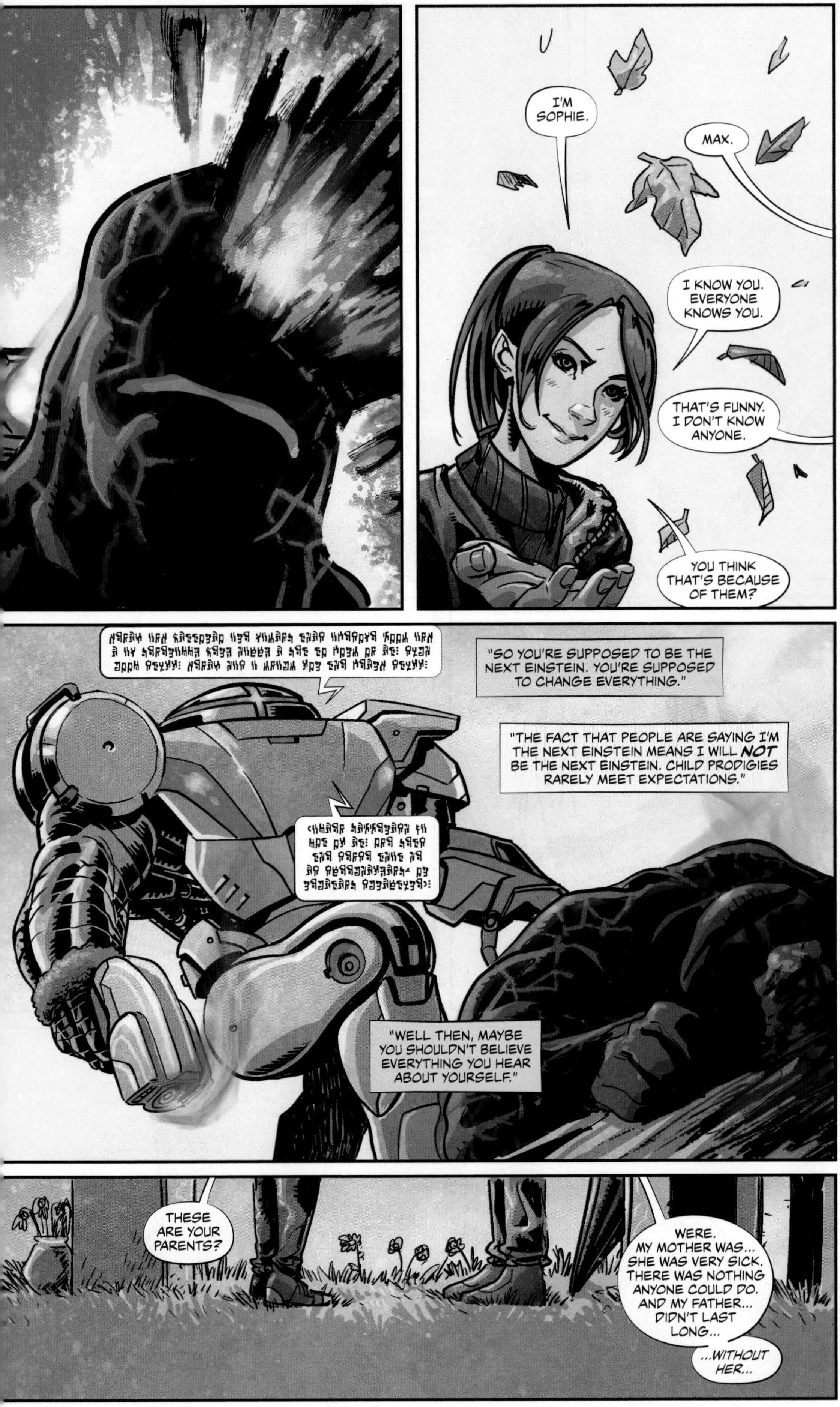

I'M SOPHIE.
MAX.
I KNOW YOU. EVERYONE KNOWS YOU.
THAT'S FUNNY. I DON'T KNOW ANYONE.
YOU THINK THAT'S BECAUSE OF THEM?
"SO YOU'RE SUPPOSED TO BE THE NEXT EINSTEIN. YOU'RE SUPPOSED TO CHANGE EVERYTHING."
"THE FACT THAT PEOPLE ARE SAYING I'M THE NEXT EINSTEIN MEANS I WILL *NOT* BE THE NEXT EINSTEIN. CHILD PRODIGIES RARELY MEET EXPECTATIONS."
"WELL THEN, MAYBE YOU SHOULDN'T BELIEVE EVERYTHING YOU HEAR ABOUT YOURSELF."
THESE ARE YOUR PARENTS?
WERE. MY MOTHER WAS... SHE WAS VERY SICK. THERE WAS NOTHING ANYONE COULD DO. AND MY FATHER... DIDN'T LAST LONG...
...WITHOUT HER...

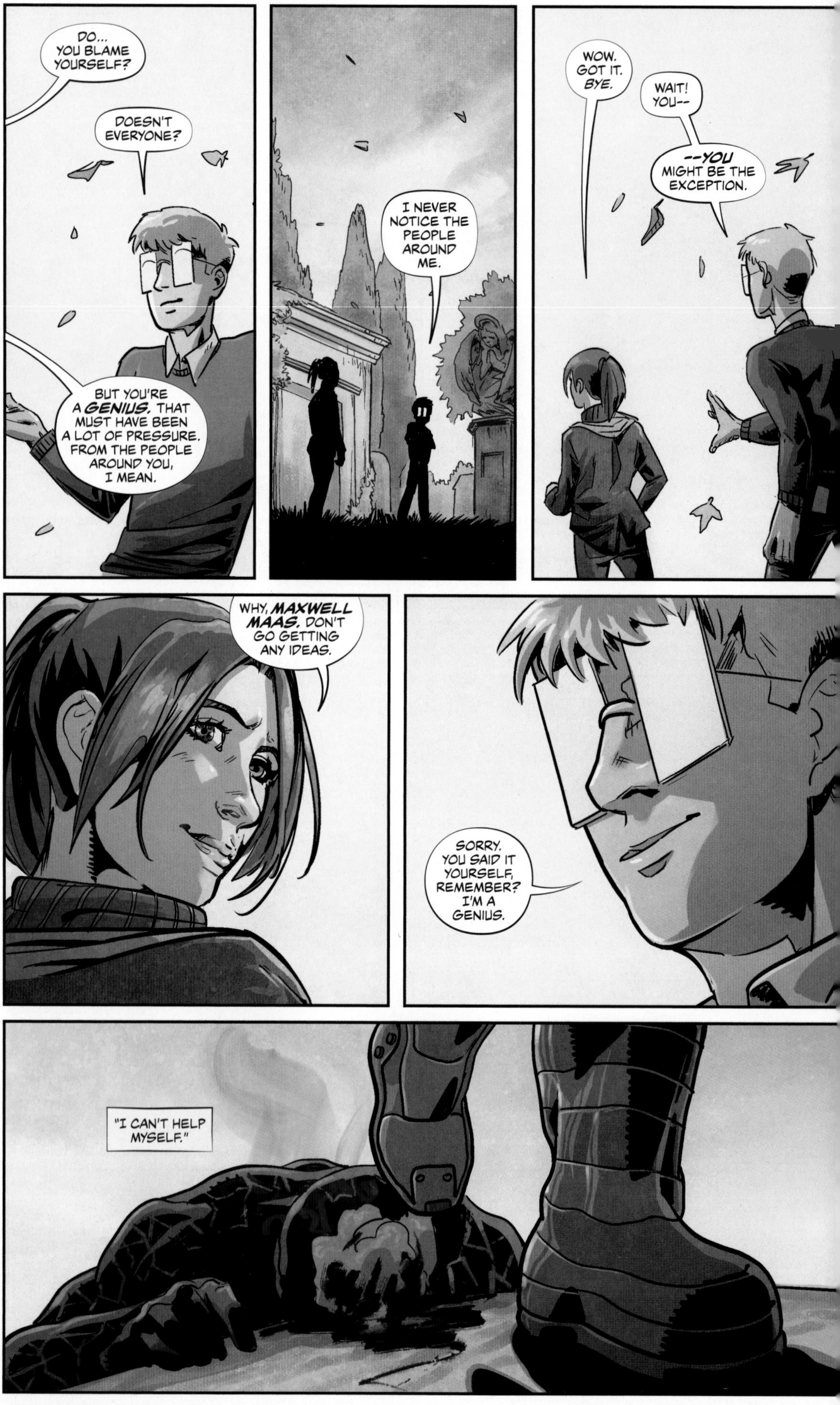
DO... YOU BLAME YOURSELF?
DOESN'T EVERYONE?
BUT YOU'RE A GENIUS. THAT MUST HAVE BEEN A LOT OF PRESSURE. FROM THE PEOPLE AROUND YOU, I MEAN.
I NEVER NOTICE THE PEOPLE AROUND ME.
WOW. GOT IT. BYE.
WAIT! YOU--
--YOU MIGHT BE THE EXCEPTION.
WHY, MAXWELL MAAS. DON'T GO GETTING ANY IDEAS.
SORRY. YOU SAID IT YOURSELF, REMEMBER? I'M A GENIUS.
"I CAN'T HELP MYSELF."

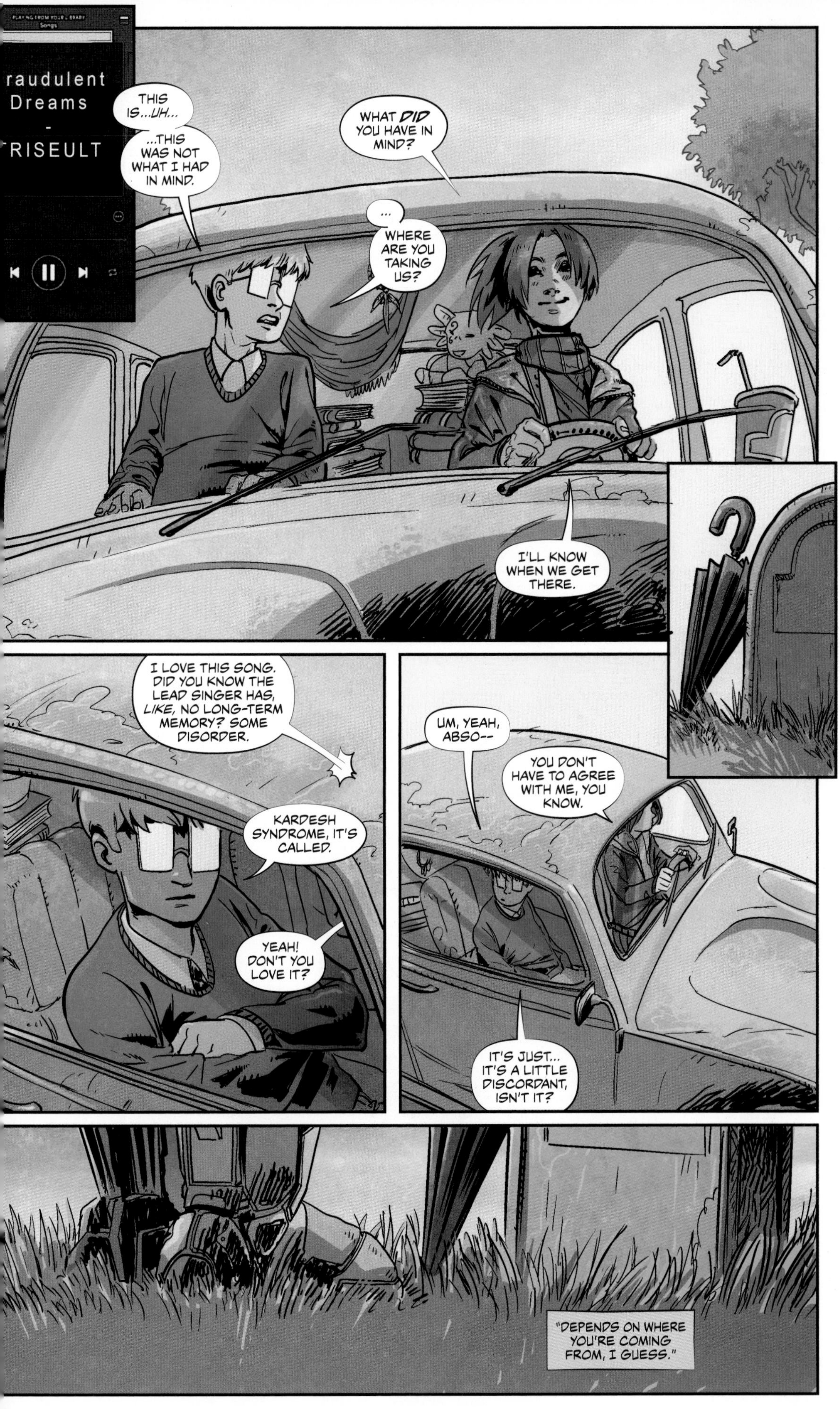
raudulent Dreams
-
RISEULT
THIS IS...UH...
...THIS WAS NOT WHAT I HAD IN MIND.
WHAT *DID* YOU HAVE IN MIND?
...
WHERE ARE YOU TAKING US?
I'LL KNOW WHEN WE GET THERE.
I LOVE THIS SONG. DID YOU KNOW THE LEAD SINGER HAS, *LIKE,* NO LONG-TERM MEMORY? SOME DISORDER.
KARDESH SYNDROME, IT'S CALLED.
YEAH! DON'T YOU LOVE IT?
UM, YEAH, ABSO--
YOU DON'T HAVE TO AGREE WITH ME, YOU KNOW.
IT'S JUST... IT'S A LITTLE DISCORDANT, ISN'T IT?
"DEPENDS ON WHERE YOU'RE COMING FROM, I GUESS."

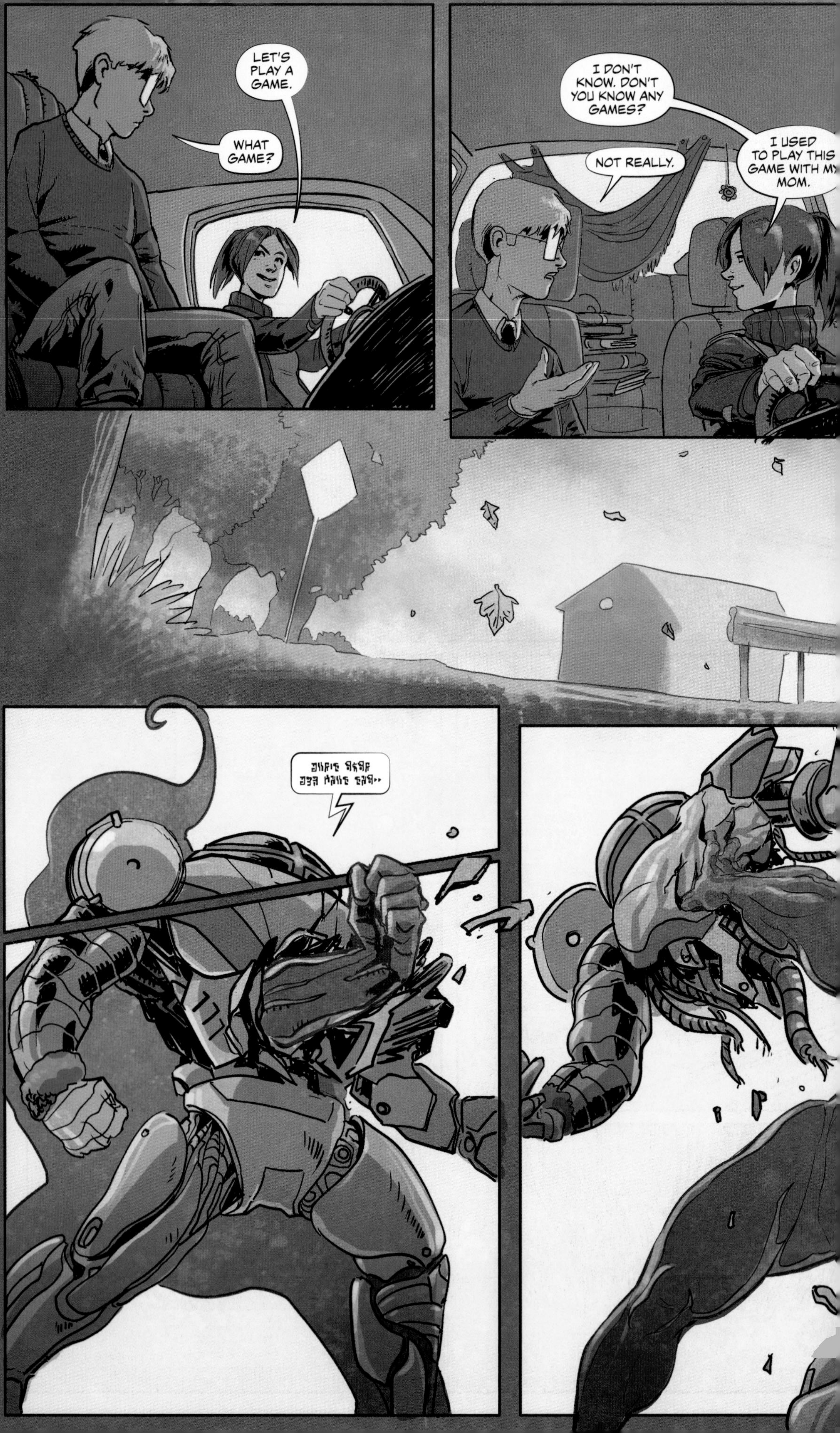
LET'S PLAY A GAME.
WHAT GAME?
I DON'T KNOW. DON'T YOU KNOW ANY GAMES?
NOT REALLY.
I USED TO PLAY THIS GAME WITH MY MOM.

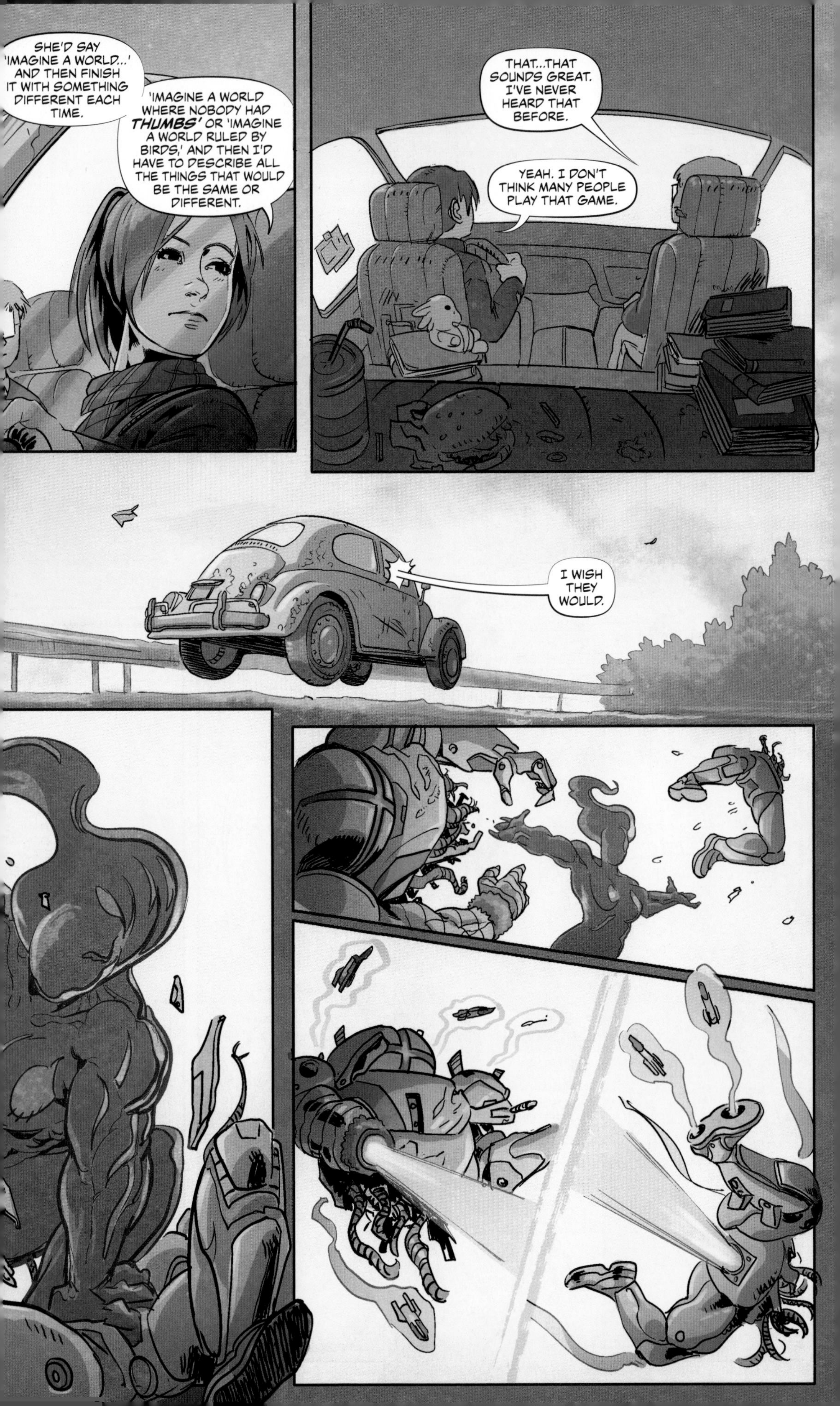
SHE'D SAY 'IMAGINE A WORLD...' AND THEN FINISH IT WITH SOMETHING DIFFERENT EACH TIME.
'IMAGINE A WORLD WHERE NOBODY HAD *THUMBS*' OR 'IMAGINE A WORLD RULED BY BIRDS,' AND THEN I'D HAVE TO DESCRIBE ALL THE THINGS THAT WOULD BE THE SAME OR DIFFERENT.
THAT...THAT SOUNDS GREAT. I'VE NEVER HEARD THAT BEFORE.
YEAH. I DON'T THINK MANY PEOPLE PLAY THAT GAME.
I WISH THEY WOULD.

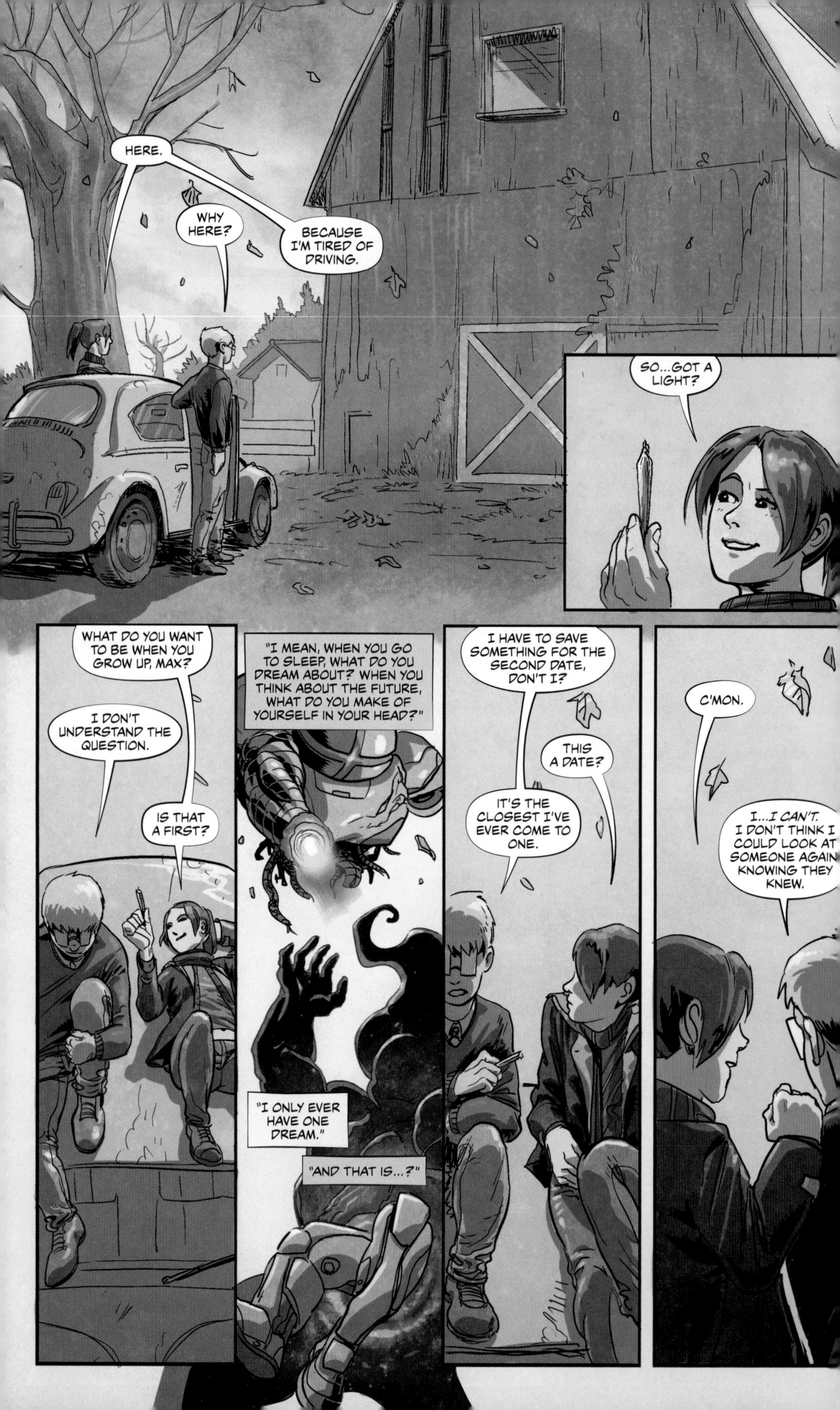
HERE.
WHY HERE?
BECAUSE I'M TIRED OF DRIVING.
SO...GOT A LIGHT?
WHAT DO YOU WANT TO BE WHEN YOU GROW UP, MAX?
I DON'T UNDERSTAND THE QUESTION.
IS THAT A FIRST?
"I MEAN, WHEN YOU GO TO SLEEP, WHAT DO YOU DREAM ABOUT? WHEN YOU THINK ABOUT THE FUTURE, WHAT DO YOU MAKE OF YOURSELF IN YOUR HEAD?"
"I ONLY EVER HAVE ONE DREAM."
"AND THAT IS...?"
I HAVE TO SAVE SOMETHING FOR THE SECOND DATE, DON'T I?
THIS A DATE?
IT'S THE CLOSEST I'VE EVER COME TO ONE.
C'MON.
I...I CAN'T. I DON'T THINK I COULD LOOK AT SOMEONE AGAIN KNOWING THEY KNEW.

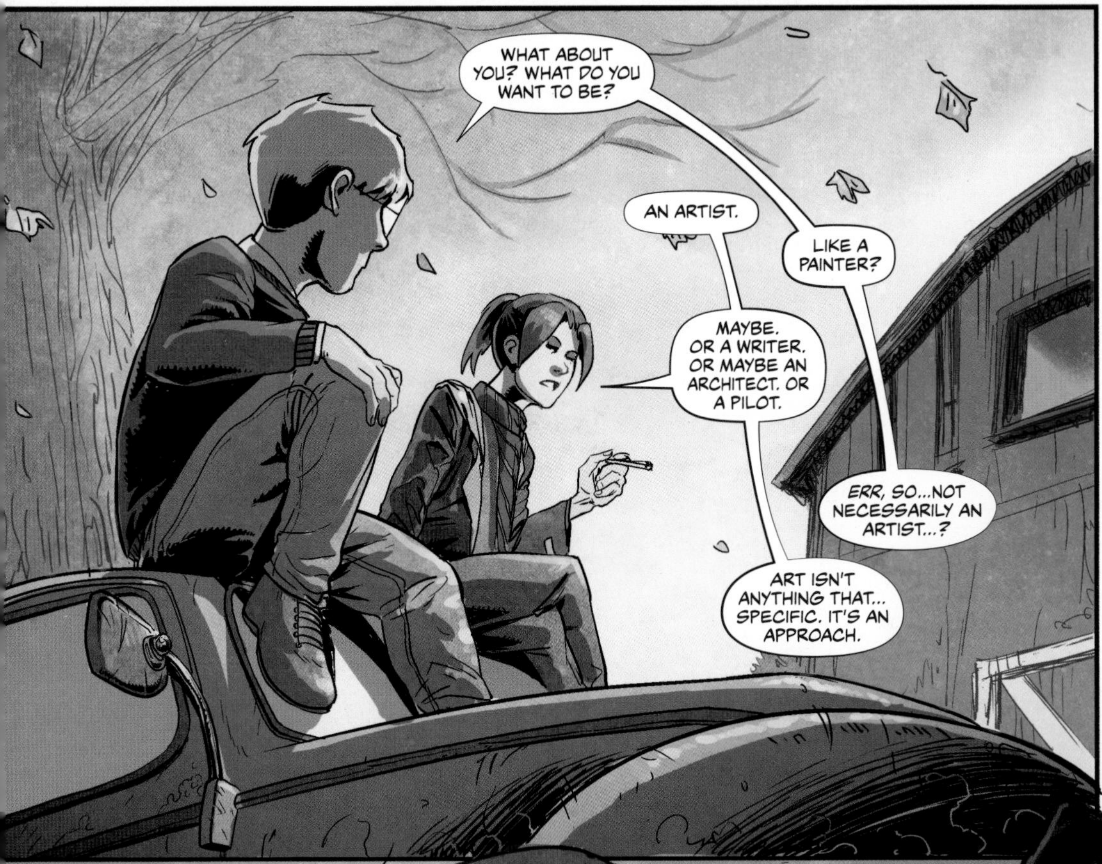
WHAT ABOUT YOU? WHAT DO YOU WANT TO BE?
AN ARTIST.
LIKE A PAINTER?
MAYBE. OR A WRITER. OR MAYBE AN ARCHITECT. OR A PILOT.
ERR, SO...NOT NECESSARILY AN ARTIST...?
ART ISN'T ANYTHING THAT... SPECIFIC. IT'S AN APPROACH.

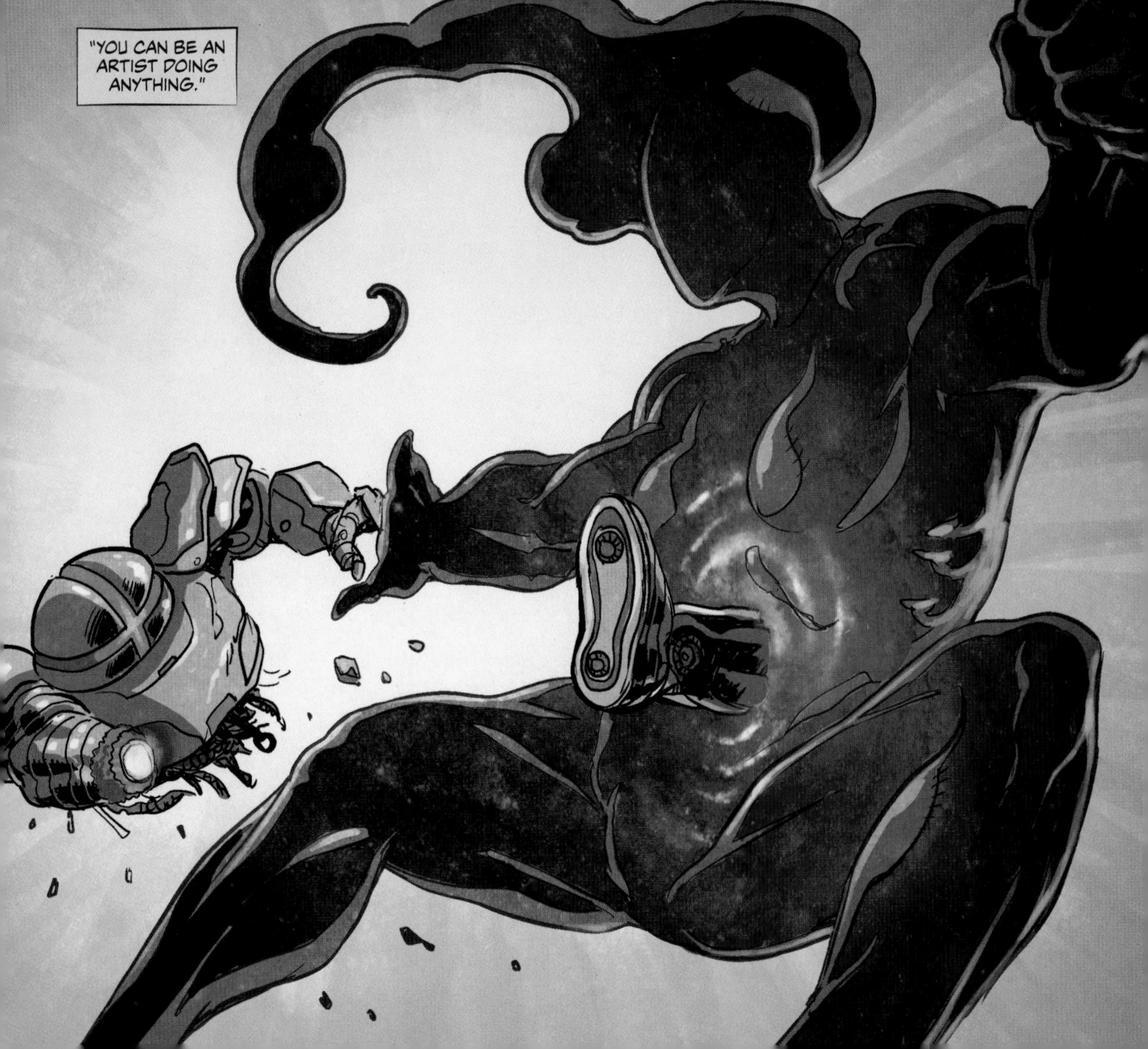
"YOU CAN BE AN ARTIST DOING ANYTHING."

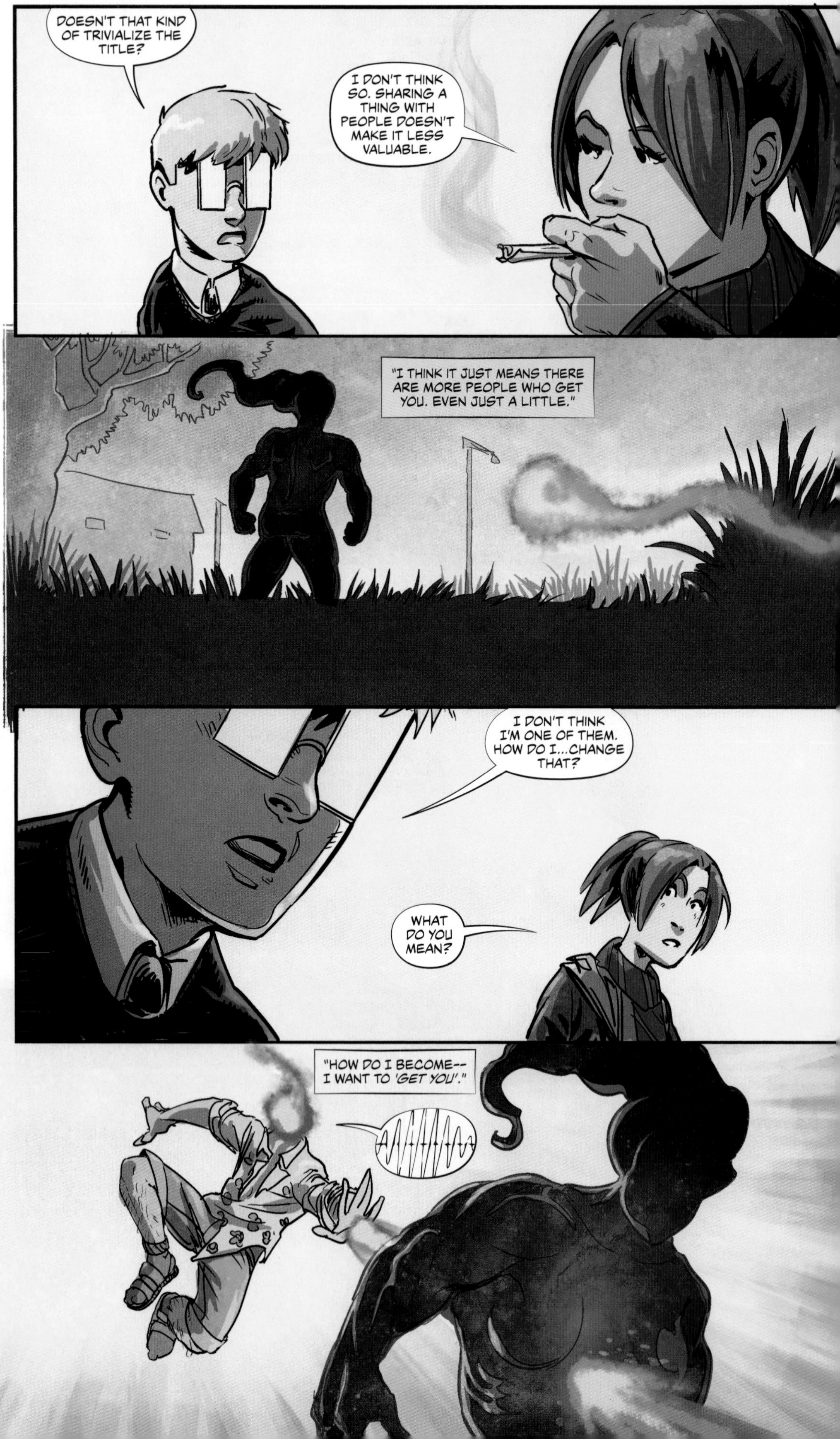
DOESN'T THAT KIND OF TRIVIALIZE THE TITLE?
I DON'T THINK SO. SHARING A THING WITH PEOPLE DOESN'T MAKE IT LESS VALUABLE.
"I THINK IT JUST MEANS THERE ARE MORE PEOPLE WHO GET YOU. EVEN JUST A LITTLE."
I DON'T THINK I'M ONE OF THEM. HOW DO I...CHANGE THAT?
WHAT DO YOU MEAN?
"HOW DO I BECOME-- I WANT TO *'GET YOU'*."

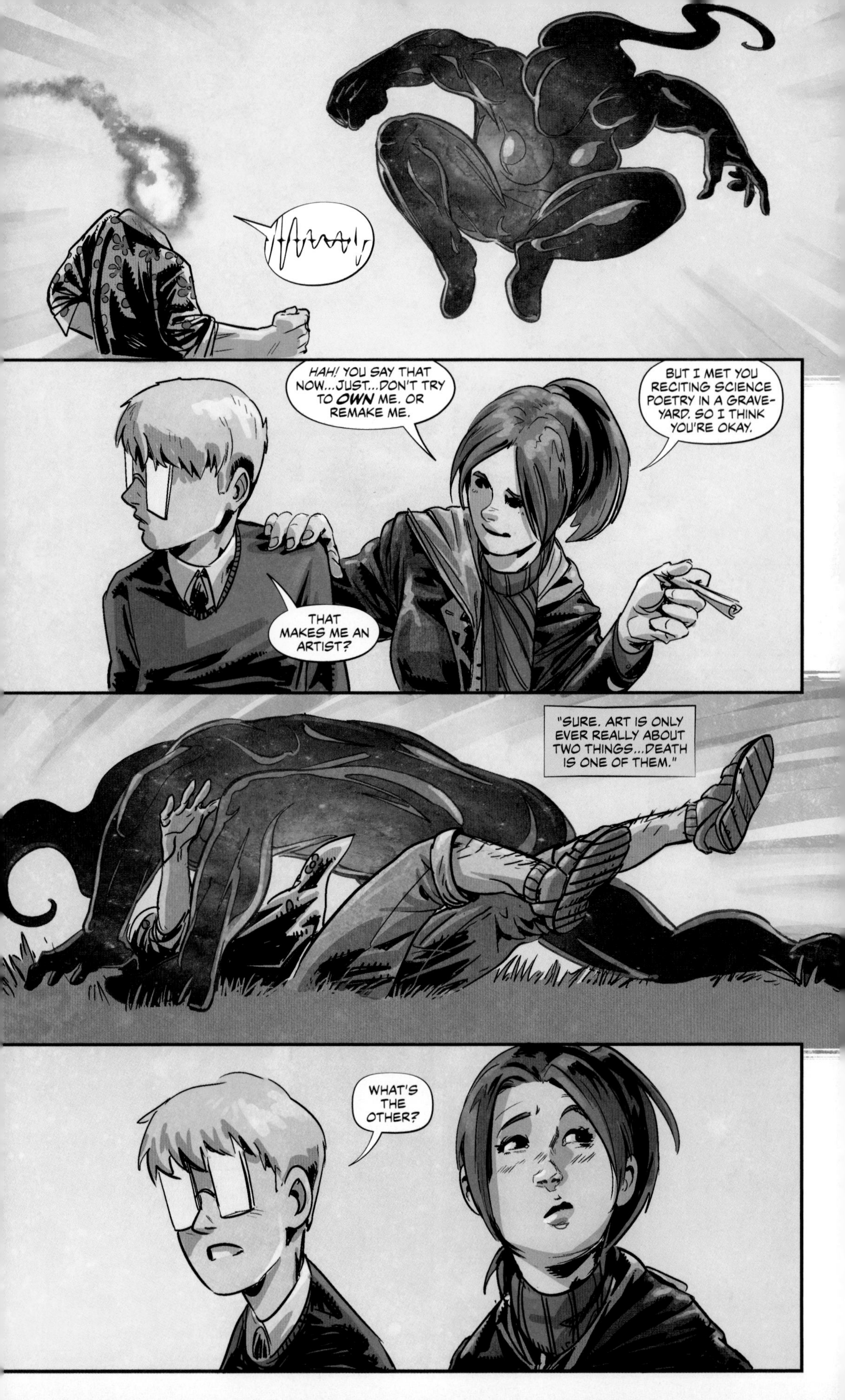
HAH! YOU SAY THAT NOW...JUST...DON'T TRY TO *OWN* ME. OR REMAKE ME.
BUT I MET YOU RECITING SCIENCE POETRY IN A GRAVE-YARD. SO I THINK YOU'RE OKAY.
THAT MAKES ME AN ARTIST?
"SURE. ART IS ONLY EVER REALLY ABOUT TWO THINGS...DEATH IS ONE OF THEM."
WHAT'S THE OTHER?

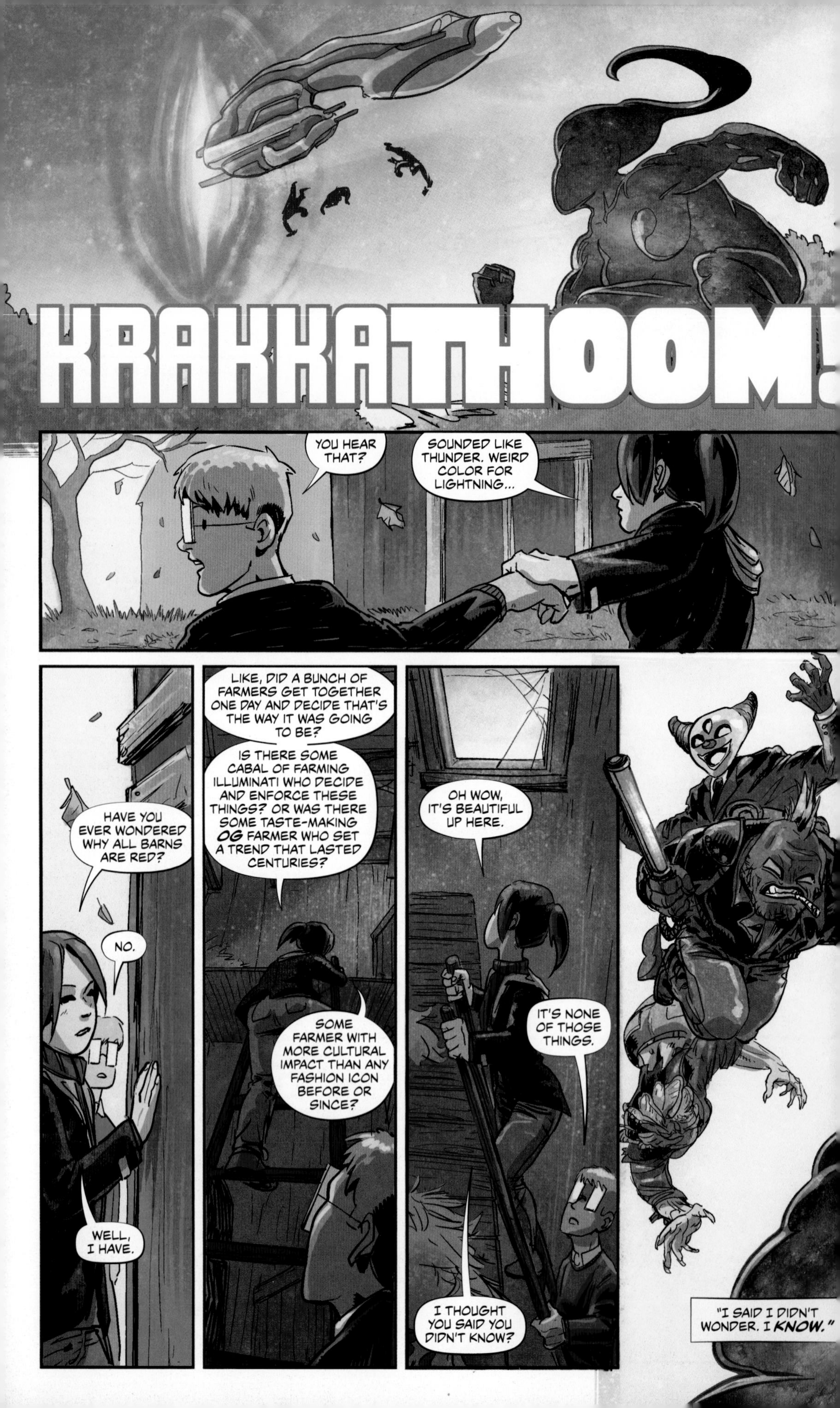
KRAKKATHOOM!
YOU HEAR THAT?
SOUNDED LIKE THUNDER. WEIRD COLOR FOR LIGHTNING...
HAVE YOU EVER WONDERED WHY ALL BARNS ARE RED?
NO.
WELL, I HAVE.
LIKE, DID A BUNCH OF FARMERS GET TOGETHER ONE DAY AND DECIDE THAT'S THE WAY IT WAS GOING TO BE?
IS THERE SOME CABAL OF FARMING ILLUMINATI WHO DECIDE AND ENFORCE THESE THINGS? OR WAS THERE SOME TASTE-MAKING OG FARMER WHO SET A TREND THAT LASTED CENTURIES?
SOME FARMER WITH MORE CULTURAL IMPACT THAN ANY FASHION ICON BEFORE OR SINCE?
OH WOW, IT'S BEAUTIFUL UP HERE.
IT'S NONE OF THOSE THINGS.
I THOUGHT YOU SAID YOU DIDN'T KNOW?
"I SAID I DIDN'T WONDER. I KNOW."

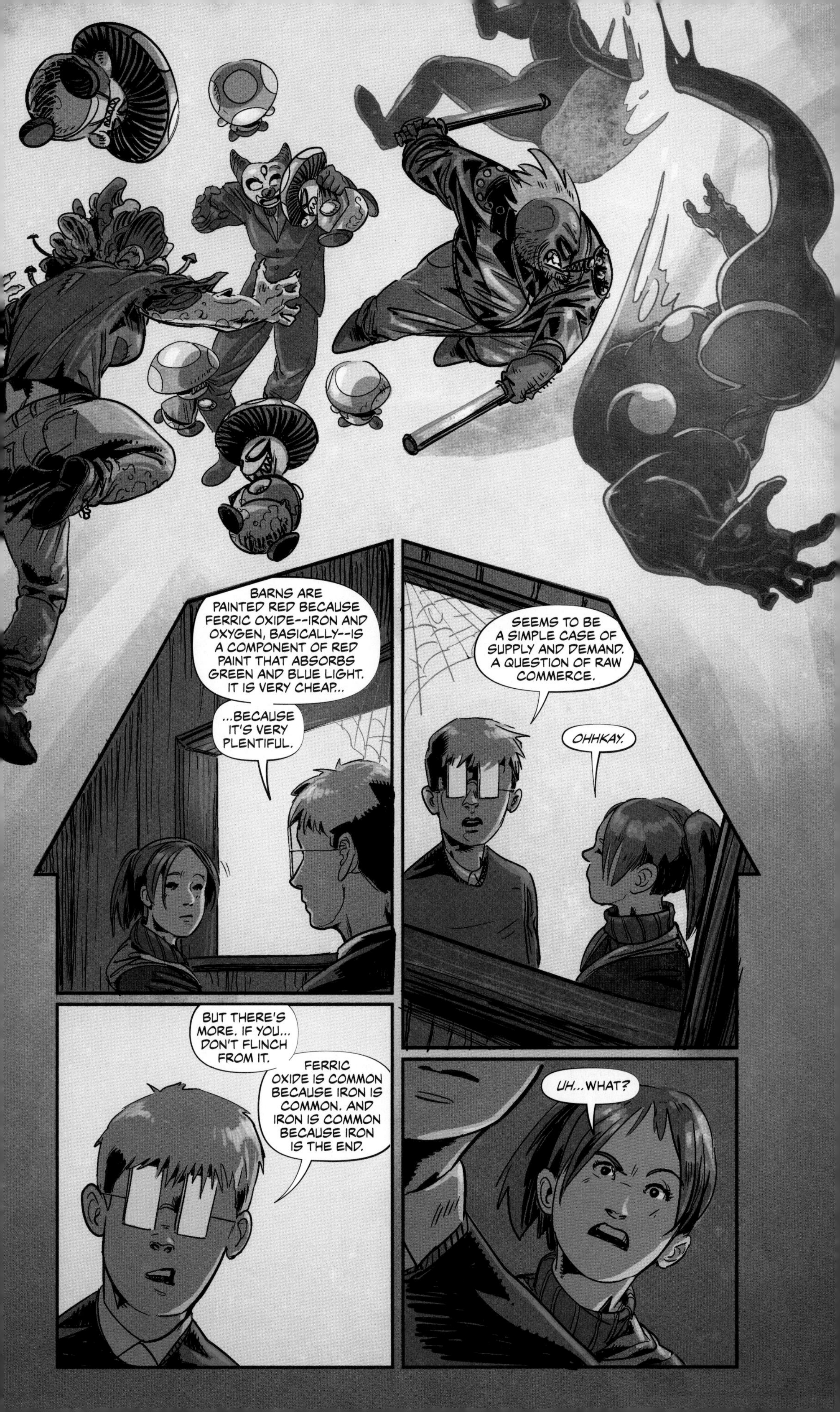
BARNS ARE PAINTED RED BECAUSE FERRIC OXIDE--IRON AND OXYGEN, BASICALLY--IS A COMPONENT OF RED PAINT THAT ABSORBS GREEN AND BLUE LIGHT. IT IS VERY CHEAP...
...BECAUSE IT'S VERY PLENTIFUL.
SEEMS TO BE A SIMPLE CASE OF SUPPLY AND DEMAND. A QUESTION OF RAW COMMERCE.
OHHKAY.
BUT THERE'S MORE. IF YOU... DON'T FLINCH FROM IT.
FERRIC OXIDE IS COMMON BECAUSE IRON IS COMMON. AND IRON IS COMMON BECAUSE IRON IS THE END.
UH...WHAT?

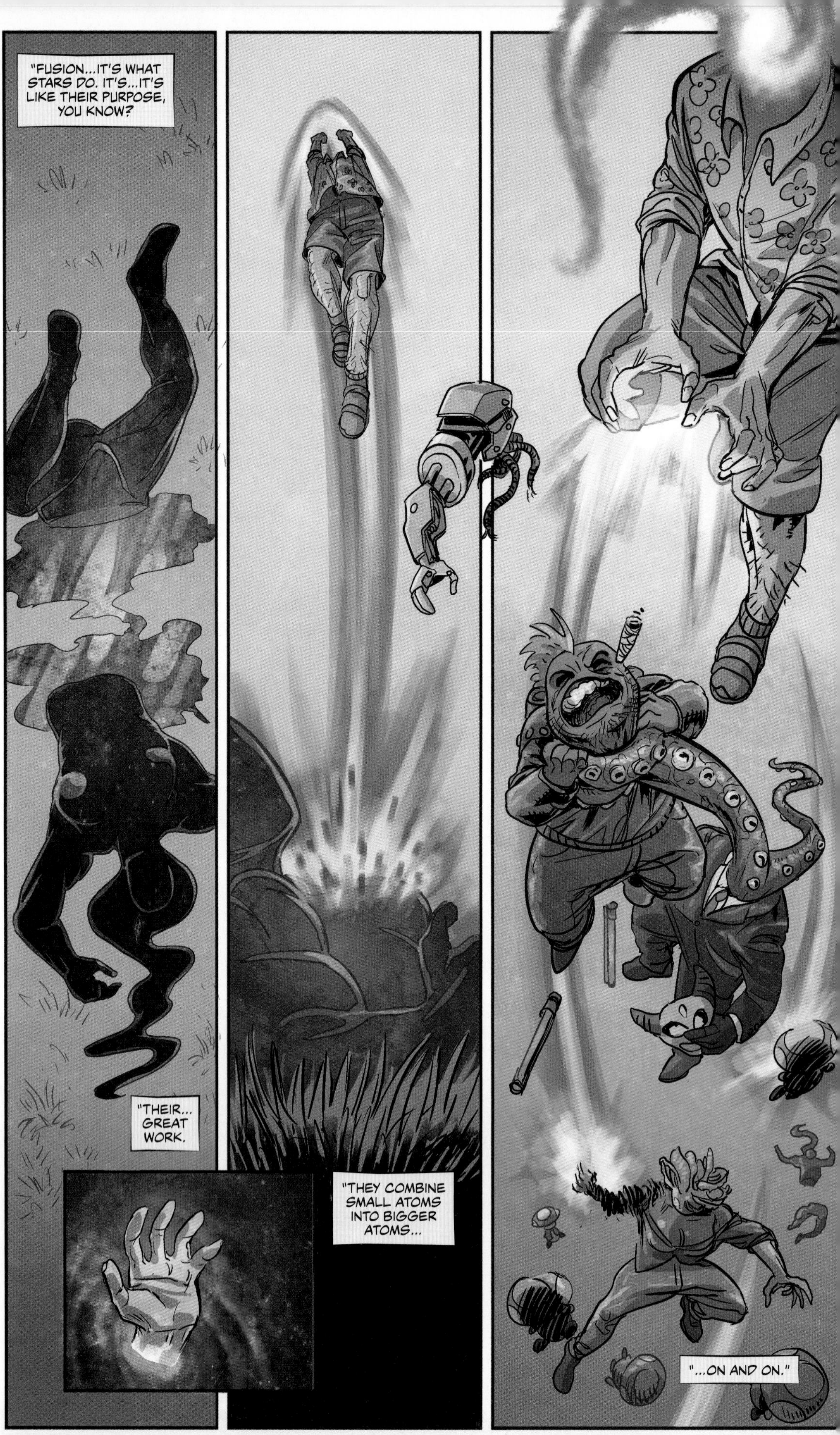
"FUSION...IT'S WHAT STARS DO. IT'S...IT'S LIKE THEIR PURPOSE, YOU KNOW?
"THEIR... GREAT WORK.
"THEY COMBINE SMALL ATOMS INTO BIGGER ATOMS...
"...ON AND ON."

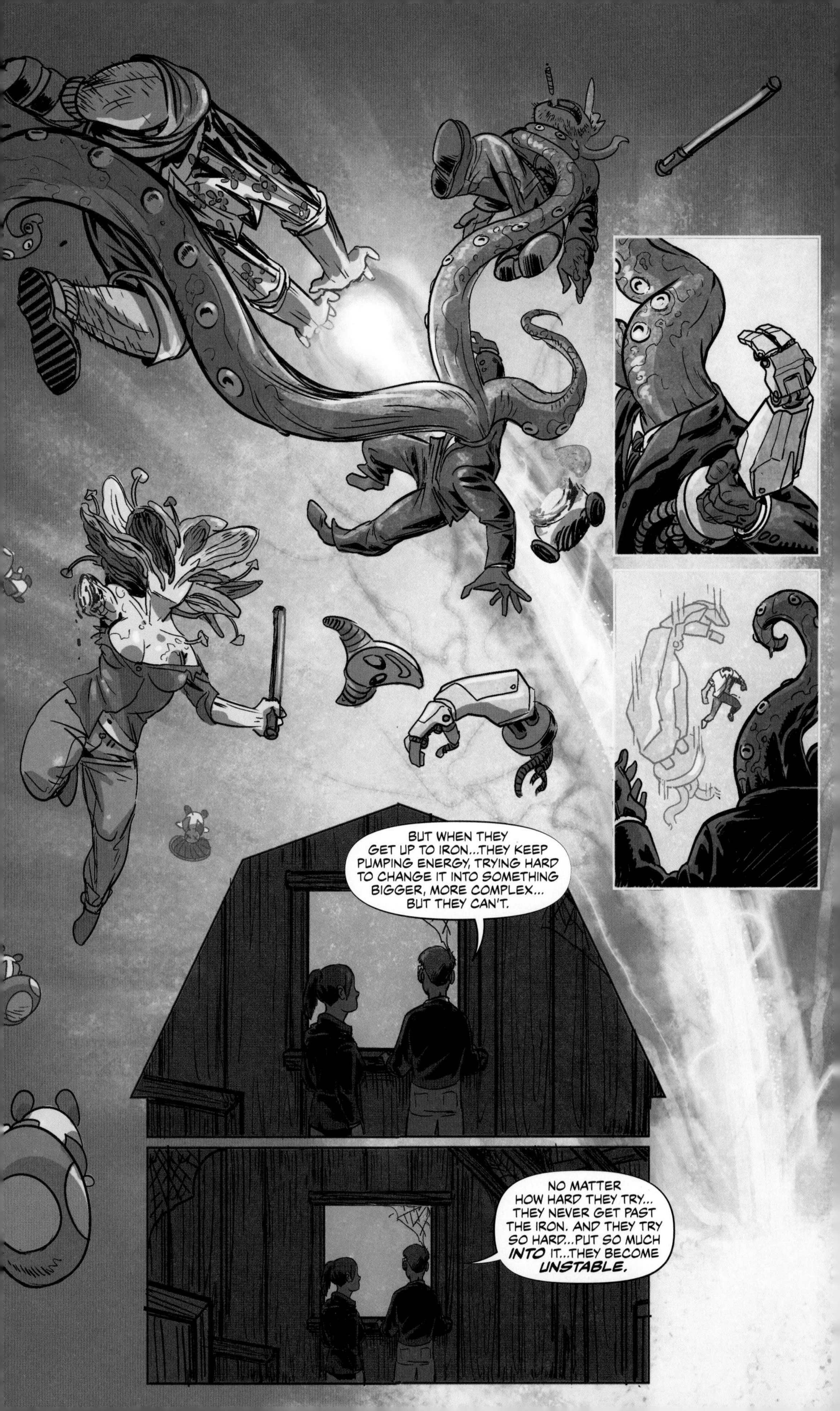
BUT WHEN THEY GET UP TO IRON...THEY KEEP PUMPING ENERGY, TRYING HARD TO CHANGE IT INTO SOMETHING BIGGER, MORE COMPLEX... BUT THEY CAN'T.
NO MATTER HOW HARD THEY TRY... THEY NEVER GET PAST THE IRON. AND THEY TRY SO HARD...PUT SO MUCH *INTO* IT...THEY BECOME ***UNSTABLE.***

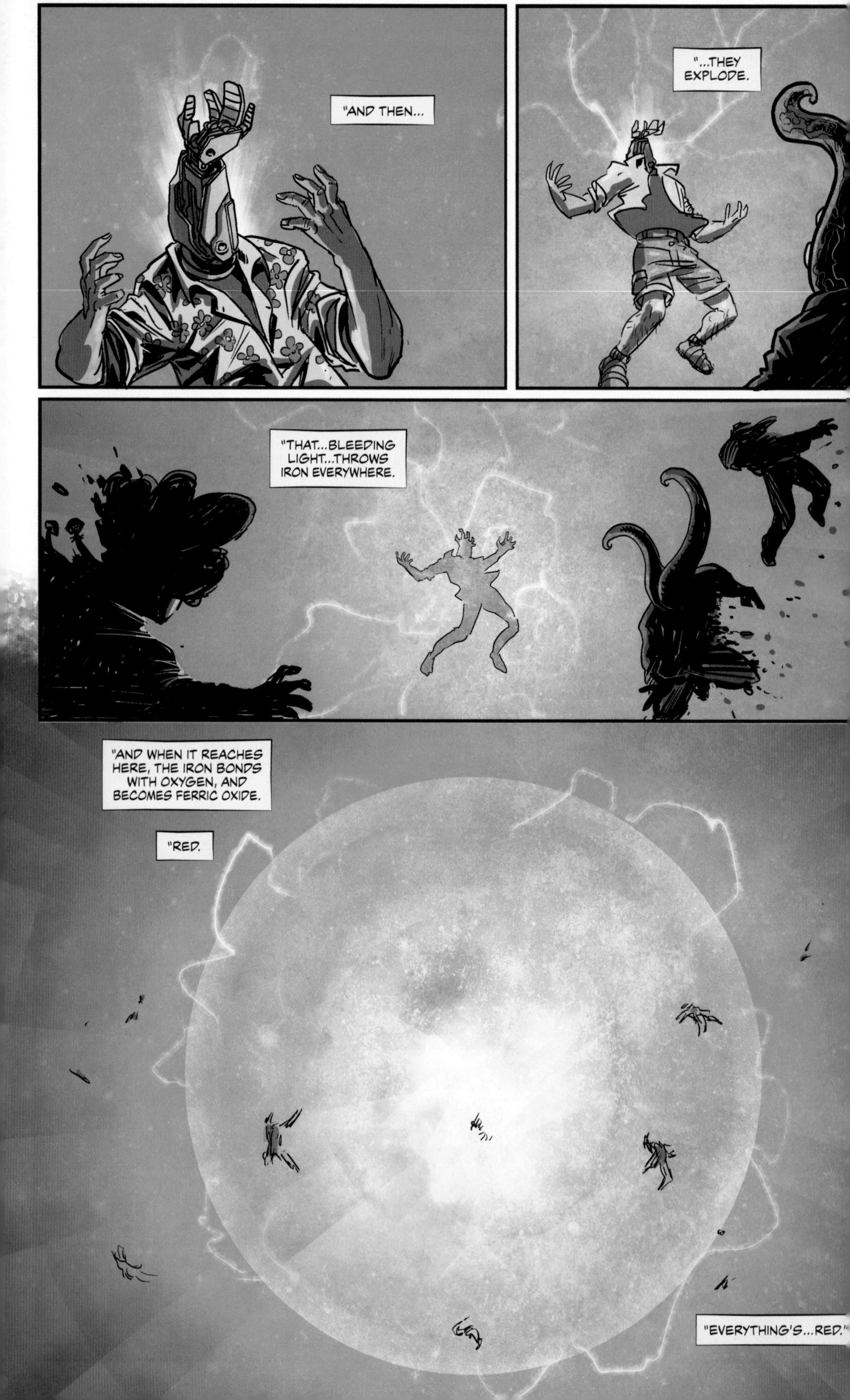
"AND THEN...
"...THEY EXPLODE.
"THAT...BLEEDING LIGHT...THROWS IRON EVERYWHERE.
"AND WHEN IT REACHES HERE, THE IRON BONDS WITH OXYGEN, AND BECOMES FERRIC OXIDE.
"RED.
"EVERYTHING'S...RED."

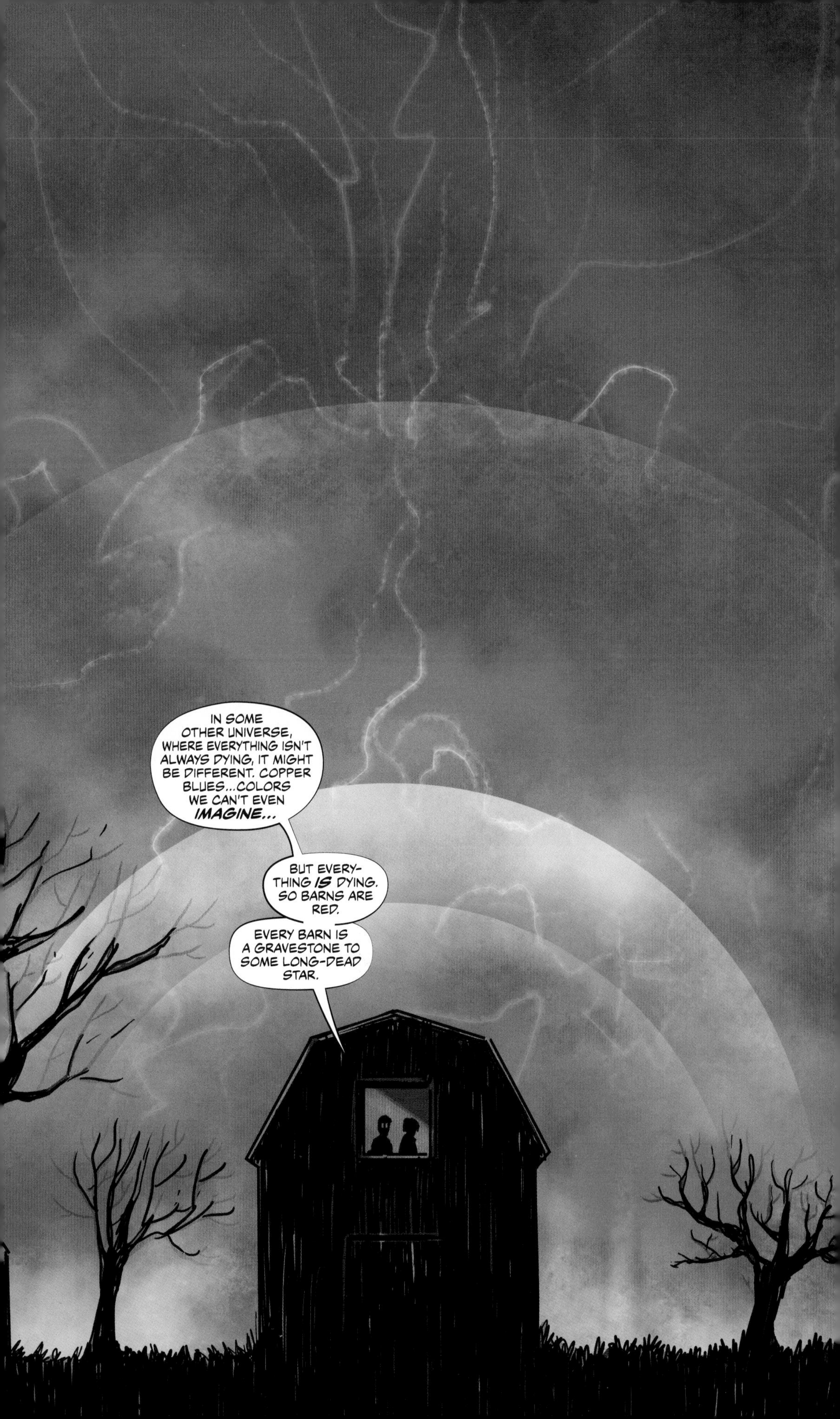
IN SOME OTHER UNIVERSE, WHERE EVERYTHING ISN'T ALWAYS DYING, IT MIGHT BE DIFFERENT. COPPER BLUES...COLORS WE CAN'T EVEN *IMAGINE...*
BUT EVERY-THING *IS* DYING. SO BARNS ARE RED.
EVERY BARN IS A GRAVESTONE TO SOME LONG-DEAD STAR.

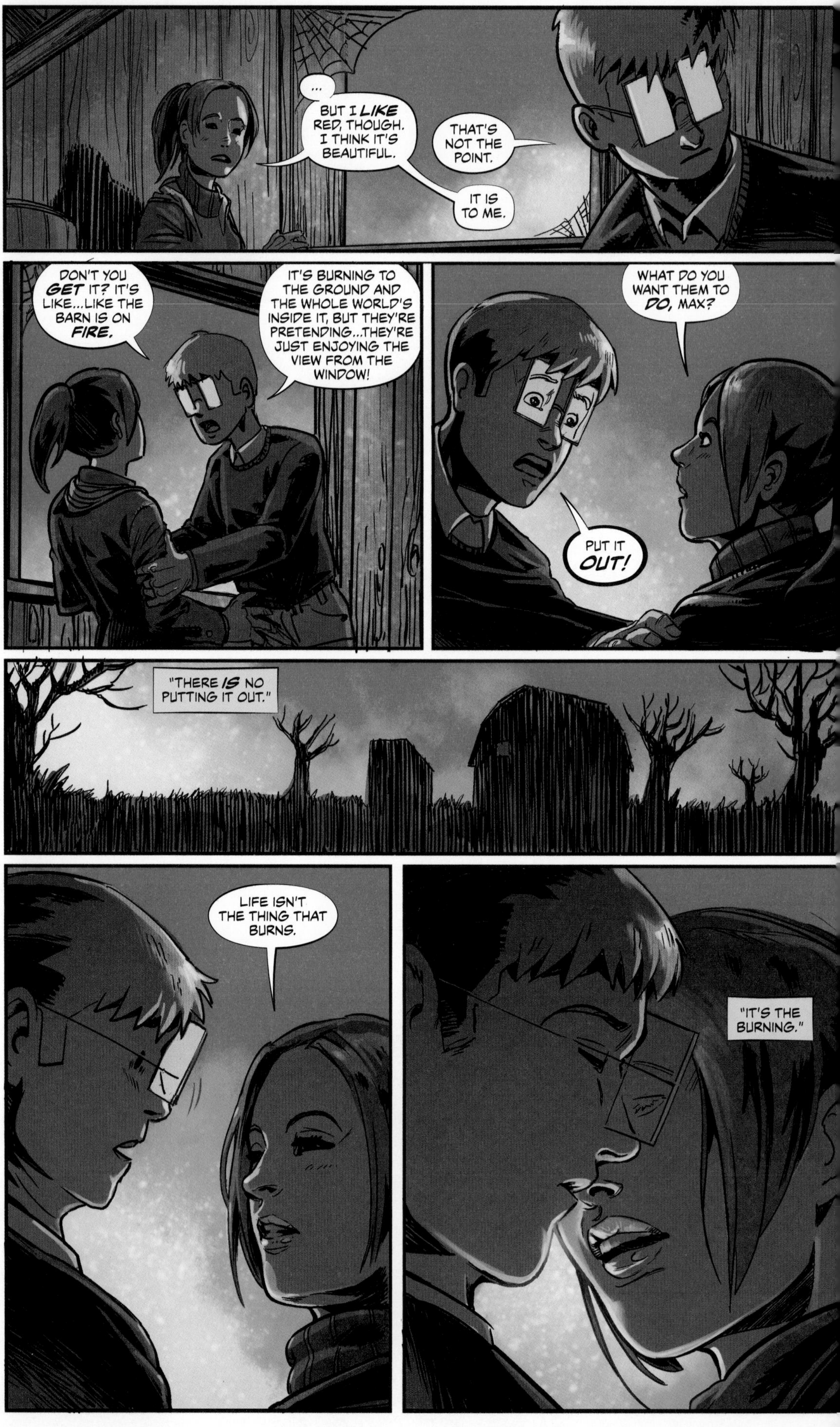
...
BUT I LIKE RED, THOUGH. I THINK IT'S BEAUTIFUL.
THAT'S NOT THE POINT.
IT IS TO ME.
DON'T YOU GET IT? IT'S LIKE...LIKE THE BARN IS ON FIRE.
IT'S BURNING TO THE GROUND AND THE WHOLE WORLD'S INSIDE IT, BUT THEY'RE PRETENDING...THEY'RE JUST ENJOYING THE VIEW FROM THE WINDOW!
WHAT DO YOU WANT THEM TO DO, MAX?
PUT IT OUT!
"THERE IS NO PUTTING IT OUT."
LIFE ISN'T THE THING THAT BURNS.
"IT'S THE BURNING."

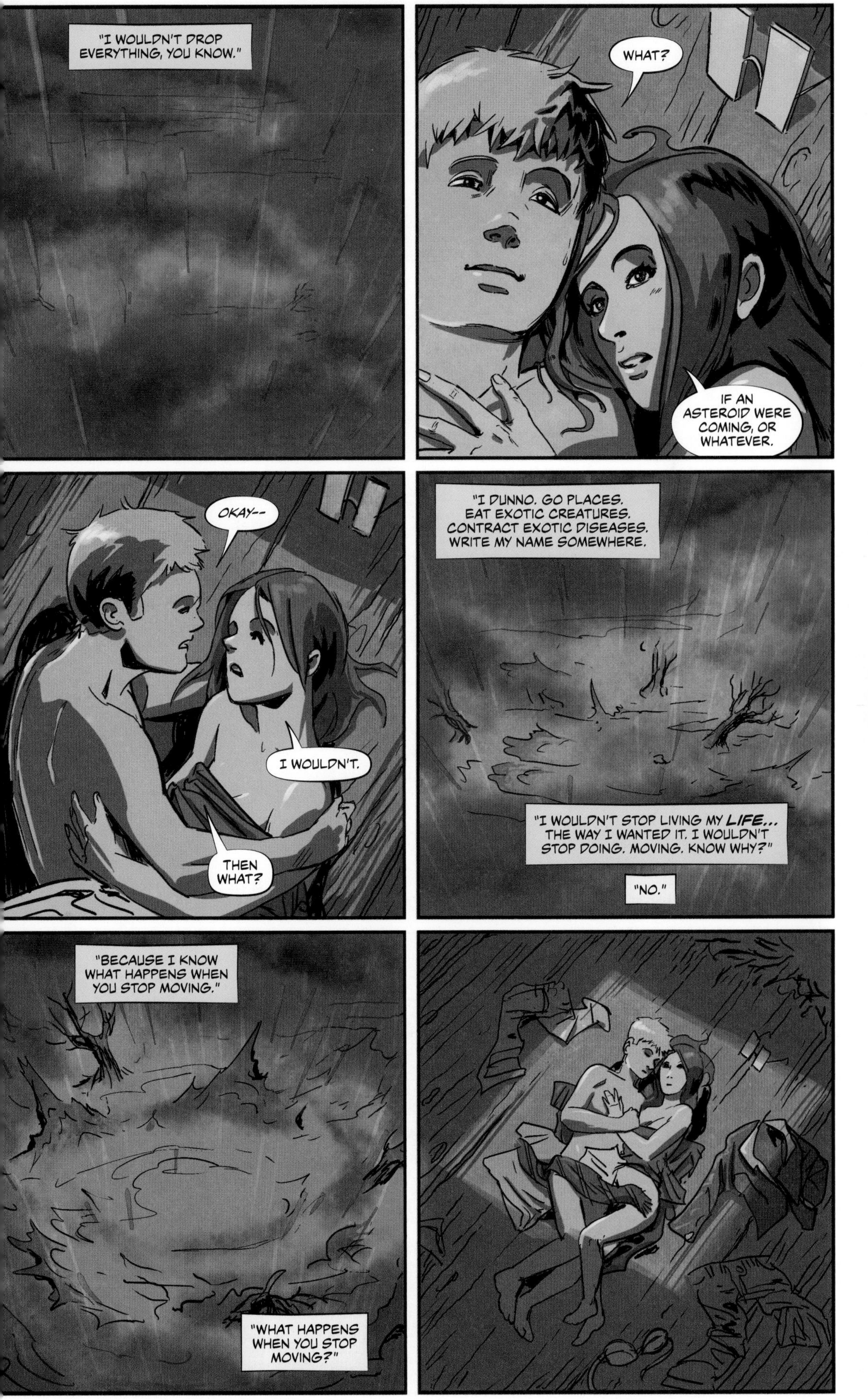
"I WOULDN'T DROP EVERYTHING, YOU KNOW."
WHAT?
IF AN ASTEROID WERE COMING, OR WHATEVER.
OKAY--
I WOULDN'T.
THEN WHAT?
"I DUNNO. GO PLACES. EAT EXOTIC CREATURES. CONTRACT EXOTIC DISEASES. WRITE MY NAME SOMEWHERE.
"I WOULDN'T STOP LIVING MY *LIFE*... THE WAY I WANTED IT. I WOULDN'T STOP DOING. MOVING. KNOW WHY?"
"NO."
"BECAUSE I KNOW WHAT HAPPENS WHEN YOU STOP MOVING."
"WHAT HAPPENS WHEN YOU STOP MOVING?"

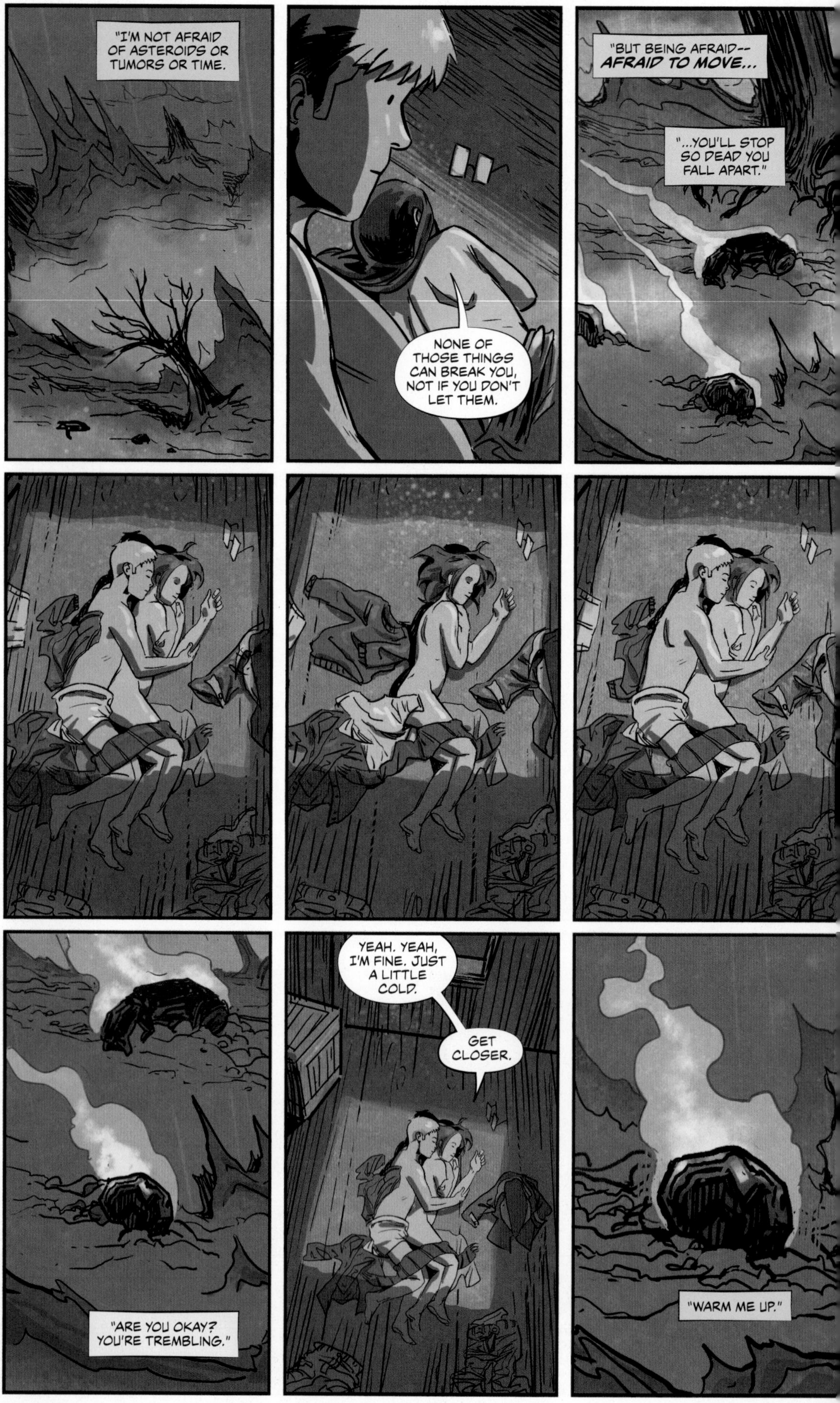
"I'M NOT AFRAID OF ASTEROIDS OR TUMORS OR TIME.
NONE OF THOSE THINGS CAN BREAK YOU, NOT IF YOU DON'T LET THEM.
"BUT BEING AFRAID-- AFRAID TO MOVE...
"...YOU'LL STOP SO DEAD YOU FALL APART."
"ARE YOU OKAY? YOU'RE TREMBLING."
YEAH. YEAH, I'M FINE. JUST A LITTLE COLD.
GET CLOSER.
"WARM ME UP."

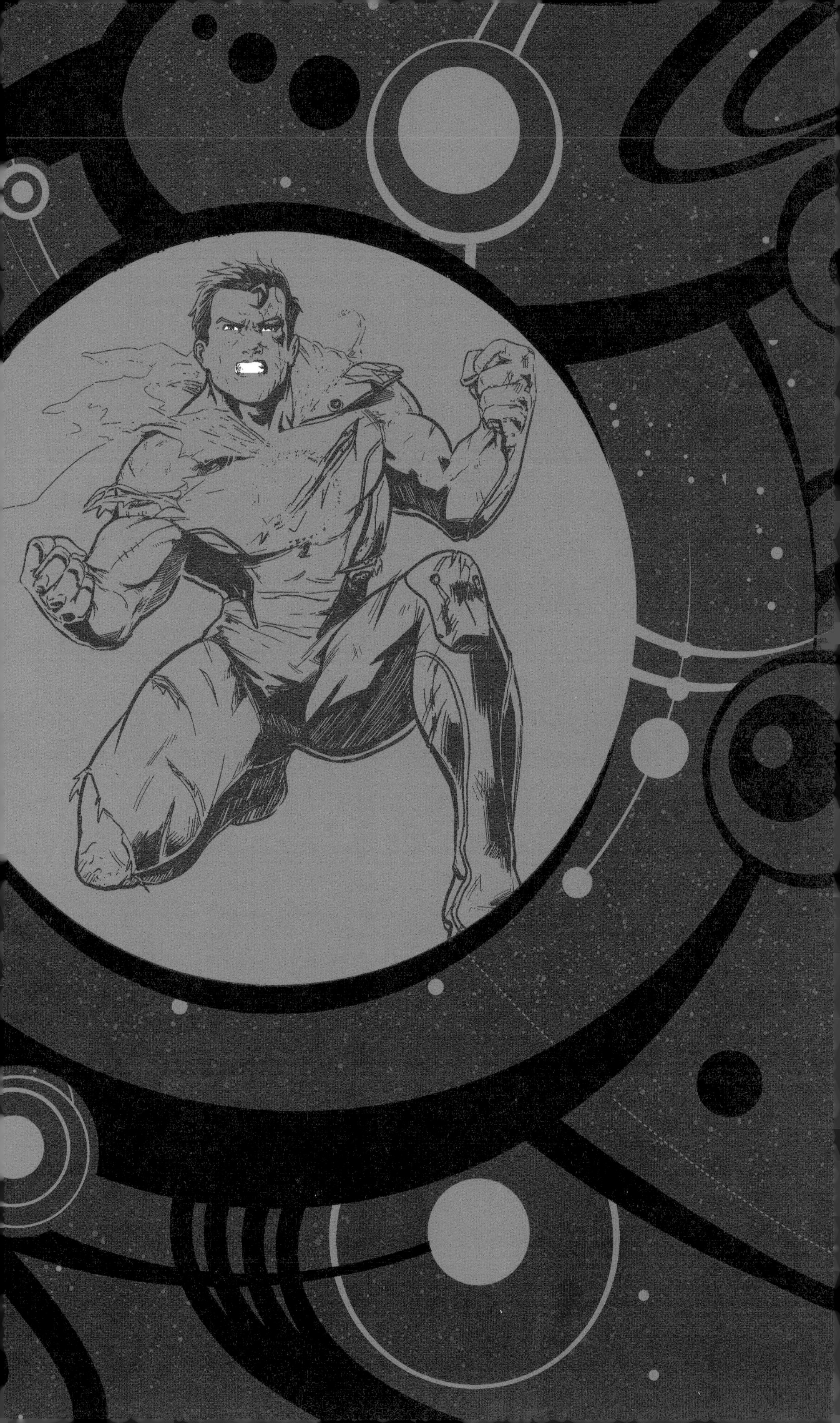

FIVE

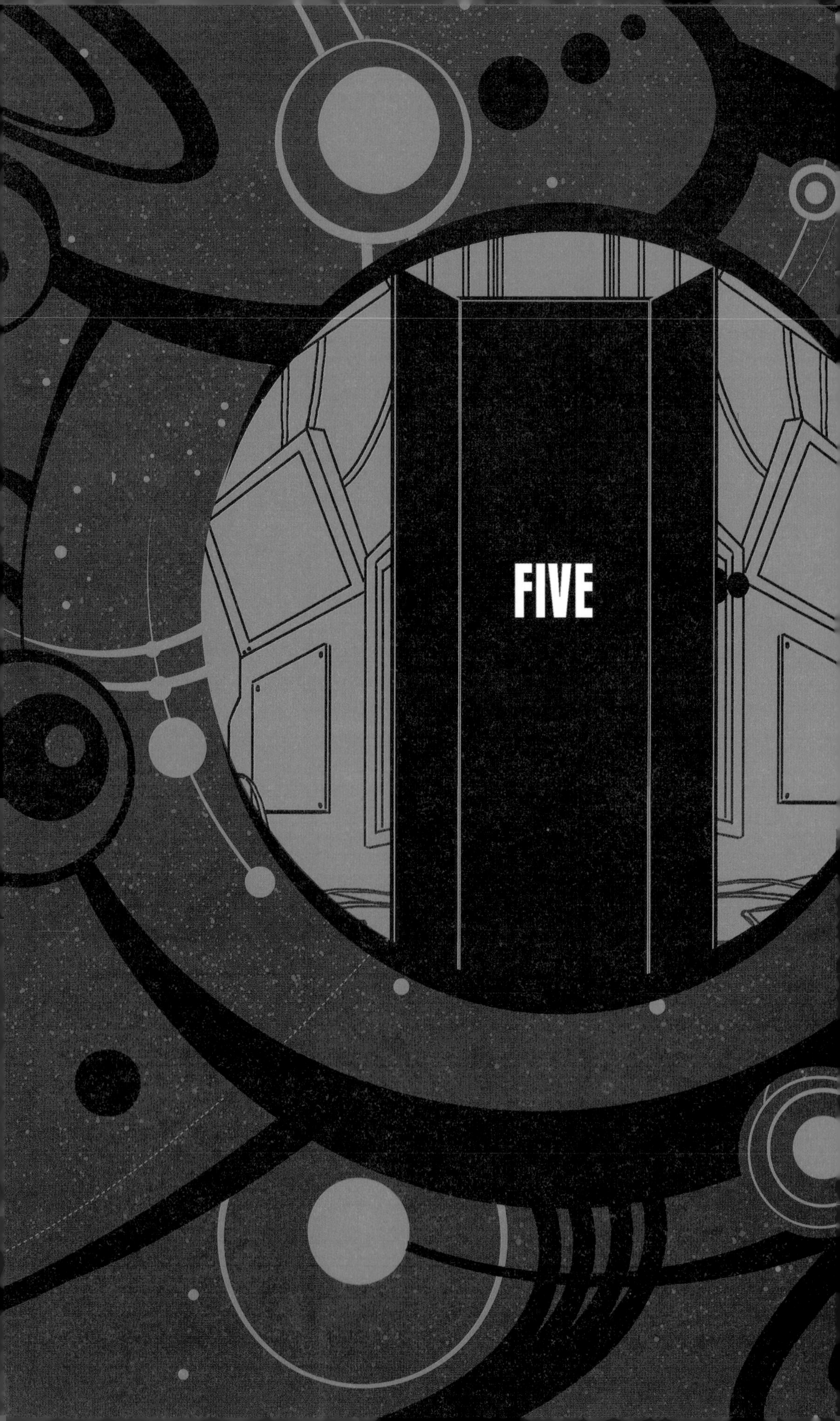

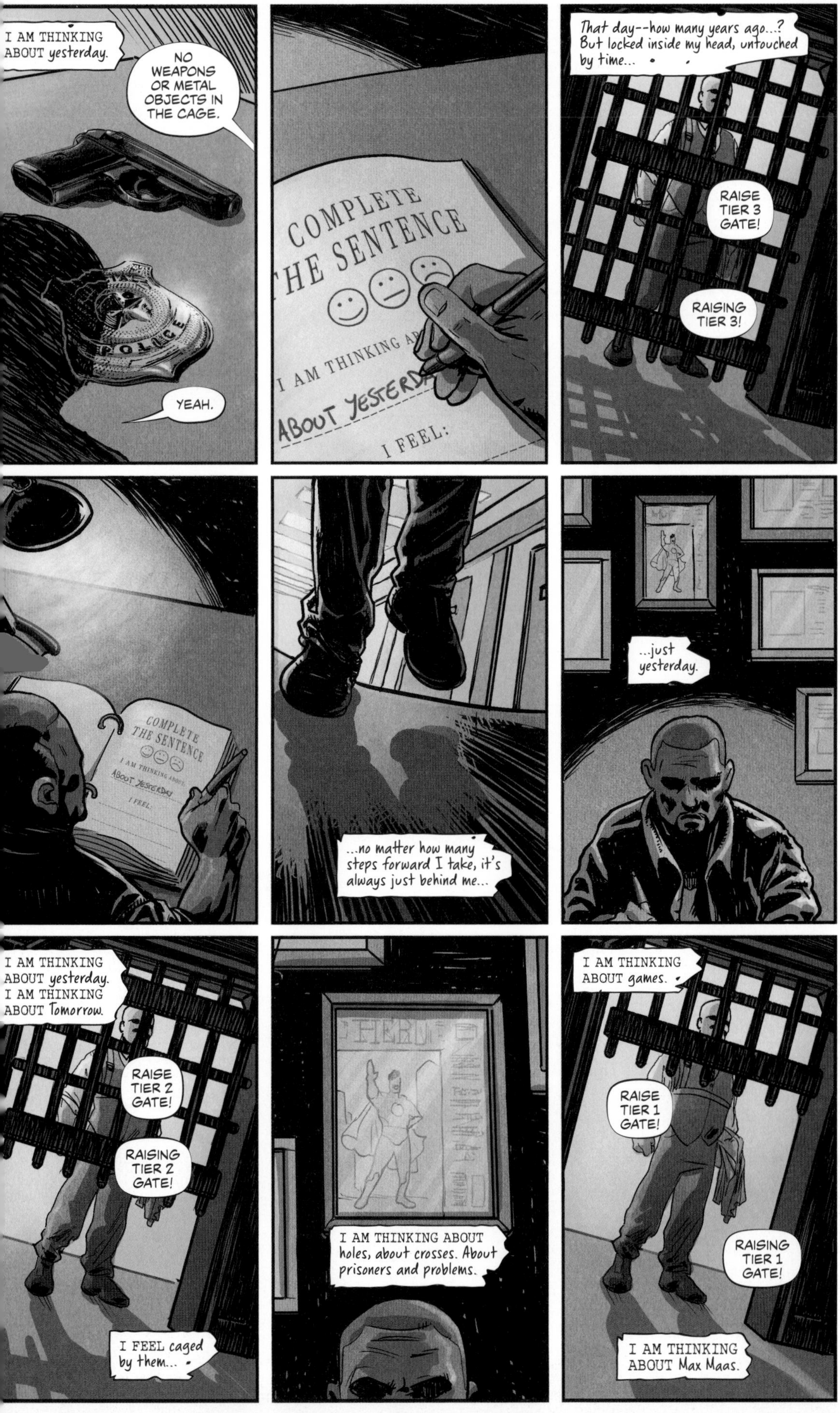
I AM THINKING ABOUT yesterday.
NO WEAPONS OR METAL OBJECTS IN THE CAGE.
POLICE
YEAH.
COMPLETE THE SENTENCE
I AM THINKING AB
ABOUT YESTERD
I FEEL:
That day--how many years ago...? But locked inside my head, untouched by time...
RAISE TIER 3 GATE!
RAISING TIER 3!
COMPLETE THE SENTENCE
I AM THINKING ABOUT
ABOUT YESTERDAY
I FEEL:
...no matter how many steps forward I take, it's always just behind me...
...just yesterday.
I AM THINKING ABOUT yesterday. I AM THINKING ABOUT Tomorrow.
RAISE TIER 2 GATE!
RAISING TIER 2 GATE!
I FEEL caged by them...
HERO
I AM THINKING ABOUT holes, about crosses. About prisoners and problems.
I AM THINKING ABOUT games.
RAISE TIER 1 GATE!
RAISING TIER 1 GATE!
I AM THINKING ABOUT Max Maas.

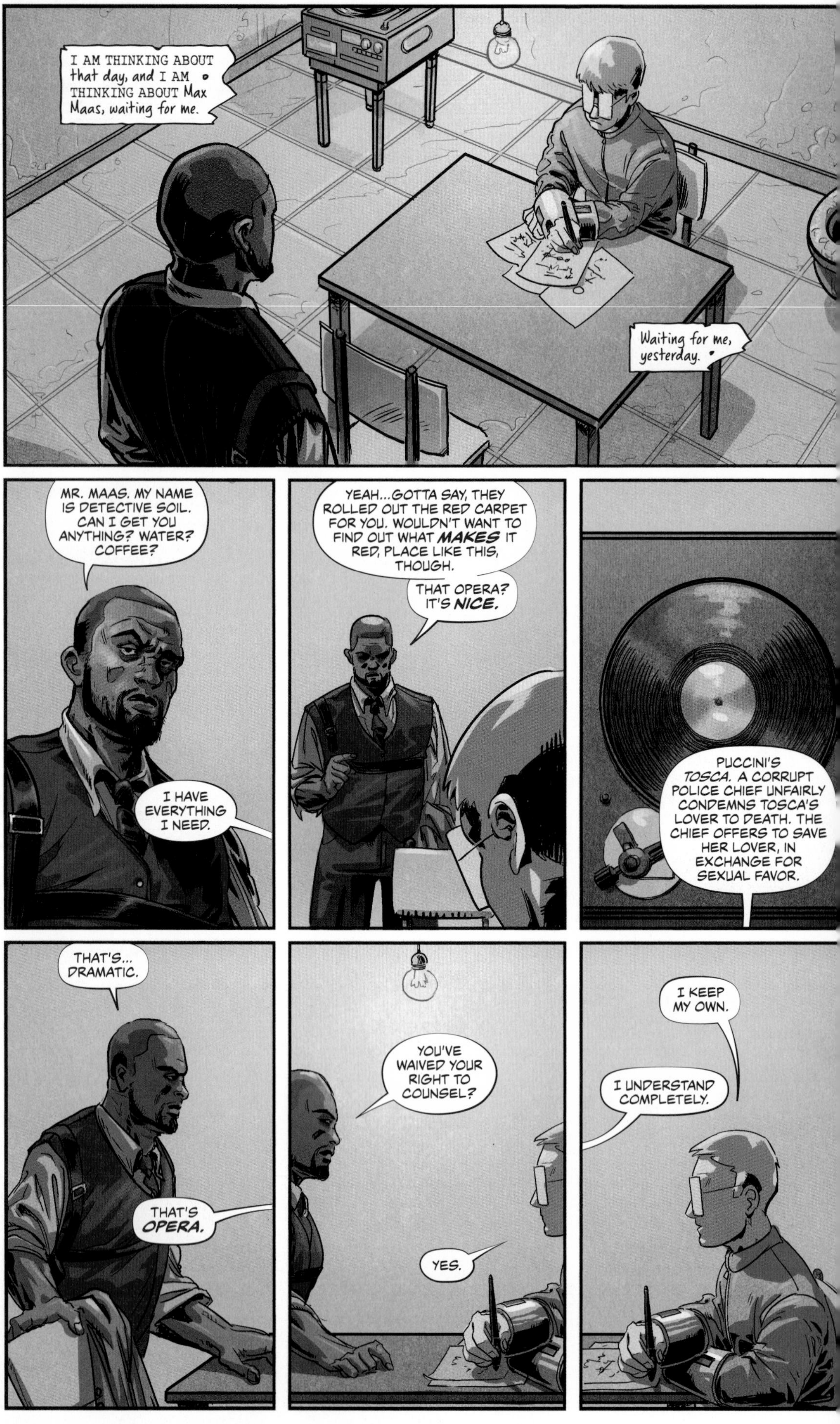
I AM THINKING ABOUT that day, and I AM THINKING ABOUT Max Maas, waiting for me.
Waiting for me, yesterday.
MR. MAAS. MY NAME IS DETECTIVE SOIL. CAN I GET YOU ANYTHING? WATER? COFFEE?
I HAVE EVERYTHING I NEED.
YEAH...GOTTA SAY, THEY ROLLED OUT THE RED CARPET FOR YOU. WOULDN'T WANT TO FIND OUT WHAT MAKES IT RED, PLACE LIKE THIS, THOUGH.
THAT OPERA? IT'S NICE.
PUCCINI'S TOSCA. A CORRUPT POLICE CHIEF UNFAIRLY CONDEMNS TOSCA'S LOVER TO DEATH. THE CHIEF OFFERS TO SAVE HER LOVER, IN EXCHANGE FOR SEXUAL FAVOR.
THAT'S... DRAMATIC.
THAT'S OPERA.
YOU'VE WAIVED YOUR RIGHT TO COUNSEL?
YES.
I KEEP MY OWN.
I UNDERSTAND COMPLETELY.

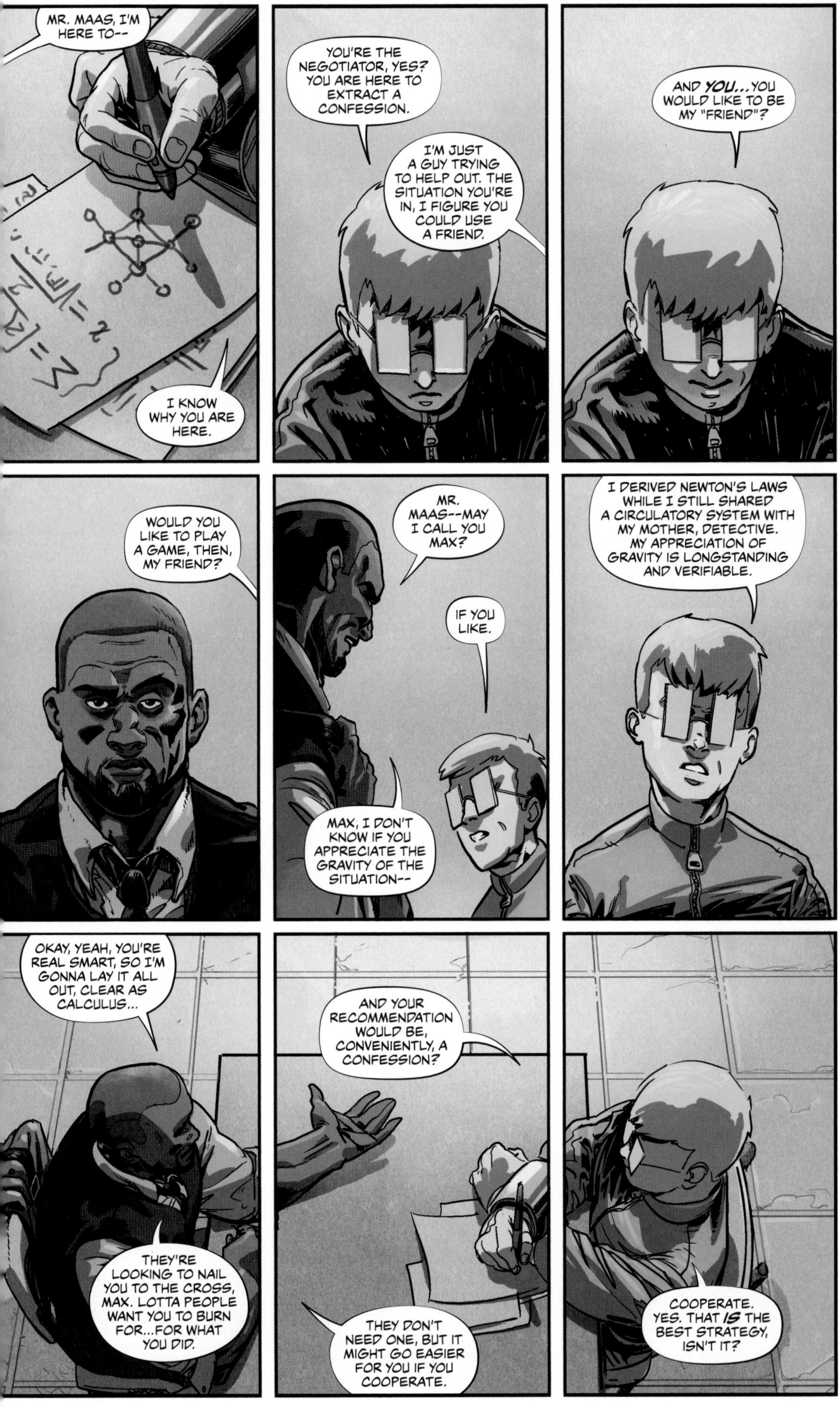
MR. MAAS, I'M HERE TO--
I KNOW WHY YOU ARE HERE.
YOU'RE THE NEGOTIATOR, YES? YOU ARE HERE TO EXTRACT A CONFESSION.
I'M JUST A GUY TRYING TO HELP OUT. THE SITUATION YOU'RE IN, I FIGURE YOU COULD USE A FRIEND.
AND YOU... YOU WOULD LIKE TO BE MY "FRIEND"?
WOULD YOU LIKE TO PLAY A GAME, THEN, MY FRIEND?
MR. MAAS--MAY I CALL YOU MAX?
IF YOU LIKE.
MAX, I DON'T KNOW IF YOU APPRECIATE THE GRAVITY OF THE SITUATION--
I DERIVED NEWTON'S LAWS WHILE I STILL SHARED A CIRCULATORY SYSTEM WITH MY MOTHER, DETECTIVE. MY APPRECIATION OF GRAVITY IS LONGSTANDING AND VERIFIABLE.
OKAY, YEAH, YOU'RE REAL SMART, SO I'M GONNA LAY IT ALL OUT, CLEAR AS CALCULUS...
THEY'RE LOOKING TO NAIL YOU TO THE CROSS, MAX. LOTTA PEOPLE WANT YOU TO BURN FOR...FOR WHAT YOU DID.
AND YOUR RECOMMENDATION WOULD BE, CONVENIENTLY, A CONFESSION?
THEY DON'T NEED ONE, BUT IT MIGHT GO EASIER FOR YOU IF YOU COOPERATE.
COOPERATE. YES. THAT IS THE BEST STRATEGY, ISN'T IT?

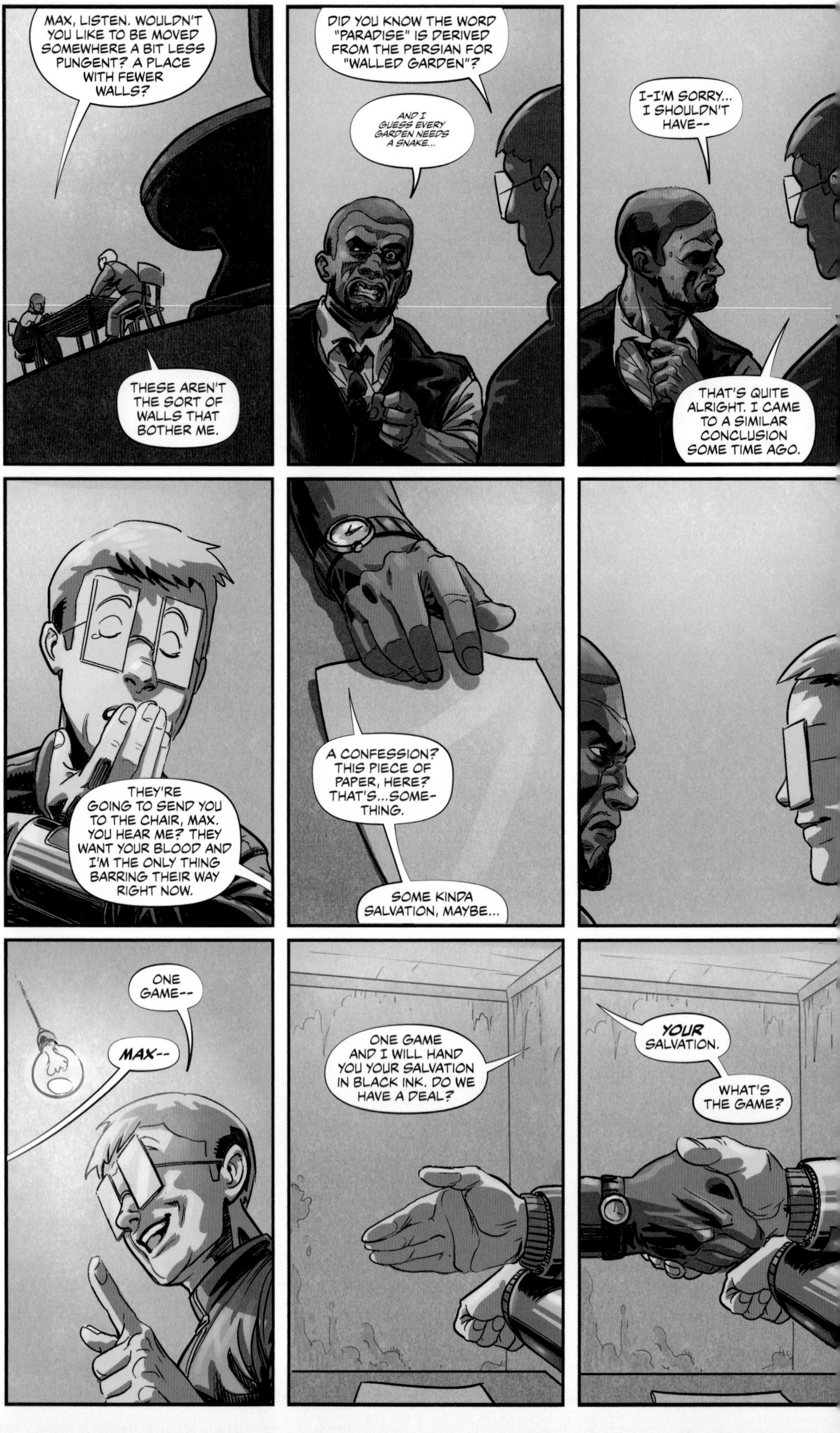
MAX, LISTEN. WOULDN'T YOU LIKE TO BE MOVED SOMEWHERE A BIT LESS PUNGENT? A PLACE WITH FEWER WALLS?
THESE AREN'T THE SORT OF WALLS THAT BOTHER ME.
DID YOU KNOW THE WORD "PARADISE" IS DERIVED FROM THE PERSIAN FOR "WALLED GARDEN"?
AND I GUESS EVERY GARDEN NEEDS A SNAKE...
I-I'M SORRY... I SHOULDN'T HAVE--
THAT'S QUITE ALRIGHT. I CAME TO A SIMILAR CONCLUSION SOME TIME AGO.
THEY'RE GOING TO SEND YOU TO THE CHAIR, MAX. YOU HEAR ME? THEY WANT YOUR BLOOD AND I'M THE ONLY THING BARRING THEIR WAY RIGHT NOW.
A CONFESSION? THIS PIECE OF PAPER, HERE? THAT'S...SOME-THING.
SOME KINDA SALVATION, MAYBE...
ONE GAME--
MAX--
ONE GAME AND I WILL HAND YOU YOUR SALVATION IN BLACK INK. DO WE HAVE A DEAL?
YOUR SALVATION.
WHAT'S THE GAME?

TIC-TAC-TOE.

...

YOU SEEM SURPRISED.

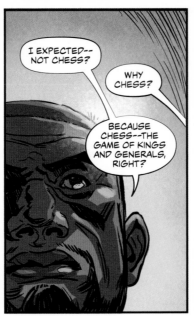

I EXPECTED-- NOT CHESS?

WHY CHESS?

BECAUSE CHESS--THE GAME OF KINGS AND GENERALS, RIGHT?

OUT OF TRADITION, NOT OUT OF ANY SPECIAL *WORTHINESS*. WARS HAVE BEEN LOST IN MISTAKING ONE FOR THE OTHER.

YOU CANNOT MODEL REAL-WORLD CONFLICT ON ZERO-SUM GAMES. IN CHESS, AS IN TIC-TAC-TOE, THERE IS ALWAYS A CORRECT WAY TO PLAY. NOT SO IN LIFE.

IT'S THE GRID, YOU SEE. IT CAN BE INSTRUCTIVE, BUT IN TIME IT WILL STOP YOU FROM MOVING IN THE NECESSARY DIRECTIONS...THINKING IN THREE DIMENSIONS.

FRAMEWORKS INVARIABLY BECOME PRISONS. AS THE GERMANS DISCOVERED WITH THEIR BELOVED WAR GAME "KRIEGSPIEL" IN WORLD WAR I.

THOSE "KINGS AND GENERALS" PLAYED GAMES AS THE WORLD CLOSED IN AROUND THEM.

WOULDN'T HAVE BEEN A PROBLEM IF THEY HADN'T INSISTED ON A WAR.

I'M SURE THEY DID WHAT THEY THOUGHT THEY HAD TO.

AND LOOK WHERE IT GOT THEM...AND EVERYONE ELSE.

MAKE YOUR MOVE.

LOOK AT YOU. RICHEST MAN IN THE WORLD. MAYBE SMARTEST, TOO. YOU COULD HAVE... YOU COULD HAVE BEEN *ANYTHING*. BUT YOU'LL ONLY BE REMEMBERED AS *THIS*.

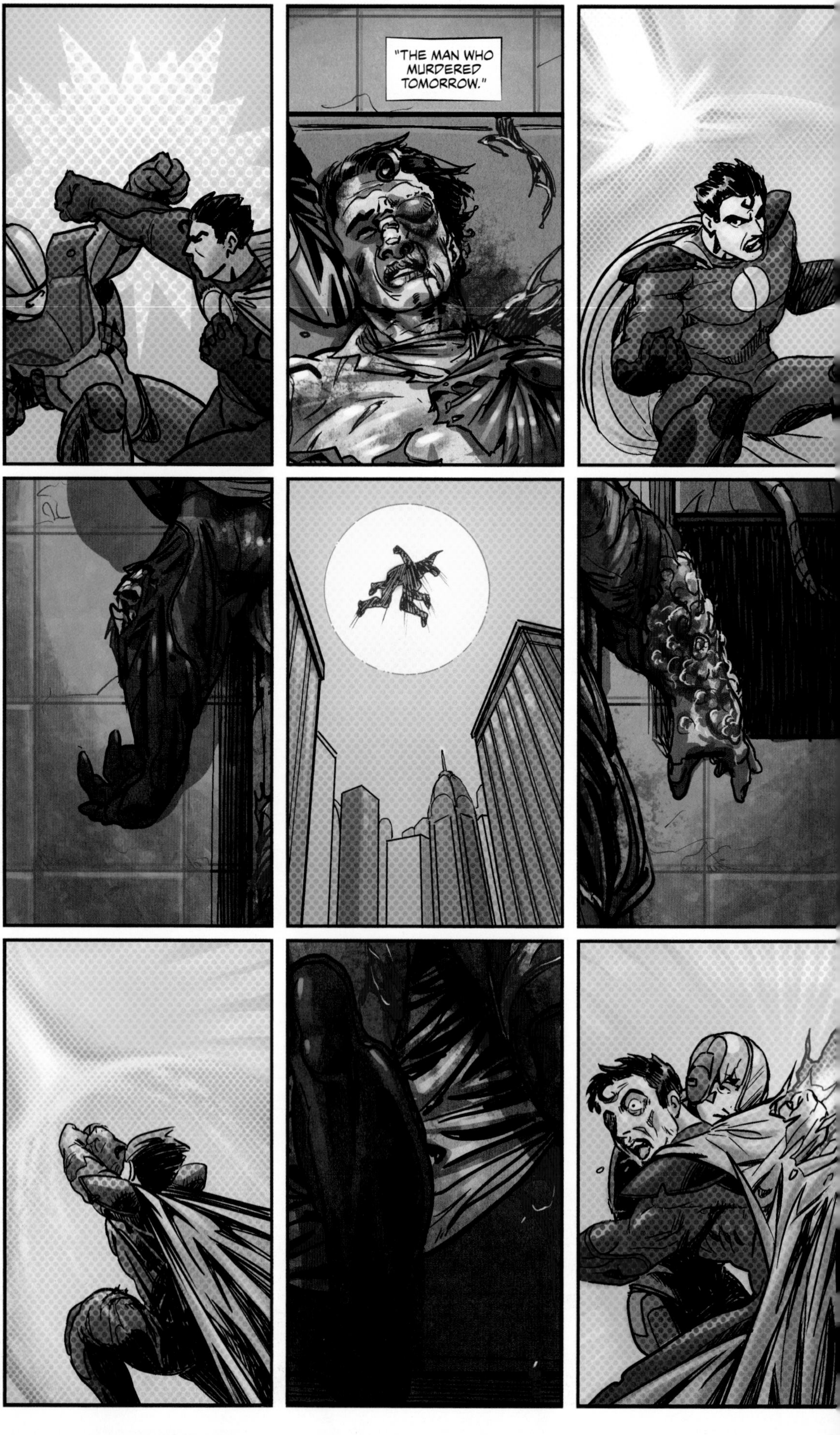
"THE MAN WHO MURDERED TOMORROW."

HISTORY IS THE MEMORY OF STATES, NOT INDIVIDUALS. ALL STATES CHANGE... WITH THE MEASURED APPLICATION OF HEAT AND PRESSURE.

I DON'T FOLLOW.

OH, BUT YOU *DO*. YOU JUST DON'T KNOW IT YET.

YOU CAN'T SERIOUSLY THINK--

HOW I AM PERCEIVED... DOES NOT CONCERN ME.

THE VIRTUES OF ANY AGE ARE LIMITED TO JUST THAT--THEIR *AGE*. ARISTOTLE HELD UP PRIDE AS THE GREATEST OF ALL VIRTUES.

LATER, THE EARTH WAS PROMISED TO THE MEEK.

WE COULD DEBATE THE DELIVERABLES.

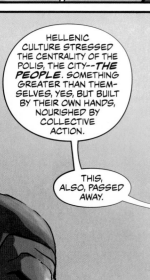

HELLENIC CULTURE STRESSED THE CENTRALITY OF THE POLIS, THE CITY--*THE PEOPLE*. SOMETHING GREATER THAN THEM-SELVES, YES, BUT BUILT BY THEIR OWN HANDS, NOURISHED BY COLLECTIVE ACTION.

THIS, ALSO, PASSED AWAY.

LEADERS BECAME SHEPHERDS. WHAT LEFT FOR THE PEOPLE...BUT TO BECOME SHEEP? THEY TOPPLED MAN AND REPLACED HIM WITH GOD.

I SUPPOSE IT WAS LESS EXHAUSTING.

VILLAIN, HERO, GOD, LEADER. THESE LABELS CHANGE MEANING WITH THEIR CONTEXT...

...AND THE CONTEXT IS CHANGING SO QUICKLY YOU DON'T HAVE THE EQUIPMENT TO MEASURE OR UNDER-STAND IT.

HISTORY WILL JUDGE ME BY ITS OWN INSCRUTABLE STANDARD.

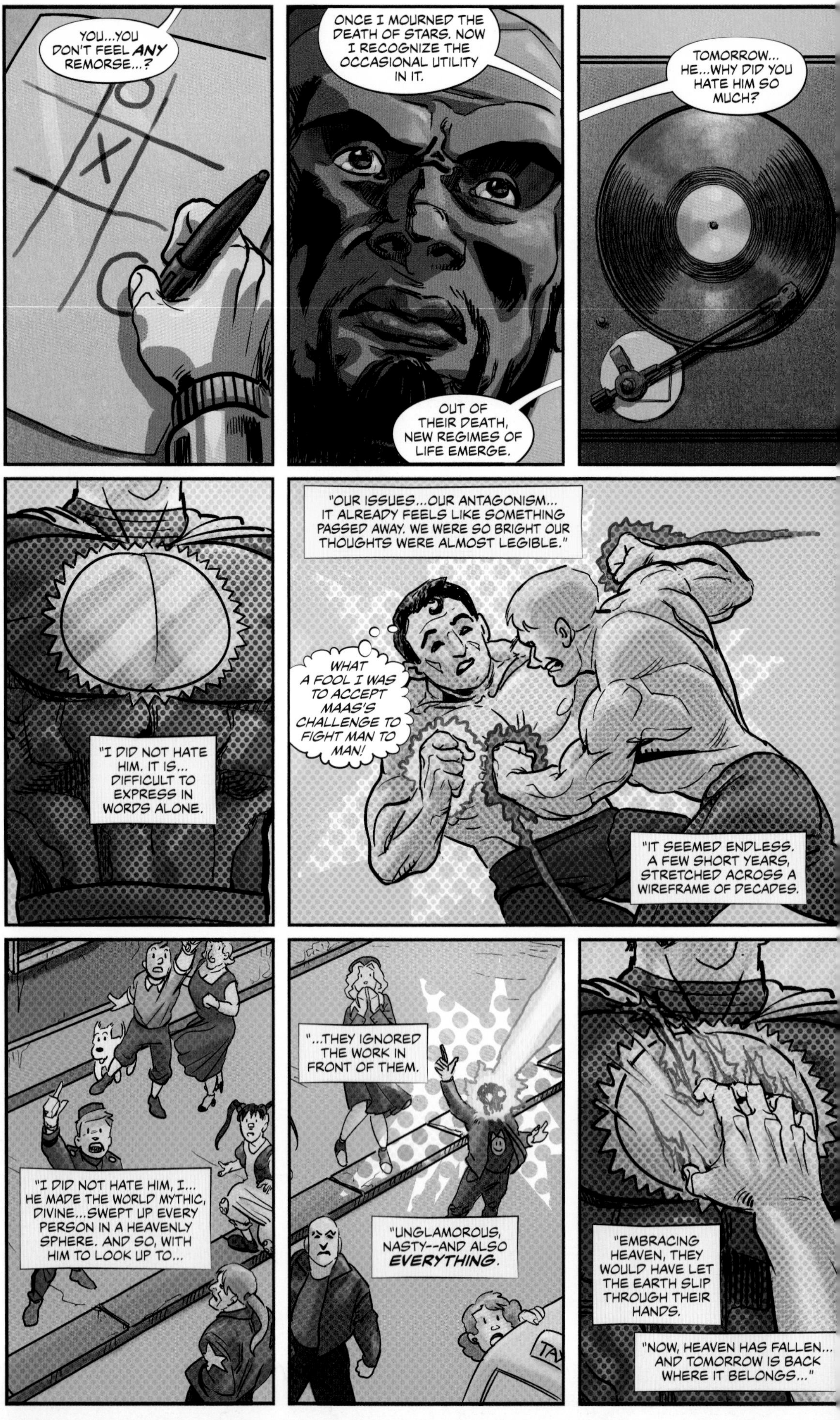
YOU...YOU DON'T FEEL ANY REMORSE...?
ONCE I MOURNED THE DEATH OF STARS. NOW I RECOGNIZE THE OCCASIONAL UTILITY IN IT.
OUT OF THEIR DEATH, NEW REGIMES OF LIFE EMERGE.
TOMORROW... HE...WHY DID YOU HATE HIM SO MUCH?
"I DID NOT HATE HIM. IT IS... DIFFICULT TO EXPRESS IN WORDS ALONE.
"OUR ISSUES...OUR ANTAGONISM... IT ALREADY FEELS LIKE SOMETHING PASSED AWAY. WE WERE SO BRIGHT OUR THOUGHTS WERE ALMOST LEGIBLE."
WHAT A FOOL I WAS TO ACCEPT MAAS'S CHALLENGE TO FIGHT MAN TO MAN!
"IT SEEMED ENDLESS. A FEW SHORT YEARS, STRETCHED ACROSS A WIREFRAME OF DECADES.
"I DID NOT HATE HIM, I... HE MADE THE WORLD MYTHIC, DIVINE...SWEPT UP EVERY PERSON IN A HEAVENLY SPHERE. AND SO, WITH HIM TO LOOK UP TO...
"...THEY IGNORED THE WORK IN FRONT OF THEM.
"UNGLAMOROUS, NASTY--AND ALSO EVERYTHING.
"EMBRACING HEAVEN, THEY WOULD HAVE LET THE EARTH SLIP THROUGH THEIR HANDS.
"NOW, HEAVEN HAS FALLEN... AND TOMORROW IS BACK WHERE IT BELONGS..."

...IN THE DIRT. WITH US.

PERHAPS WE'LL START TO SEE THE WORLD AGAIN.

PERHAPS WE'LL EVEN THINK TO CHANGE IT.

OR MAYBE... MAYBE WE'LL JUST BASH EACH OTHER'S HEADS IN.

IS THAT ALL LIFE IS? A ZERO-SUM GAME?

SMARTER MEN THAN ME HAVE TRIED TO ANSWER THAT, I'M SURE.

WOULD THAT I COULD SAY THE SAME.

LISTEN... IMAGINE THE WORLD...IMAGINE EVERY AGE OF HUMAN THOUGHT AS A VAST TRELLIS.

VAST, BUT NOT INFINITE.

THE STRUCTURE OF THIS GRID DEFINES WHAT CAN BE KNOWN, THROUGH INSTITUTIONS, CULTURE...

IT'S ALL BUILT ON "FUNDAMENTAL TRUTHS"...IDEAS NEVER DISCRETELY PERCEIVED...

...AND SO NEVER CONSCIOUSLY *QUESTIONED*.

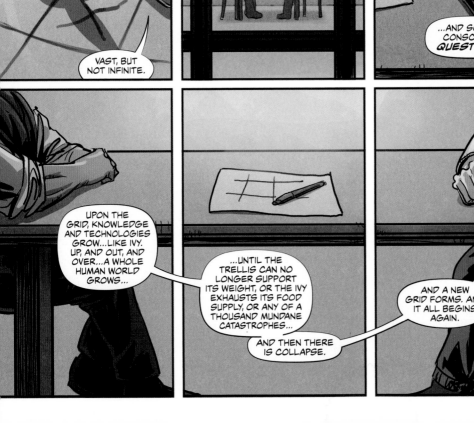

UPON THE GRID, KNOWLEDGE AND TECHNOLOGIES GROW...LIKE IVY. UP, AND OUT, AND OVER...A WHOLE HUMAN WORLD GROWS...

...UNTIL THE TRELLIS CAN NO LONGER SUPPORT ITS WEIGHT, OR THE IVY EXHAUSTS ITS FOOD SUPPLY, OR ANY OF A THOUSAND MUNDANE CATASTROPHES...

AND THEN THERE IS COLLAPSE.

AND A NEW GRID FORMS. AND IT ALL BEGINS AGAIN.

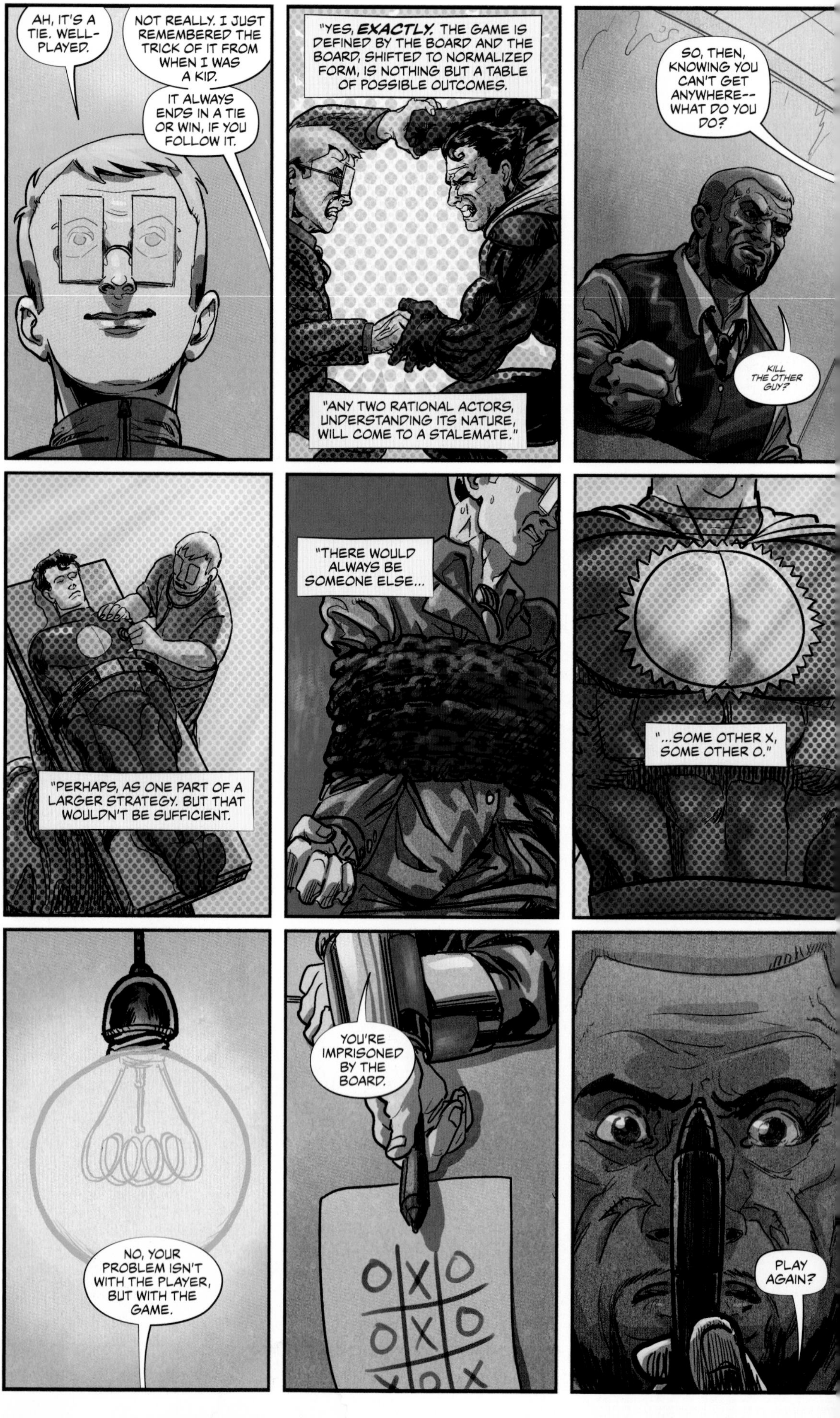
AH, IT'S A TIE. WELL-PLAYED.
NOT REALLY. I JUST REMEMBERED THE TRICK OF IT FROM WHEN I WAS A KID.
IT ALWAYS ENDS IN A TIE OR WIN, IF YOU FOLLOW IT.
"YES, EXACTLY. THE GAME IS DEFINED BY THE BOARD AND THE BOARD, SHIFTED TO NORMALIZED FORM, IS NOTHING BUT A TABLE OF POSSIBLE OUTCOMES.
"ANY TWO RATIONAL ACTORS, UNDERSTANDING ITS NATURE, WILL COME TO A STALEMATE."
SO, THEN, KNOWING YOU CAN'T GET ANYWHERE-- WHAT DO YOU DO?
KILL THE OTHER GUY?
"PERHAPS, AS ONE PART OF A LARGER STRATEGY. BUT THAT WOULDN'T BE SUFFICIENT.
"THERE WOULD ALWAYS BE SOMEONE ELSE...
"...SOME OTHER X, SOME OTHER O."
NO, YOUR PROBLEM ISN'T WITH THE PLAYER, BUT WITH THE GAME.
YOU'RE IMPRISONED BY THE BOARD.
PLAY AGAIN?

GET OUTTA MY FACE!

WHAT...?

A TOY...

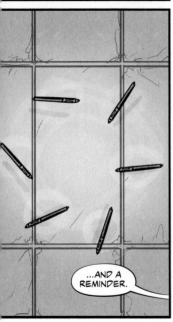

...AND A REMINDER.

ZERO μ SHEATHING-- NO FRICTION. NOT EVEN AGAINST GRAVITY.

LEFT ALONE, IT'LL SPIN UNTIL THE LAST BLACK STAR SWALLOWS THE FINAL PHOTON.

IT'S...IT'S INCREDIBLE...

YES. BUT IT NEVER REALLY GOES ANYWHERE...

...DOES IT?

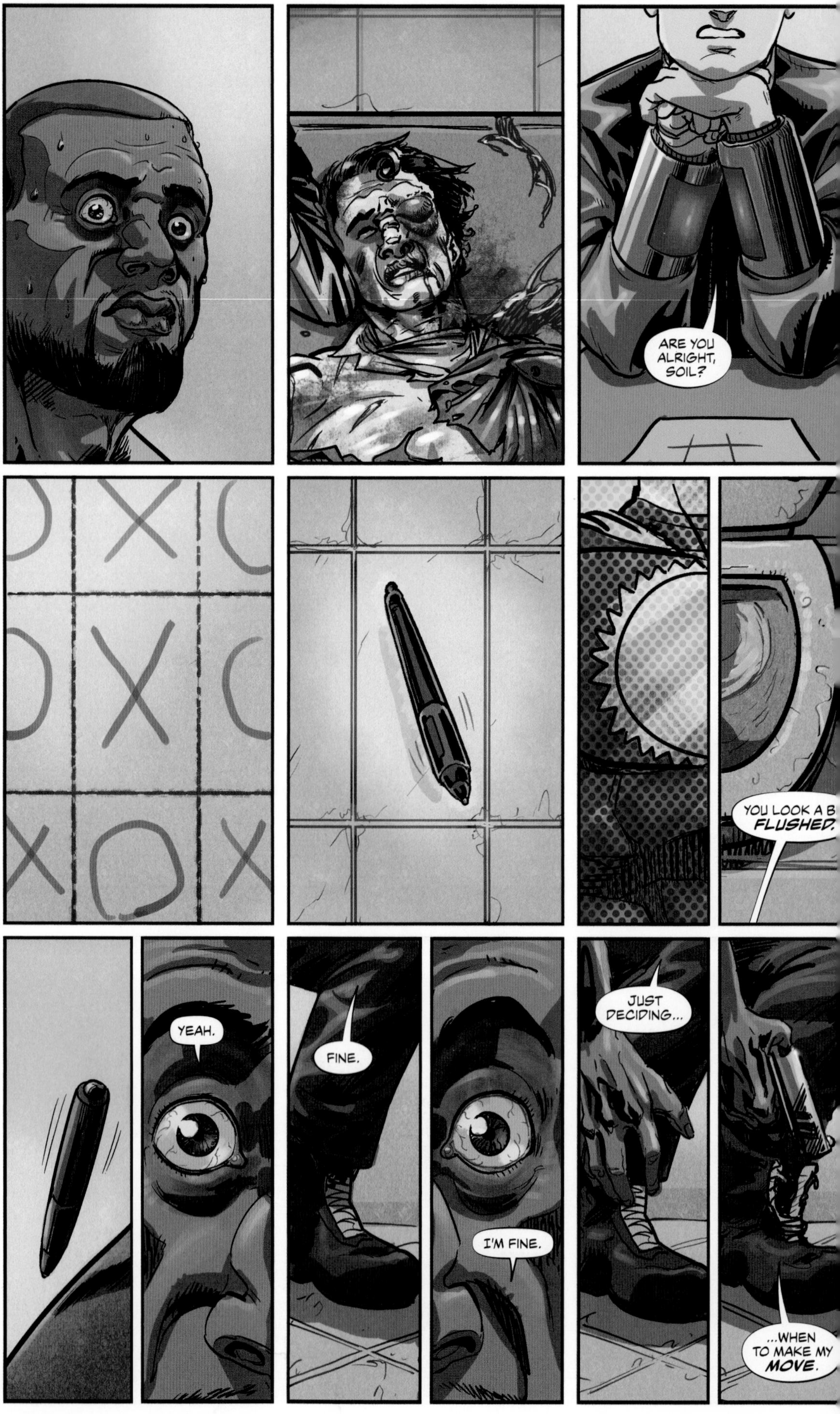
ARE YOU ALRIGHT, SOIL?
YOU LOOK A B FLUSHED.
YEAH.
FINE.
I'M FINE.
JUST DECIDING...
...WHEN TO MAKE MY MOVE.

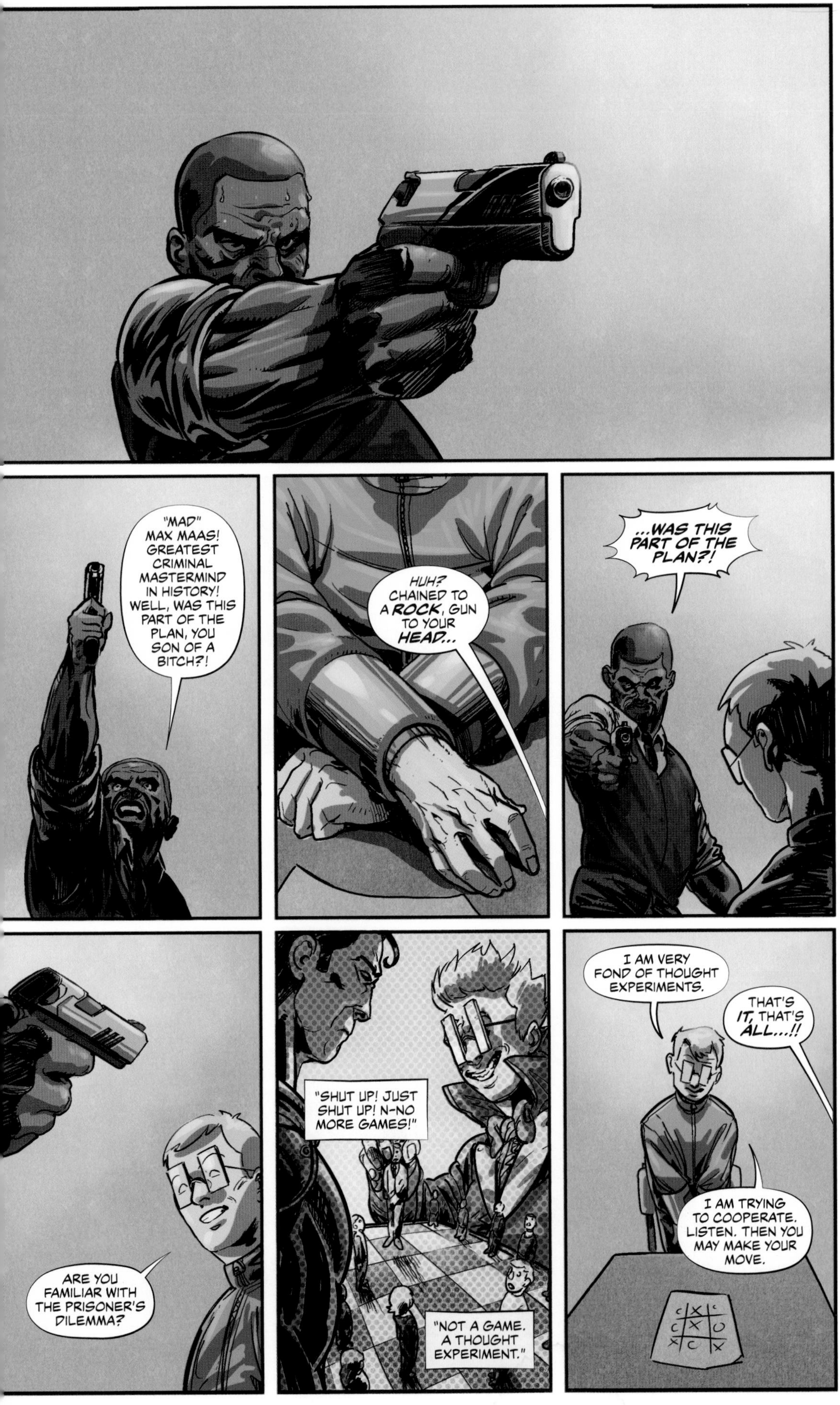
"MAD" MAX MAAS! GREATEST CRIMINAL MASTERMIND IN HISTORY! WELL, WAS THIS PART OF THE PLAN, YOU SON OF A BITCH?!
HUH? CHAINED TO A ROCK, GUN TO YOUR HEAD...
...WAS THIS PART OF THE PLAN?!
ARE YOU FAMILIAR WITH THE PRISONER'S DILEMMA?
"SHUT UP! JUST SHUT UP! N-NO MORE GAMES!"
"NOT A GAME. A THOUGHT EXPERIMENT."
I AM VERY FOND OF THOUGHT EXPERIMENTS.
THAT'S IT, THAT'S ALL...!!
I AM TRYING TO COOPERATE. LISTEN. THEN YOU MAY MAKE YOUR MOVE.

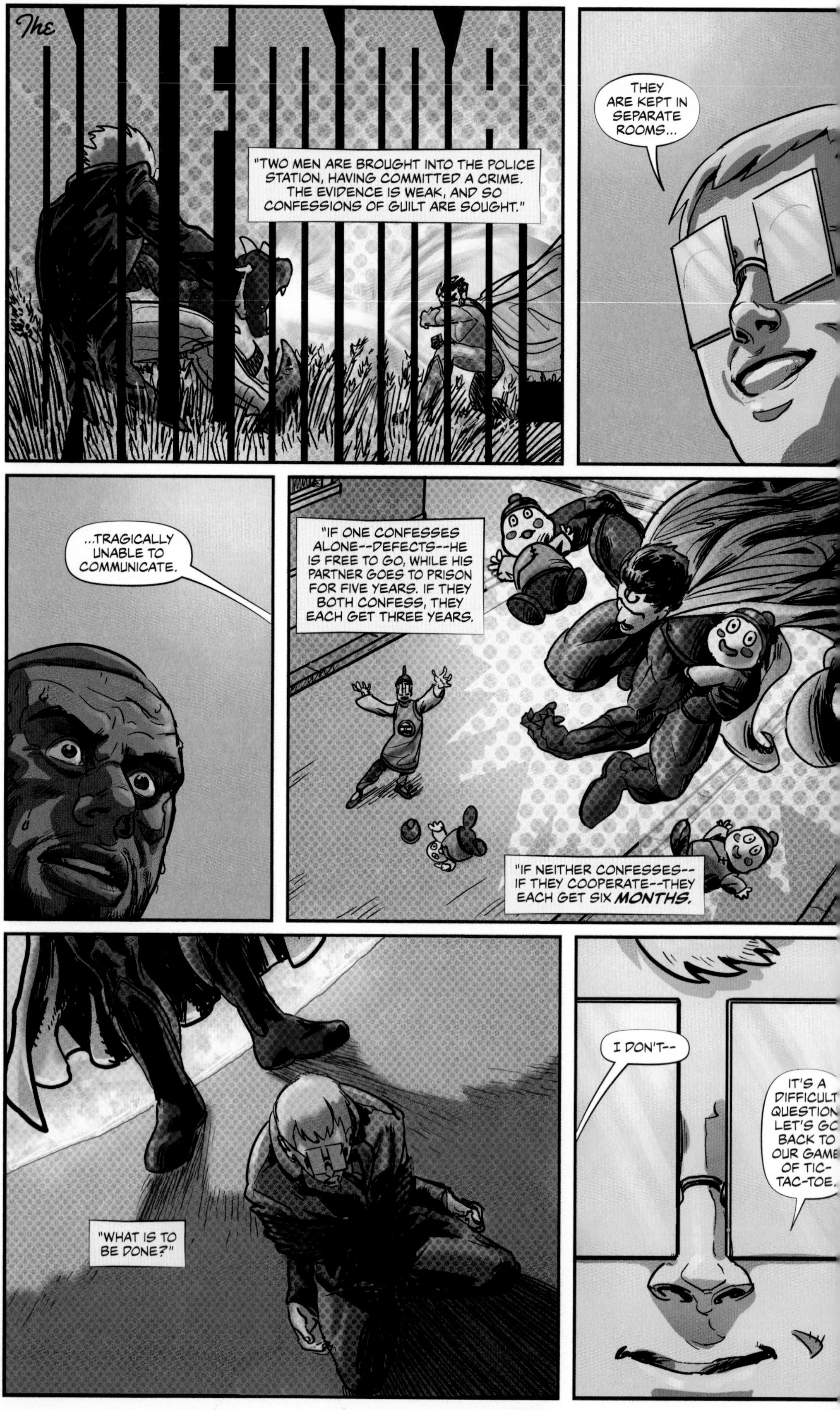
The
"TWO MEN ARE BROUGHT INTO THE POLICE STATION, HAVING COMMITTED A CRIME. THE EVIDENCE IS WEAK, AND SO CONFESSIONS OF GUILT ARE SOUGHT."
THEY ARE KEPT IN SEPARATE ROOMS...
...TRAGICALLY UNABLE TO COMMUNICATE.
"IF ONE CONFESSES ALONE--DEFECTS--HE IS FREE TO GO, WHILE HIS PARTNER GOES TO PRISON FOR FIVE YEARS. IF THEY BOTH CONFESS, THEY EACH GET THREE YEARS.
"IF NEITHER CONFESSES--IF THEY COOPERATE--THEY EACH GET SIX *MONTHS.*
"WHAT IS TO BE DONE?"
I DON'T--
IT'S A DIFFICULT QUESTION LET'S GO BACK TO OUR GAME OF TIC-TAC-TOE.

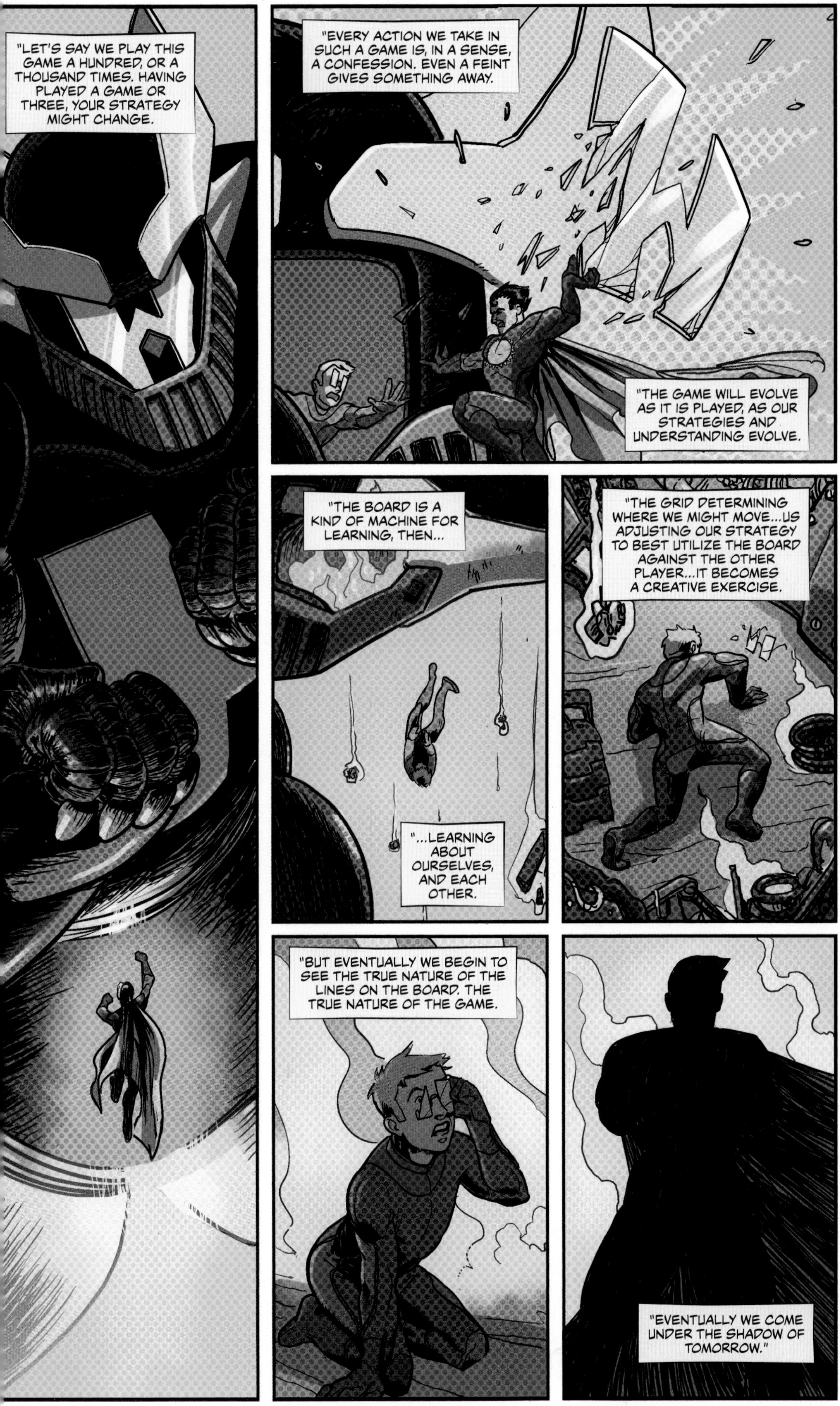
"LET'S SAY WE PLAY THIS GAME A HUNDRED, OR A THOUSAND TIMES. HAVING PLAYED A GAME OR THREE, YOUR STRATEGY MIGHT CHANGE.
"EVERY ACTION WE TAKE IN SUCH A GAME IS, IN A SENSE, A CONFESSION. EVEN A FEINT GIVES SOMETHING AWAY.
"THE GAME WILL EVOLVE AS IT IS PLAYED, AS OUR STRATEGIES AND UNDERSTANDING EVOLVE.
"THE BOARD IS A KIND OF MACHINE FOR LEARNING, THEN...
"...LEARNING ABOUT OURSELVES, AND EACH OTHER.
"THE GRID DETERMINING WHERE WE MIGHT MOVE...US ADJUSTING OUR STRATEGY TO BEST UTILIZE THE BOARD AGAINST THE OTHER PLAYER...IT BECOMES A CREATIVE EXERCISE.
"BUT EVENTUALLY WE BEGIN TO SEE THE TRUE NATURE OF THE LINES ON THE BOARD. THE TRUE NATURE OF THE GAME.
"EVENTUALLY WE COME UNDER THE SHADOW OF TOMORROW."

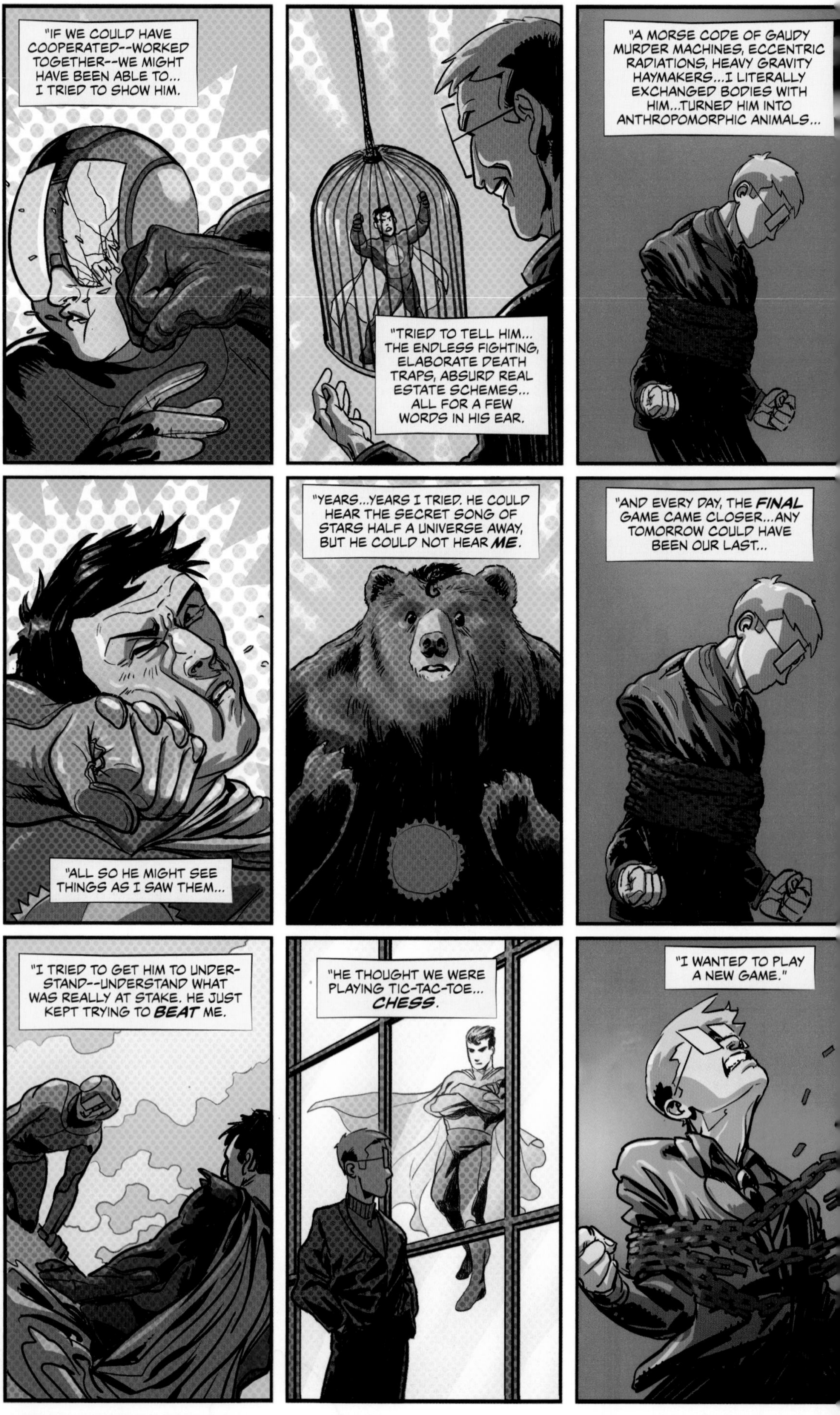
"IF WE COULD HAVE COOPERATED--WORKED TOGETHER--WE MIGHT HAVE BEEN ABLE TO... I TRIED TO SHOW HIM.
"TRIED TO TELL HIM... THE ENDLESS FIGHTING, ELABORATE DEATH TRAPS, ABSURD REAL ESTATE SCHEMES... ALL FOR A FEW WORDS IN HIS EAR.
"A MORSE CODE OF GAUDY MURDER MACHINES, ECCENTRIC RADIATIONS, HEAVY GRAVITY HAYMAKERS...I LITERALLY EXCHANGED BODIES WITH HIM...TURNED HIM INTO ANTHROPOMORPHIC ANIMALS...
"ALL SO HE MIGHT SEE THINGS AS I SAW THEM...
"YEARS...YEARS I TRIED. HE COULD HEAR THE SECRET SONG OF STARS HALF A UNIVERSE AWAY, BUT HE COULD NOT HEAR ***ME***.
"AND EVERY DAY, THE ***FINAL*** GAME CAME CLOSER...ANY TOMORROW COULD HAVE BEEN OUR LAST...
"I TRIED TO GET HIM TO UNDER-STAND--UNDERSTAND WHAT WAS REALLY AT STAKE. HE JUST KEPT TRYING TO ***BEAT*** ME.
"HE THOUGHT WE WERE PLAYING TIC-TAC-TOE... ***CHESS***.
"I WANTED TO PLAY A NEW GAME."

THE THING ABOUT THE PRISONER'S DILEMMA-- IN THE END, PEOPLE ALWAYS DEFECT.

ALWAYS.

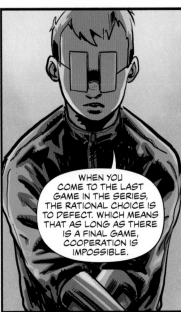

WHEN YOU COME TO THE LAST GAME IN THE SERIES, THE RATIONAL CHOICE IS TO DEFECT. WHICH MEANS THAT AS LONG AS THERE IS A FINAL GAME, COOPERATION IS IMPOSSIBLE.

WHAT CHOICE DID I HAVE? GODS, IN THEIR ETERNAL INFINITY, CAN COOPERATE. THEY CAN AFFORD TO. BUT FOR MEN--THE GAME IS FINITE.

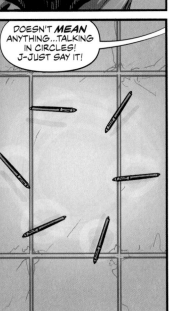

DOESN'T *MEAN* ANYTHING...TALKING IN CIRCLES! J-JUST SAY IT!

"BEFORE WE CAN WORK TOGETHER--BEFORE WE CAN BUILD A HEAVEN OF OUR *OWN*--WE MUST FIRST CONQUER DEATH."

"THAT...THAT'S INSANE."

NO. IT IS POSSIBLE. BUT NOT WITHOUT SOME DRASTIC... *RESTRUCTURING*.

WRITE THE CONFESSION.

klick

YOU LOVED HIM, I KNOW.

W-WHO?

TOMORROW.

Y-YEAH.

YES.

EVERYBODY LO--

NO. THEY LOVED THE SUN.

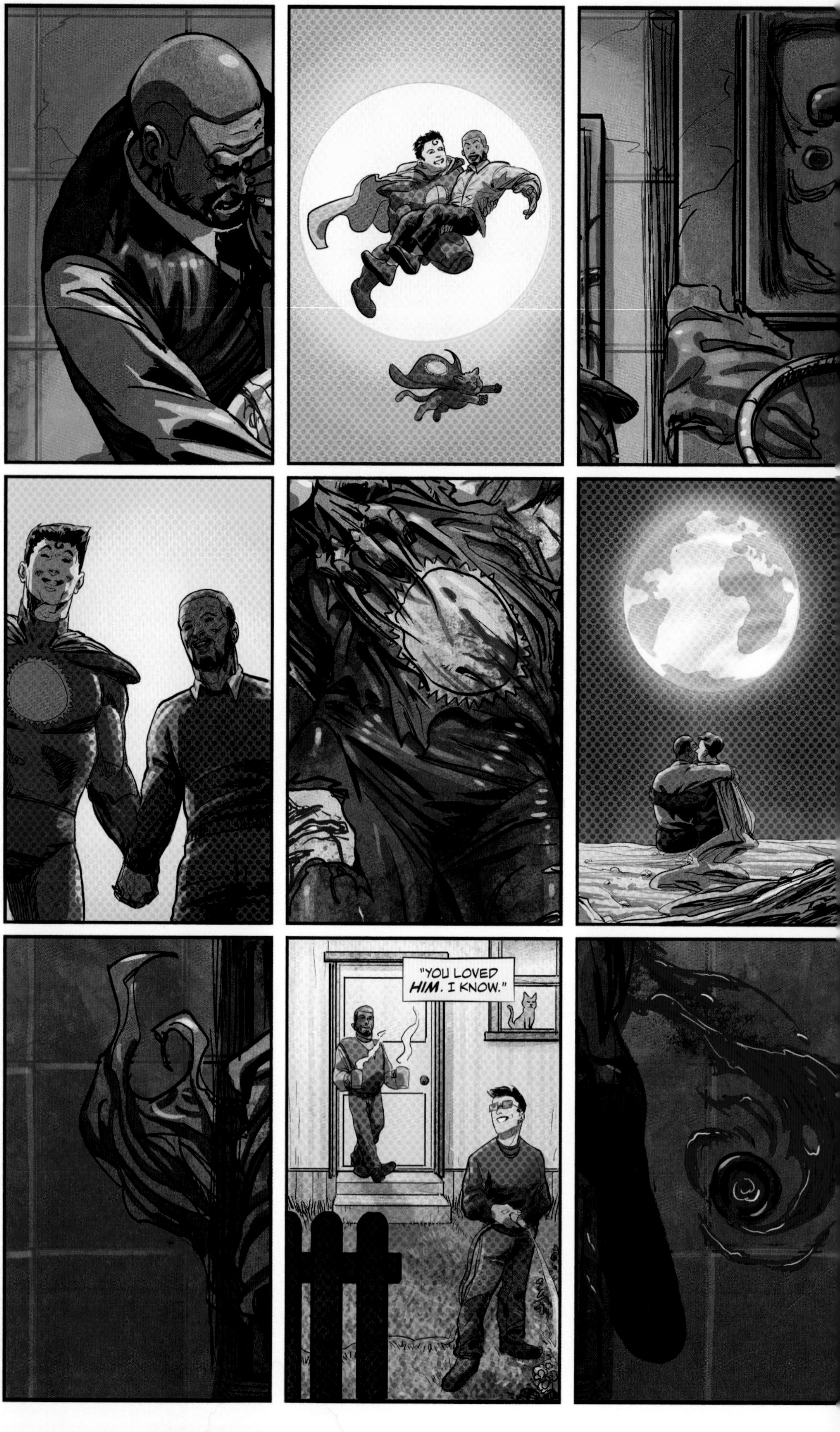
"YOU LOVED HIM. I KNOW."

NOW *YOU* KNOW. MAKE YOUR MOVE.

KNOW?! DON'T-- I DON'T KNOW *ANYTHING*... I DON'T KNOW *WHY*...

WHY *HIM*? H-HE CAME FROM THE SKY...HE DID ONLY *GOOD*.

SOMETIMES YOU CAN MAKE ALL THE RIGHT MOVES... AND STILL LOSE IN THE END.

"HE BRACED THE DECAYING STRUCTURE OF A BOARD THAT HAD LONG AGO OUTLIVED ITS USEFULNESS. I AIM TO TEAR IT DOWN."

"AND REPLACE IT WITH WHAT?"

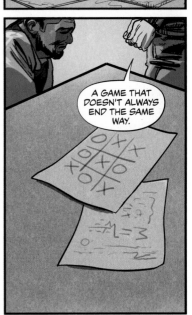

A GAME THAT DOESN'T ALWAYS END THE SAME WAY.

YOU'RE... *AFRAID.*

YES.

WHAT ARE YOU SO AFRAID OF?

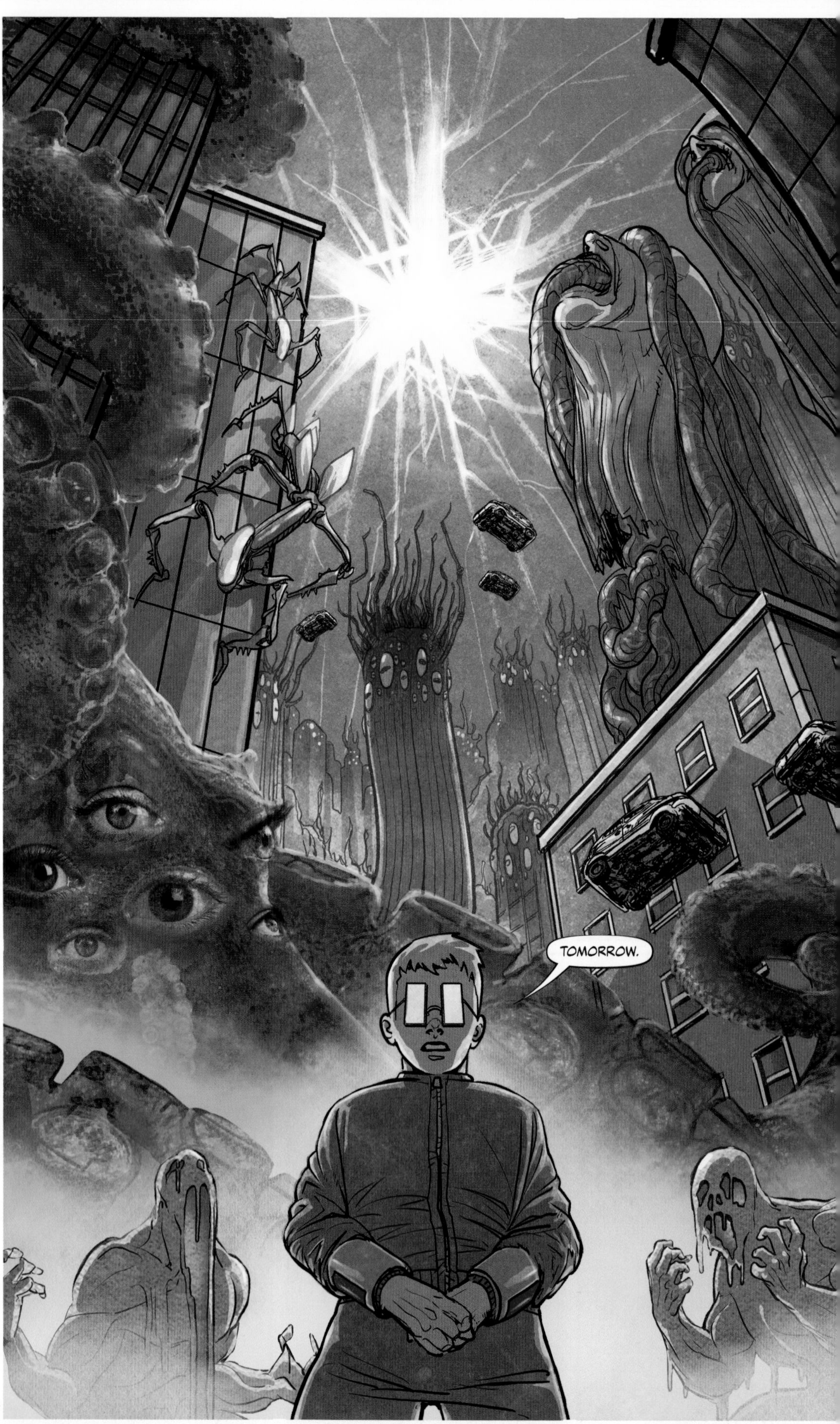
TOMORROW.

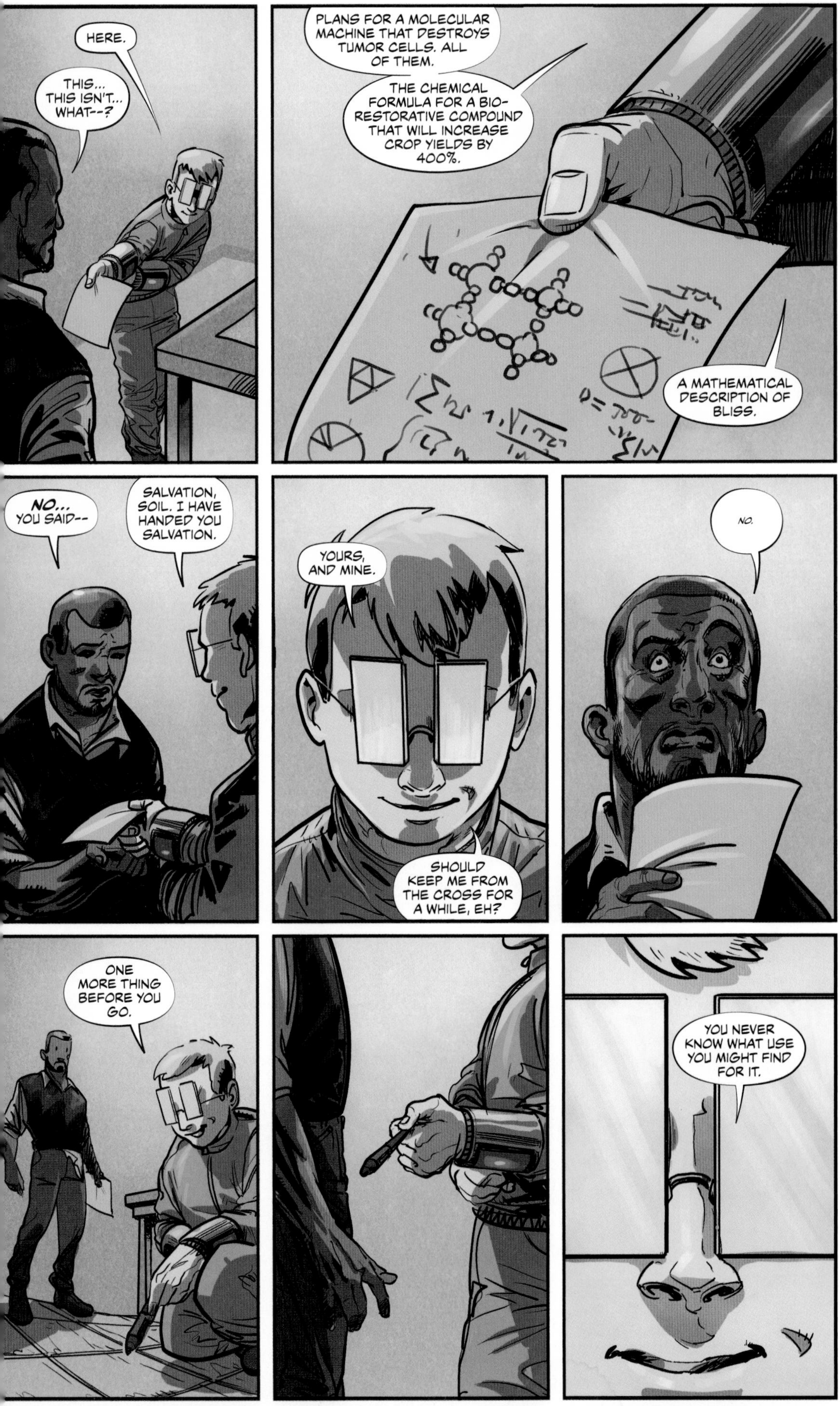
HERE.
THIS... THIS ISN'T... WHAT--?
PLANS FOR A MOLECULAR MACHINE THAT DESTROYS TUMOR CELLS. ALL OF THEM.
THE CHEMICAL FORMULA FOR A BIO-RESTORATIVE COMPOUND THAT WILL INCREASE CROP YIELDS BY 400%.
A MATHEMATICAL DESCRIPTION OF BLISS.
NO... YOU SAID--
SALVATION, SOIL. I HAVE HANDED YOU SALVATION.
YOURS, AND MINE.
SHOULD KEEP ME FROM THE CROSS FOR A WHILE, EH?
NO.
ONE MORE THING BEFORE YOU GO.
YOU NEVER KNOW WHAT USE YOU MIGHT FIND FOR IT.

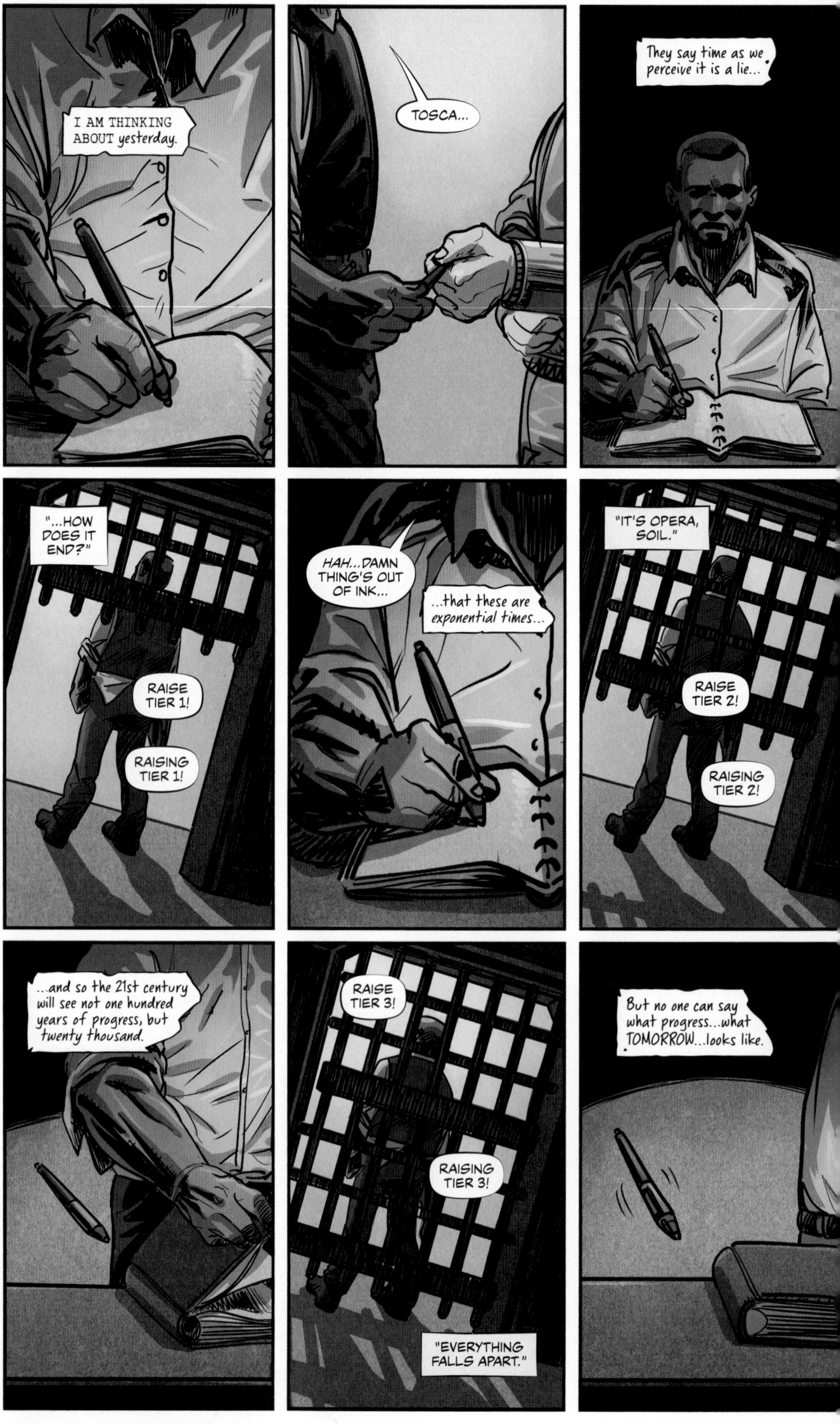
I AM THINKING ABOUT yesterday.
TOSCA...
They say time as we perceive it is a lie...
"...HOW DOES IT END?"
RAISE TIER 1!
RAISING TIER 1!
HAH...DAMN THING'S OUT OF INK...
...that these are exponential times...
"IT'S OPERA, SOIL."
RAISE TIER 2!
RAISING TIER 2!
...and so the 21st century will see not one hundred years of progress, but twenty thousand.
RAISE TIER 3!
RAISING TIER 3!
"EVERYTHING FALLS APART."
But no one can say what progress...what TOMORROW...looks like.

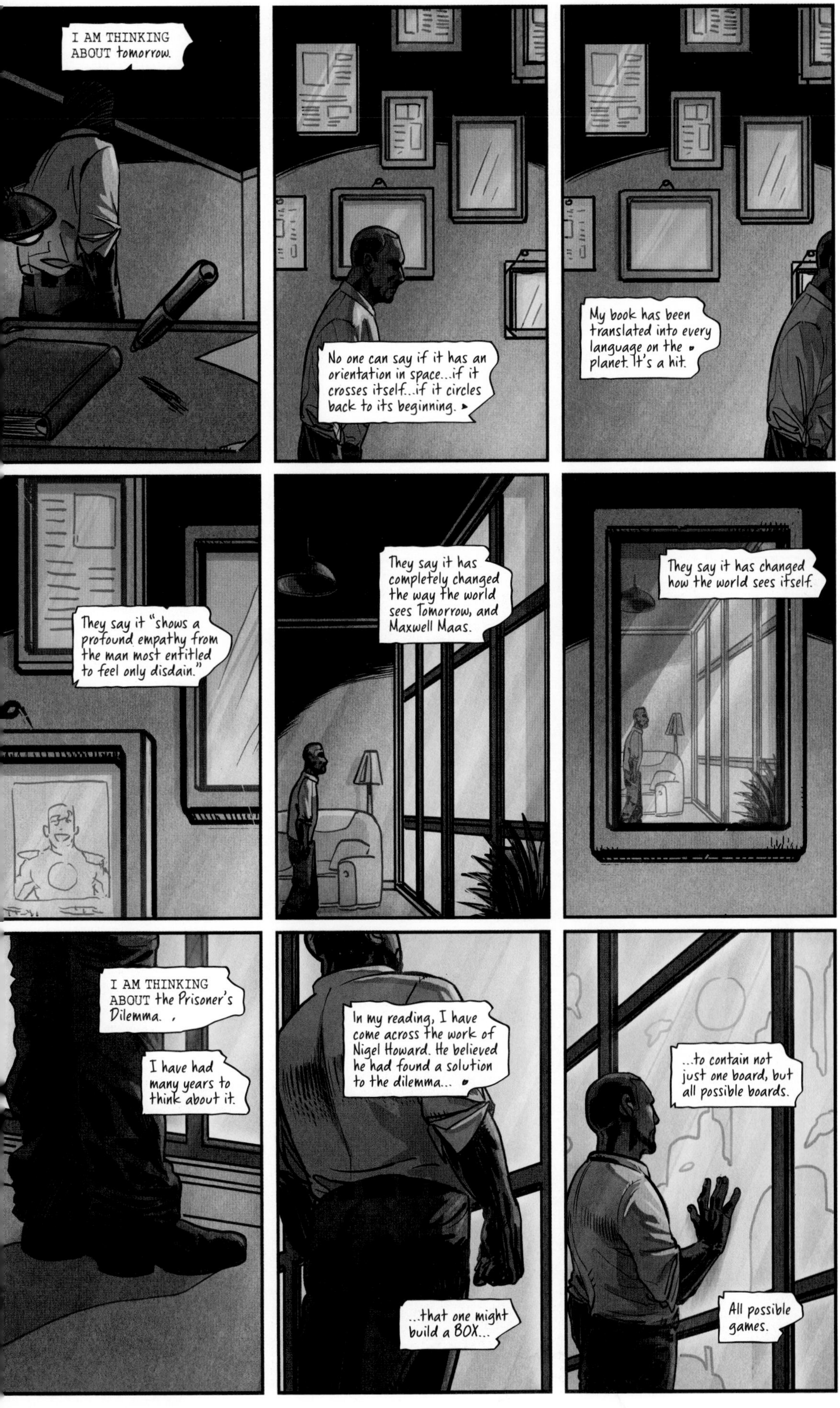
I AM THINKING ABOUT tomorrow.
No one can say if it has an orientation in space...if it crosses itself...if it circles back to its beginning.
My book has been translated into every language on the planet. It's a hit.
They say it "shows a profound empathy from the man most entitled to feel only disdain."
They say it has completely changed the way the world sees Tomorrow, and Maxwell Maas.
They say it has changed how the world sees itself.
I AM THINKING ABOUT the Prisoner's Dilemma.
I have had many years to think about it.
In my reading, I have come across the work of Nigel Howard. He believed he had found a solution to the dilemma...
...that one might build a BOX...
...to contain not just one board, but all possible boards.
All possible games.

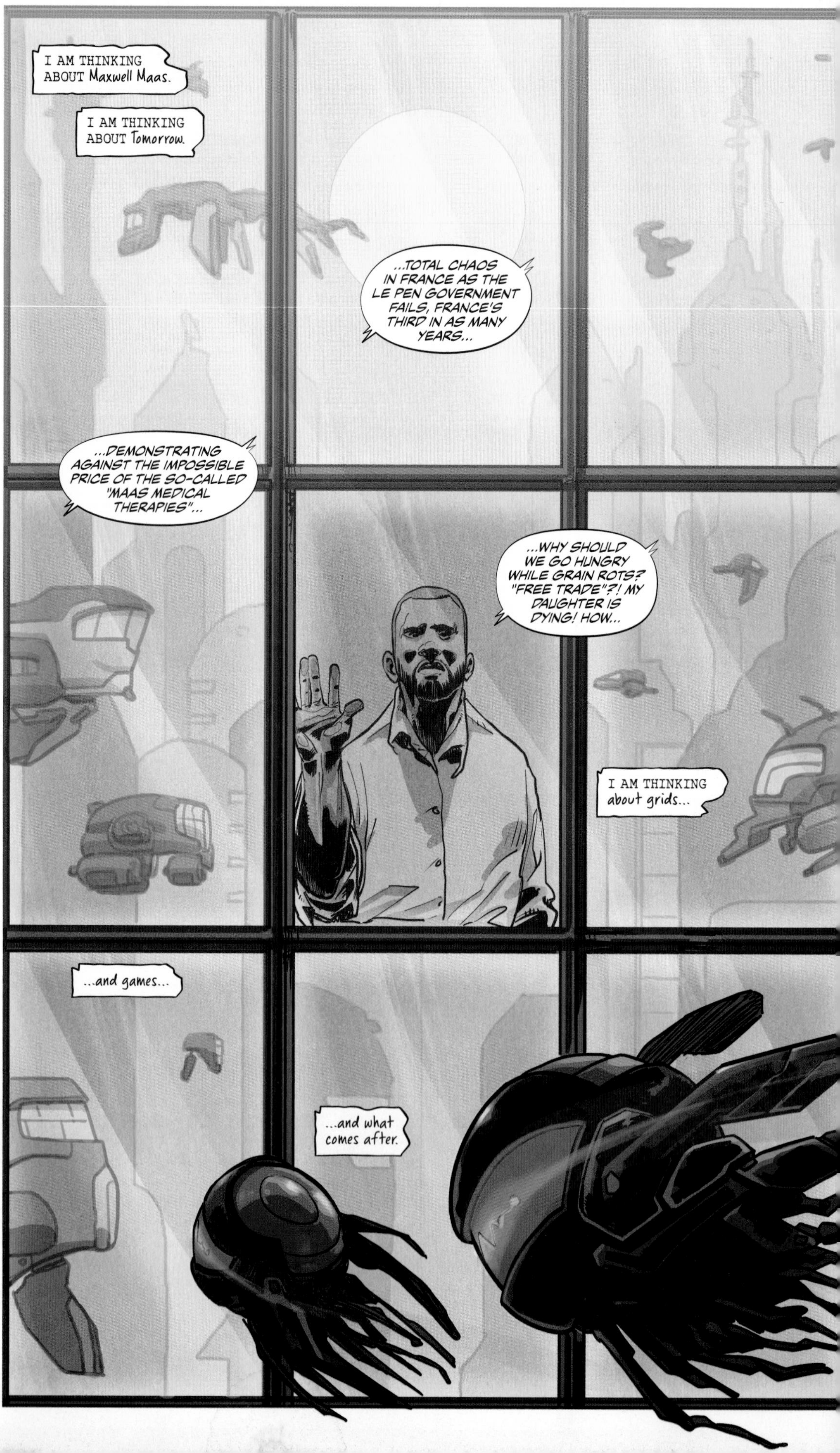
I AM THINKING ABOUT Maxwell Maas.
I AM THINKING ABOUT Tomorrow.
...TOTAL CHAOS IN FRANCE AS THE LE PEN GOVERNMENT FAILS, FRANCE'S THIRD IN AS MANY YEARS...
...DEMONSTRATING AGAINST THE IMPOSSIBLE PRICE OF THE SO-CALLED "MAAS MEDICAL THERAPIES"...
...WHY SHOULD WE GO HUNGRY WHILE GRAIN ROTS? "FREE TRADE"?! MY DAUGHTER IS DYING! HOW...
I AM THINKING about grids...
...and games...
...and what comes after.

THE ART OF

MAXWELL'S DEMONS

COVER GALLERY

FEATURING
VITTORIO ASTONE

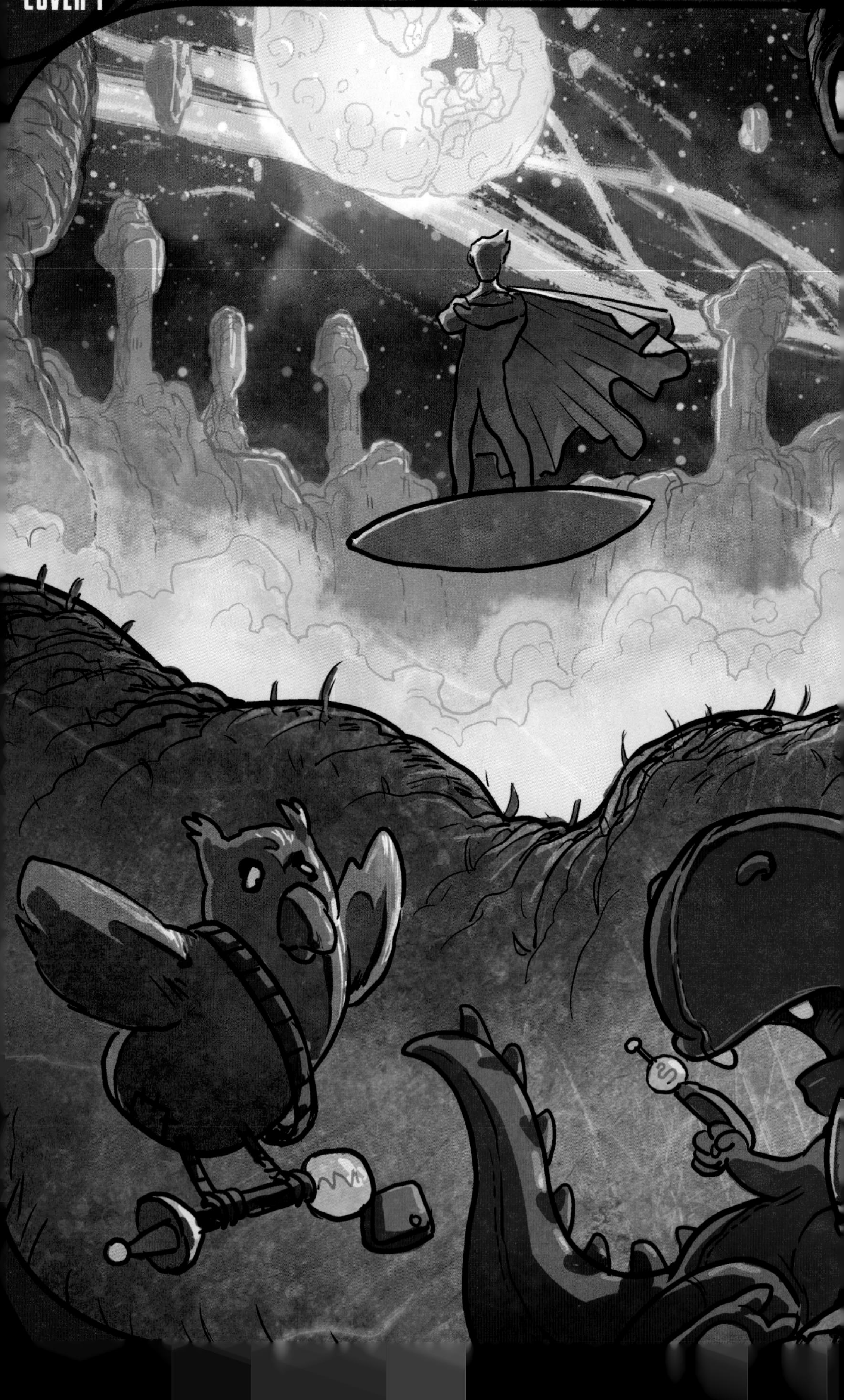

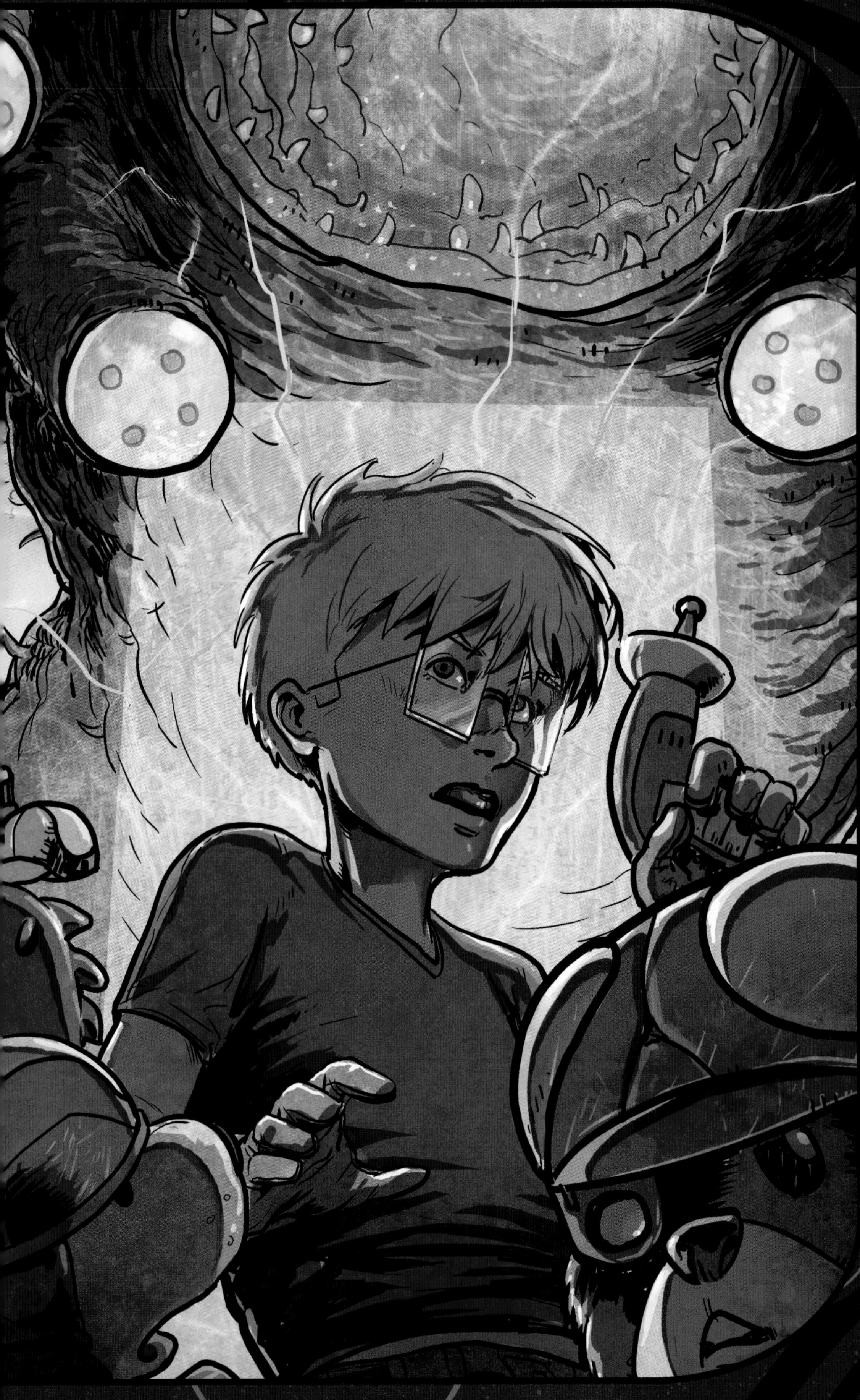

COVER 2

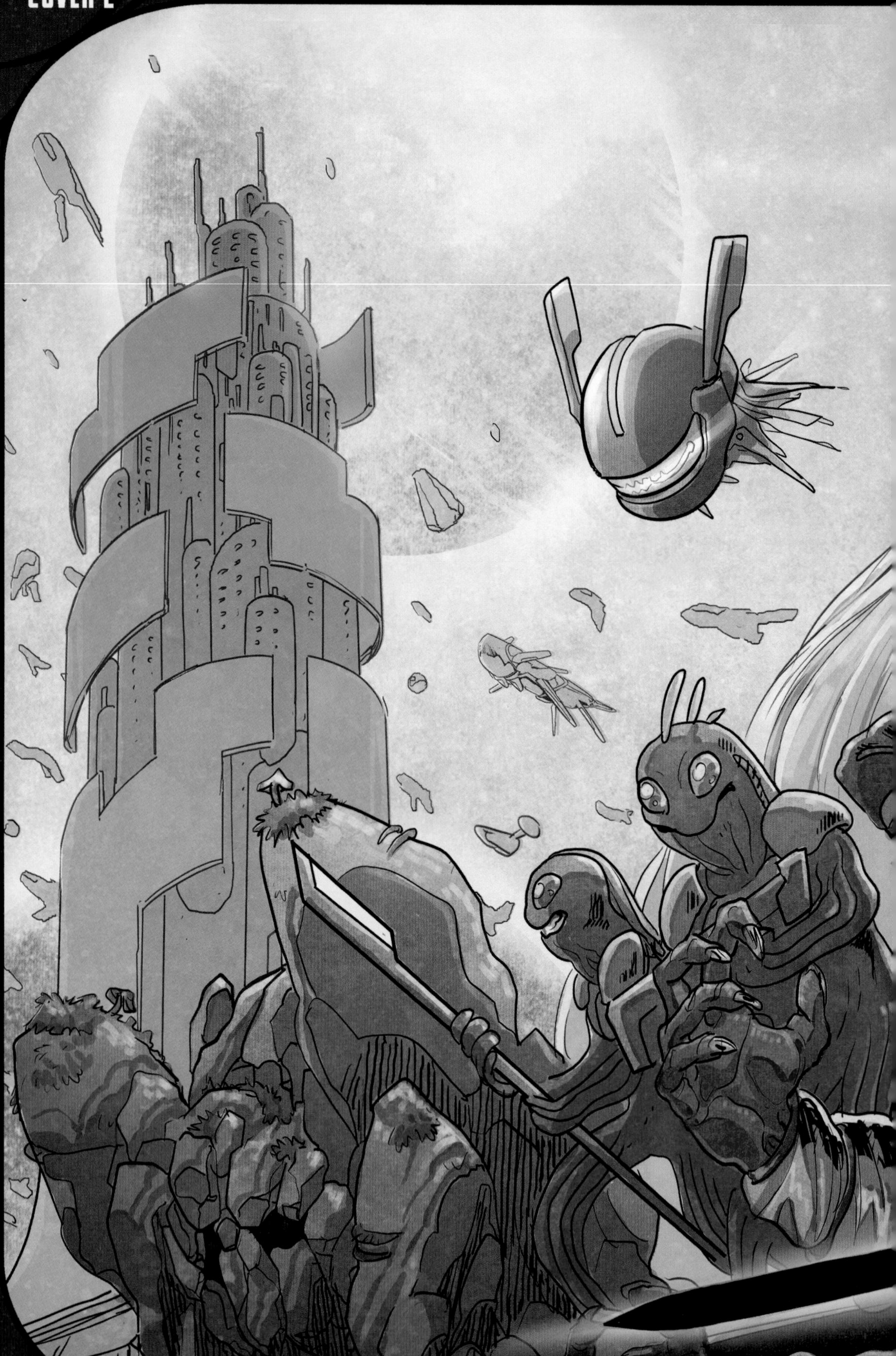

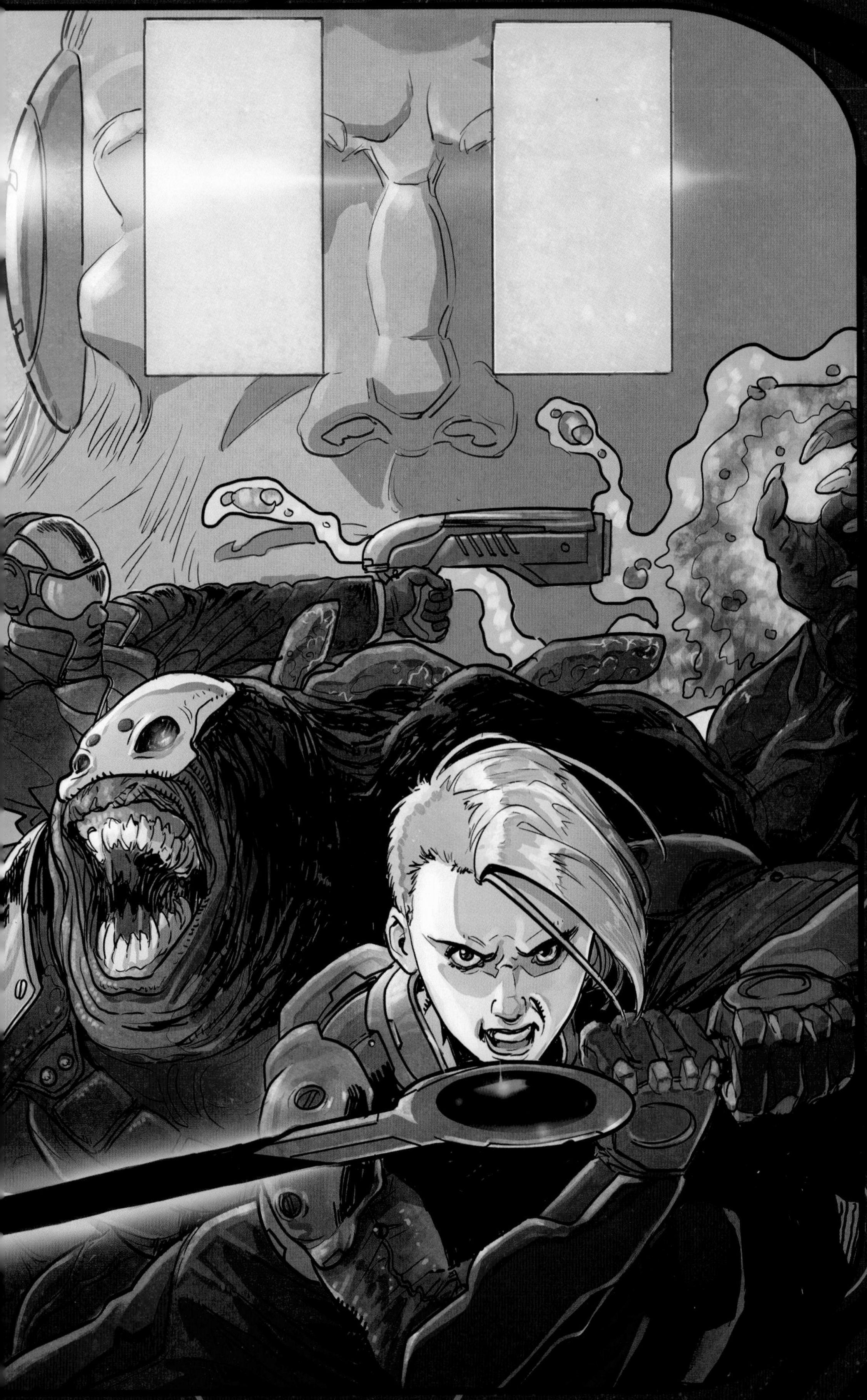

COVER 3

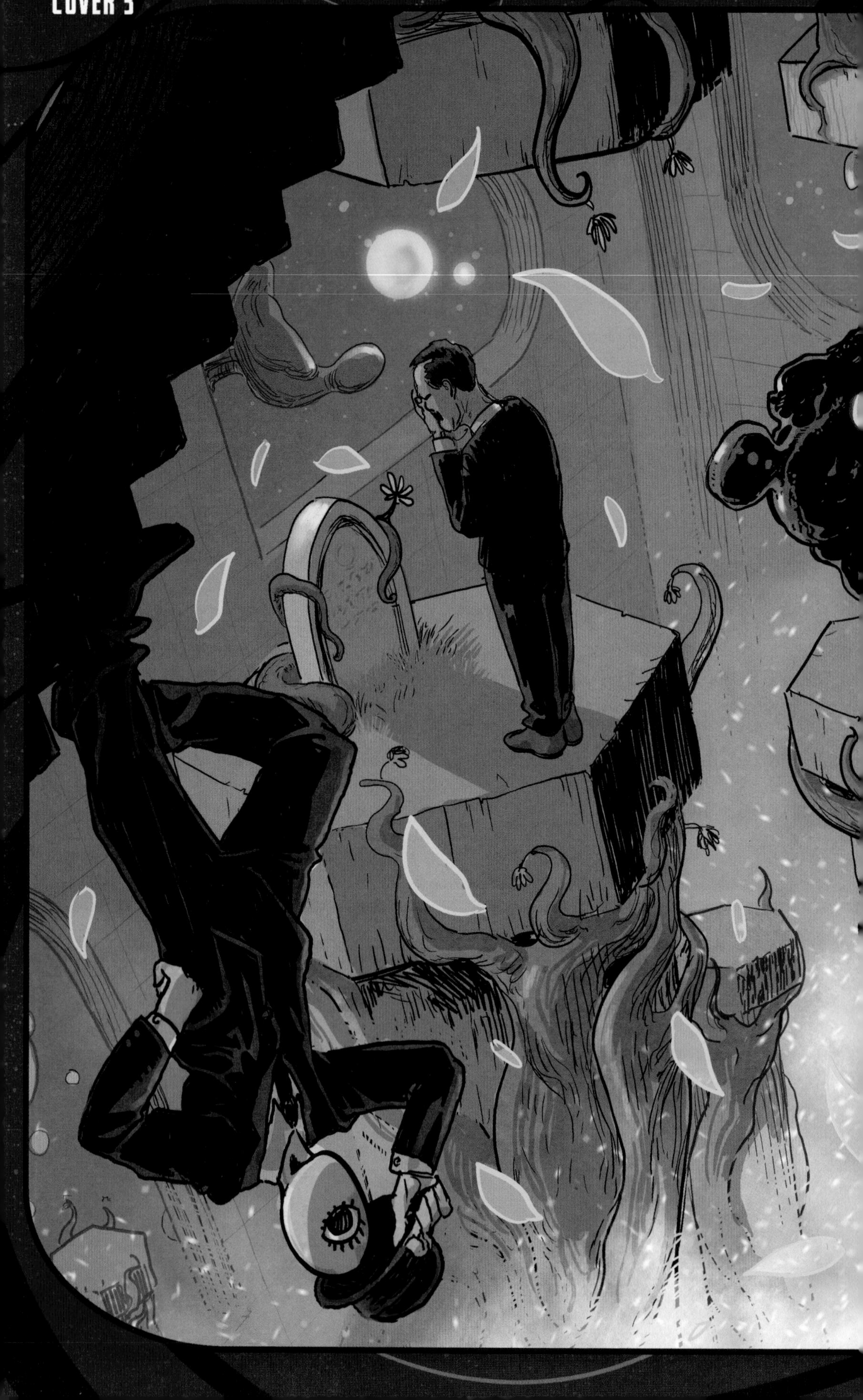

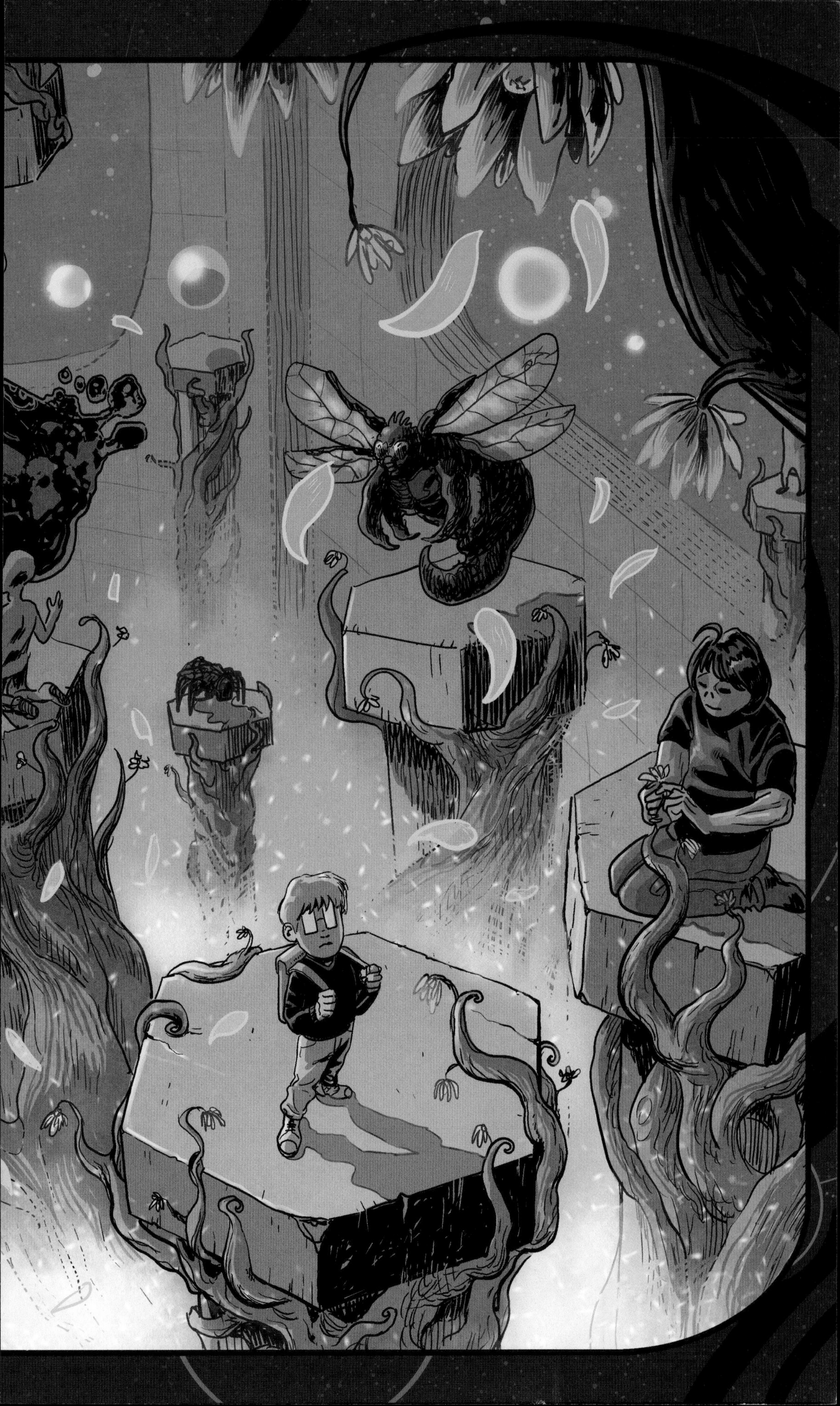

COVER 4

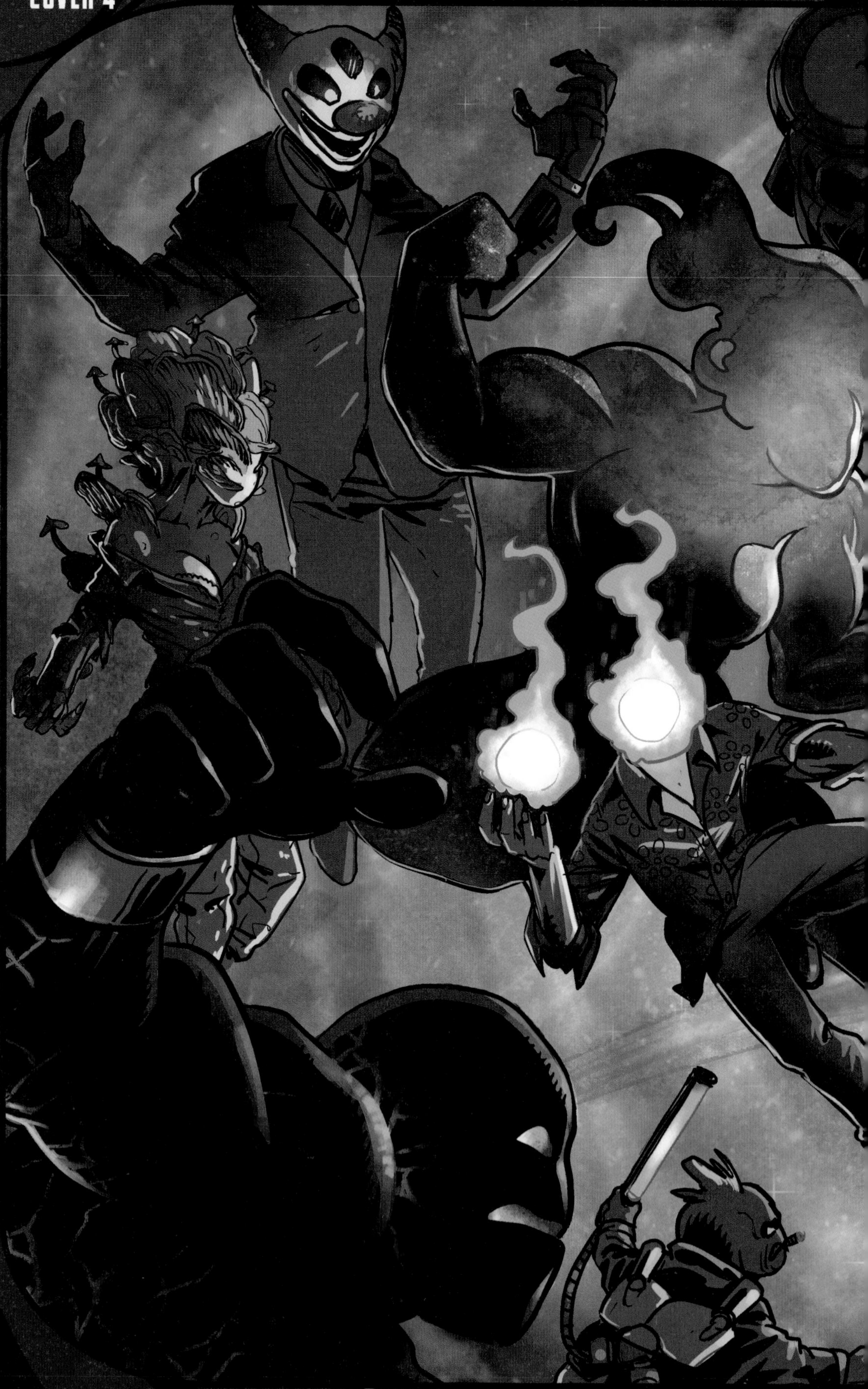

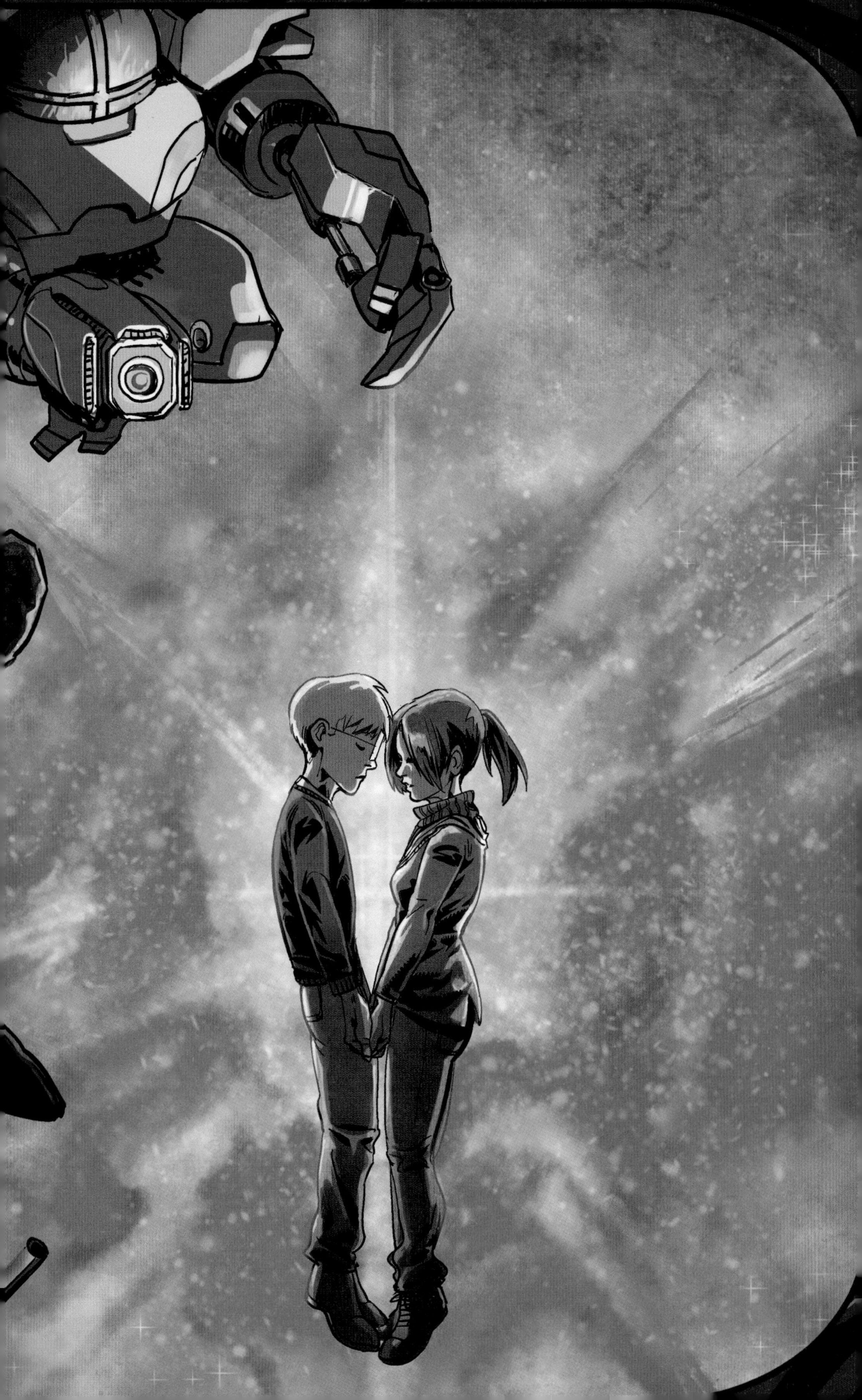

COVER 5

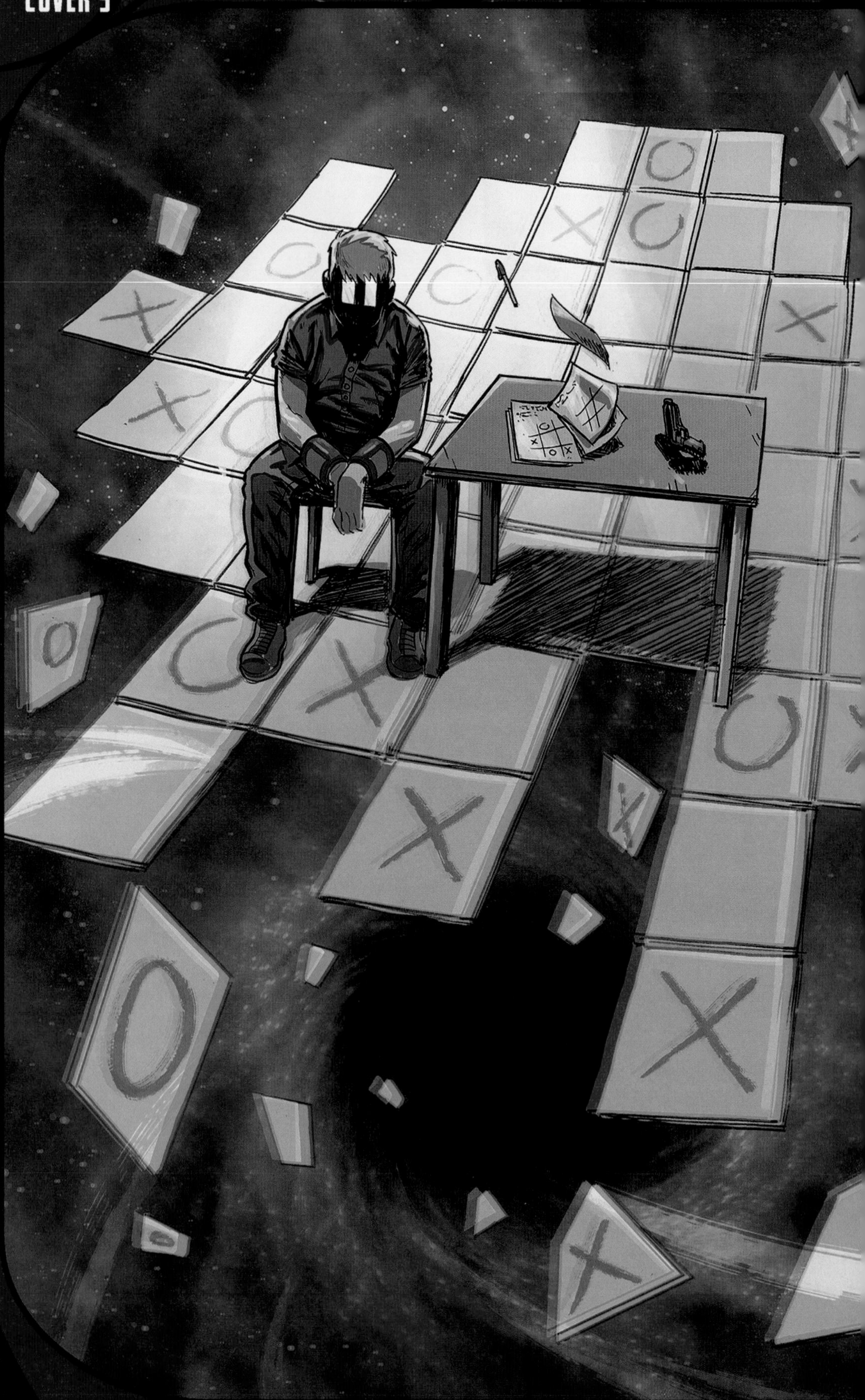

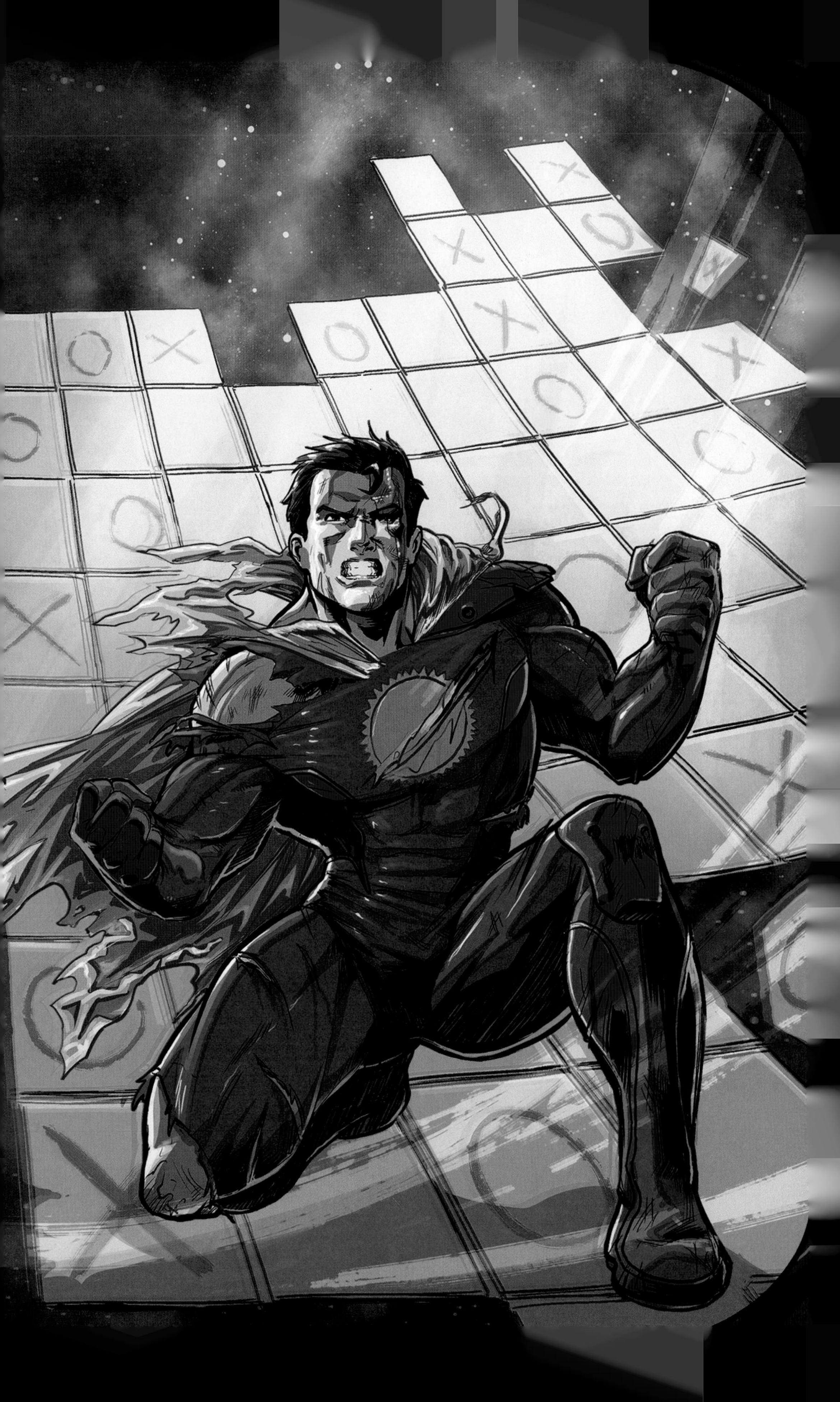

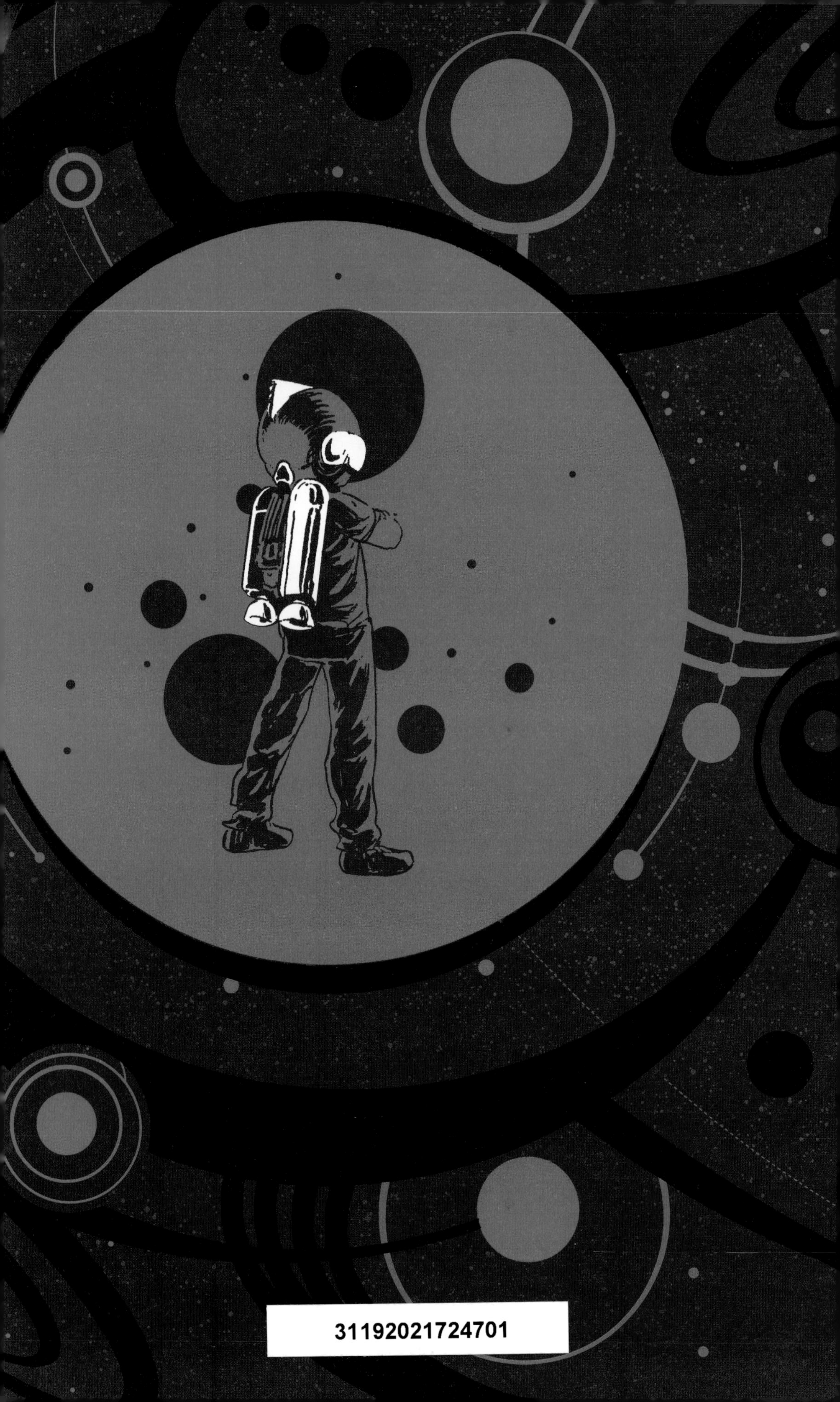